BUILDING ON A BORROWED PAST

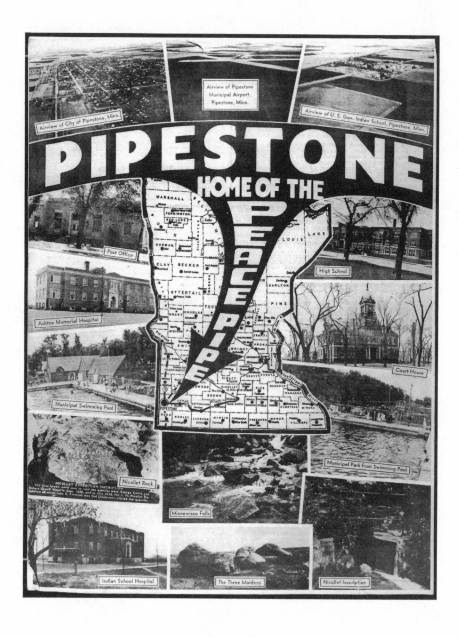

Airview of City of Pipestone, Minn.

Airview of Pipestone Municipal Airport, Pipestone, Minn.

Airview of U. S. Gov. Indian School, Pipestone, Minn.

PIPESTONE
HOME OF THE
PEACE PIPE

Post Office

High School

Ashton Memorial Hospital

Court House

Municipal Swimming Pool

Municipal Park from Swimming Pool

Nicollet Rock

NICOLLET EXPEDITION INSCRIPTION

Minnewissa Falls

Indian School Hospital

The Three Maidens

Nicollet Inscription

BUILDING ON A
BORROWED PAST

Place and Identity
in Pipestone, Minnesota

SALLY J. SOUTHWICK

Ohio University Press • Athens

Ohio University Press, Athens, Ohio 45701
www.ohio.edu/oupress
© 2005 by Ohio University Press
Printed in the United States of America
All rights reserved

12 11 10 09 08 07 06 05   5 4 3 2 1

Library of Congress Cataloging-in-Publication Data

Southwick, Sally J.
    Building on a borrowed past : place and identity in Pipestone, Minnesota
/ Sally J. Southwick.
        p. cm.
    Includes bibliographical references (p.   ) and index.
    ISBN 0-8214-1617-0 (acid-free paper) — ISBN 0-8214-1618-9 (pbk. :
acid-free paper)
    1. Pipestone (Minn.)—History. 2. Pipestone (Minn.)—Ethnic relations.
3. Whites—Minnesota—Pipestone—History. 4. Indians of North America—
Minnesota—Pipestone—History. 5. Pipestone National Monument
(Minn.)—History. 6. Group identity—Minnesota—Pipestone. 7. Monuments—Social aspects—Minnesota—Pipestone. 8. Public history—Political
aspects—Minnesota—Pipestone. I. Title.
    F614.P5S68 2005
    977.6'26—dc22
                                                        2004026581

In memory of Hilke Hebisch, 1963–1991

CONTENTS

List of Illustrations   ix

Acknowledgments   xi

Introduction   1

1   Creating the National Image of the Quarries   12

2   Building on the Image   32

3   Institutionalizing the Place   62

4   Enshrining the Quarries   88

5   Re-creating the Image   121

Conclusion   144

Notes   151

Bibliography   185

Index   199

ILLUSTRATIONS

Following Page 120

1. Local residents at the base of Catlin Ledge, 1889

2. Children on the steps of the Pipestone Indian Training School, 1893

3. Charles H. Bennett with pictographs on rocks from the Three Maidens, 1902

4. Men and tourist markings at Winnewissa Falls, ca. 1908

5. Olive Street, looking east, Pipestone, ca. 1914

6. Children at the Three Maidens, ca. 1935

7. Nicollet expedition marker, ca. 1940

8. Roe's Trading Post and Indian Museum, postcard, ca. 1960

9. Roe's Indian Trading Post brochure, ca. 1937

10. Civic and Commerce Association stationery, ca. 1941

11. Pipestone National Monument map, late 1940s

12. Roe's Indian Trading Post brochure, early 1950s

ACKNOWLEDGMENTS

Many people made this project, and its place in my life, possible and more enjoyable. Throughout the research and writing, the staff at the Minnesota Historical Society provided invaluable assistance; Alan Woolworth understood my focus and offered me access to his private collection of Pipestone-related materials, and Dallas Lindgren oriented me to the archives. As research supervisor, Debbie Miller provided not only research space in the Knight suites but also a welcome into a community of historians and an atmosphere that stimulated scholarly discussion and the spirited exchange of ideas; I thank Deb for her consistent interest, keen suggestions, years of friendship, perennials, and inimitable humor. My research benefited from the support of the James J. Hill Reference Library, the American Heritage Center, and the Graduate College of the University of Arizona. I appreciate the generous help I received at archives, including that of Michael Brodhead and Clara Rollen at the National Archives in Kansas City, Tom White and Eileen McCormick at the James J. Hill Reference Library in St. Paul, Herbert Hoover and Margaret Quintal at the University of South Dakota, Betty McSwain at Pipestone National Monument, and David Rambow and Chris Roelfsema-Hummel at the Pipestone County Historical Society.

At an early stage in the work, Hal Rothman, Tsianina Lomawaima, and William Corbett expressed interest in my subject and interpretation. Juan R. García at the University of Arizona directed the dissertation from which this work is adapted and offered encouragement throughout the project. Brian L. Job at the University of British Columbia taught me always to devote myself first to the things that matter most. Friends and colleagues at Carleton College provided critical feedback as the manuscript developed; my thanks go to Sigi Leonhard, Stacy Beckwith, Helena Kaufman, Timothy Raylor, and Michael McNally for their advice and affirmation. I appreciate Joan Sherman's careful copyediting and the editorial guidance and enthusiasm of Gillian Berchowitz and Sharon Rose at Ohio University Press.

Many dear friends deserve my heartfelt gratitude for sustaining me in recent years—Beth Kautz, Eva and Winfried Hebisch, Martyna Tchorz, Manisha Shendge, Donald Boatman, Deb Chaulk, Barry Stentiford, Mimi Anzel, Todd Reasinger, Michael Barbee, Marci French, and Dixie. In Cambridge, Massachusetts, Tim and Nikki Boyle indulged my pilgrimage to Longfellow's grave. Special recognition goes to Sally Kaiser and to Mary Alice and Bob Diebel, who opened their homes to me, particularly on my research trips; Jordan Holiday, Lukas Kautz Koester, and Rebecca Southwick, who surprised me with joy; John Whalen, who stayed around for the conclusion and nagged me as needed; and Christina Rabe Seger, who provided exceptional support, intelligent and insightful critiques, thoughts about generic Indians, emergency aid, travel companionship, vitamins, and unparalleled friendship. Finally, I am deeply grateful to H. Duane Hampton for his steadfast encouragement and friendship, for a mountain sanctuary when I tired of the prairie, and for believing all along that I could—and should—do this; to my late father, Hiram, who, among much else, shared with me his love of both the natural world and good writing; and to my mother, Peggy, who has readily provided all manner of assistance, including rhubarb pies. For this and much, much more, she has my greatest thanks.

Introduction

Those who lack links with a place must forge an
identity through other pasts.

—David Lowenthal, *The Past Is a Foreign Country*

In 1932 the Pipestone Indian Shrine Association published a brochure to explain and enhance the appeal of the catlinite quarries in southwestern Minnesota. Local interpretation claimed the site attracted visitors because of its
"Indian store of fascinating legend and tradition," said to exist "among all the
plains tribes from earliest time, and, little by little, disclosed by them to the
white explorers who won the Indians' confidence." Almost a century earlier,
in summer 1838, Joseph N. Nicollet, one of the first explorers, arrived near the
place and described what he saw around him: "It is a high, grand, and beautiful prairie . . . the view to the south seems limitless, the verdure losing itself
far away in the azure of the sky. The spectacle is full of grandeur because of
its simplicity." A French cartographer, Nicollet explored the lands west of the
upper Mississippi River in an expedition sponsored by the U.S. government.
Crossing the western prairies of what eleven years later became Minnesota
Territory, he eagerly anticipated ascending the Côteau des Prairies, an area
about which he had read in other explorers' narratives. This plateau, compris-
ing a series of gentle ridges, lies nearly a thousand feet above the surrounding
flatter land and divides the watersheds of the Mississippi River to the northeast and the Missouri River basin to the southwest. On reaching the area,
Nicollet extolled the elemental beauties of the vast prairie of undulating tall
grasses interlaced with wetlands and streams.[1]

On the slopes of the Côteau the European explorer approached the most
anticipated destination on his expedition—the pipestone quarries of which

much had been written, mostly by explorers who had never visited the site. Along a shallow stream in a regionally typical expanse of prairie, imposing bluffs of crystalline red Sioux quartzite rose from the grassy earth, accompanied by a small waterfall and pond. At the base of the ridge the surface layer of hard metamorphic rock cracked and exposed lengthy parallel veins of a darker, softer sedimentary stone, prized by several Plains tribes for its deep red hue and suitability for carving. Nicollet marveled at the incongruity of the rock formations and colors on the otherwise unbroken, waving sea of prairie grasses. He noted, "The play of light across the escarpments and the jagged, nearly perpendicular flanks of the valley produce an effect of ravishing beauty . . . the sight is as agreeable as it is unexpected." Sensing the imaginative potential of this landscape, he concluded, "This admirable hill awaits the poet and the painter."[2] In his comments Nicollet proved himself an accurate observer of both geography and American culture. He realized that the quarries would attract visitors from the East, drawn to the place's human history and geological peculiarities. Unlike others who sought to represent the site in static artistic and literary images, Nicollet viewed the landscape at the quarries as an active presence, its abiding character shaping perception and emotion. In this he was the least typical of the nontribal visitors to the place, the one with a perspective closest to the indigenous experience of the land.

During the nineteenth century the unusual natural and tribal history of the quarries entered public awareness in the United States, culminating in 1874 with the founding of the town of Pipestone near the site. Since the seventeenth century Europeans had known of the significance of carved red pipes to many tribes across North America. But not until Meriwether Lewis and William Clark's explorations of the upper Missouri River in 1804 did U.S. citizens encounter tribes living near the source of the stone; their expedition spurred a national fascination with both the pipestone quarries and their associated Indian creation legends.

This study traces over a century of non-Native interest in this tribal place and analyzes how the founders and residents of the town of Pipestone adopted and adapted images of the quarries as "the legendary home of peace to all tribes" for their own purposes. The ways in which European Americans interpreted and portrayed the place's human heritage demonstrated their own personal and communal needs rather than an interest in actual tribal history at the site or respect for tribal beliefs and practices. Pipestone provides a significant example of the larger American process of creating local and national identity

[handwritten marginalia: Nicollet viewed the landscape as an active presence]

through the use of landscape and association with a mythological Indian past. Not an exhaustive or definitive local history, this book is an exploration of how certain characteristic themes in American historical identity developed in this particular place.

When middle-class Yankee businessmen founded the town of Pipestone near the quarries in 1874, they chose the location because of what they perceived as its natural, spiritual, and historical attributes. After his 1836 visit to the area George Catlin's artistic and literary representations of the site "upon the mystic horizon" made the area famous. In the 1850s Henry Wadsworth Longfellow's widely read poetic interpretations of tribal mythology offered a romantic depiction of the quarries—as a timeless place sacred to all tribes and unique on the North American continent—that appealed to the industrializing East. The town's founders and early residents accepted these prevailing images as ethnographically accurate and imbued the landscape with useful meanings that stressed the symbol of the "peace pipe" and the quarries' creation legends. In the late nineteenth century, they adapted elements of Native people's beliefs that met their own cultural needs for a peaceful, historical place considered truly American. They actively used imagery from various tribes' legends of the quarries, divested of their original indigenous meanings, to create a special local identity within a national context and to promote the town beyond the region. The emphasis they placed on the quarries as a site that was central to America's Indian heritage helped Pipestone grow as an agricultural market center and gain both a federal Indian boarding school in the 1890s and, during the New Deal years, a national monument to protect the quarries for future generations.

This book seeks an understanding of the meanings of the popular interest in tribal mythologies and how that interest shaped broader perceptions of the past and the landscape. Pipestone's residents exemplified the national ambivalence immanent in white relations with tribes and in responses to America's rapid industrialization. The local effort to ameliorate that tension identified a revered common ground while relegating tribal spiritual traditions to a safely distant, compressed prehistory—an approach that helped form community and contributed to the growth of American nationalism throughout the late nineteenth and early twentieth centuries.

Pipestone's founders and later residents continuously adapted their conceptions of the quarries' traditions in order to generate a usable past on which to base and promote an identity that was both local and American. Their uses of tribal imagery developed from Catlin's early influential representations and evolved through the town's development and on to the first productions of the town's annual *Song of Hiawatha* pageant in the 1940s and 1950s, which enshrined Longfellow's version of tribal spiritual beliefs about the quarries. Throughout this period members of regional tribes continued visiting the quarries to extract stone and to maintain their traditions. With diverse perspectives on the site's relevance, Native Americans remained present and active on the periphery of Pipestone throughout its history. Tribal members subtly influenced nontribal interpretations of the place and its past, some by cooperating in the town's promotion of Indian imagery and others by seeking more direct control of the quarries and their traditions.

The historical study of a community such as Pipestone reveals much about the formation of American identities as an ongoing process of negotiating collective social meanings of cultural, spiritual, and racial symbols and creating useful forms of national heritage. European Americans' prolonged fascination with aspects of other cultures, especially indigenous ones, indicated points of ambivalence and unsettled definitions within their own communal identity. Following the Civil War, northern Americans sought to recover a sense of national unity by emphasizing values of commercial growth and progress and celebrating historic landscapes. At the same time, nascent concerns about the excesses of industrialization began to erode some middle-class Americans' sense of confidence. Popularly designated as the Indian site of creation and the source of the so-called peace pipe, the quarries filled these needs by serving as a uniquely American place with a usable past. Pipestone's development also reflected the pervasive unease about the place of Native Americans in national society and culture. Reification of and identification with dehistoricized tribal legends helped absorb positive elements of a perceived uncorrupted Indian past into the greater scope of U.S. history. Pipestone illustrates the persistent tension inherent in American attempts to adapt the continent's past for use as a foundation on which to build a cohesive identity. The selective use of a Native sense of sacred traditions made the landscape historically meaningful and worth preserving without compromising secular cultural beliefs in American material progress.

Prior to the visits of Catlin and Nicollet, samples of carved pipestone and vague tales about its source circulated throughout the East. From traders and explorers European Americans increasingly heard of the quarries as the sacred place where many tribes, despite intergroup conflicts, met in peace to extract the revered stone variously associated with tribal creation stories. Successive tales of the quarries as a unique, mystical site prompted Catlin and others to cross the prairie in search of it. Interpretations of the legends that these non-tribal visitors recorded after their encounters with the Dakota and other Plains tribes became the accepted—and expected—representations of the quarries and the basis for claims about their significance. Unlike the oral histories of the quarries, passed down through generations of the tribes whose cultural practices included various pipe ceremonies, the repeated literary descriptions of the site established it as a place of significance for European Americans who otherwise had no personal or cultural reason to be interested in it. Viewing tribes as homogeneous, whites condensed versions of tribal histories and be-liefs and extracted imagery without seeking any Native verification. The repe-tition of the static images removed them from their sources in tribal living cultures and rendered them useful for nontribal purposes. This process of creating "imaginary Indians" warrants analysis because it continues to shape perceptions of tribes and relations among people of different cultures.

Most of the legends presented to the reading public depicted the quarries as the sacred place of creation of the first pipe and, often, of the first tribal people. The main variations on this genesis theme produced similar senses of significance. According to one general legend, a beneficent Great Spirit cre-ated humans out of the deep red stone at the site and taught them to carve and smoke the pipe in reverent remembrance. Other versions tell of horrible warfare in the area, the bloodshed of which turned the surrounding stone red, or of the slaughter of buffalo that soaked the ground with their blood. Some variations recount a drowning flood after the warfare, with a few survivors hiding near the quarries under boulders—a collection of massive granite rocks known later as the Three Maidens. With or without a deluge, the Great Spirit is said to have instructed the remaining people to revere the stone and its source, to create the pipe from the stone, and to use it to settle their differ-ences peacefully in a sacramental ceremony. Writers such as Catlin and Long-fellow and later settlers at Pipestone embraced and embellished these themes, generalizing to make them culturally applicable for all tribes on the North American continent and readily making comparisons to their own cultural ref-erence points in phrases such as "Indian Eden" or depictions of the Great Spirit as a Christlike figure. Such descriptions made the site both safe and exotic, ap-pealing because of its distant past associations with a noble, vanishing people, subdued by their romantic spiritual beliefs.

By the time U.S. exploration west of the Mississippi began, the Dakota peoples had established political hegemony on the northern Plains and the prairie surrounding the Côteau. With Ojibwe expansion into the northern woods in the seventeenth century, the Dakota bands had moved westward and developed a horse-centered culture that allowed them to dominate the sparsely populated grasslands. For several centuries early Plains tribes, including the Oto, Omaha, Pawnee, Iowa, and other descendants of the Oasis and Mississippian cultures, had visited the quarries and extracted stone for ceremonial purposes and for trading, but until the arrival of the Dakota no tribes resided permanently in the area. Different bands within the larger Dakota group had their own beliefs about the quarries, as did other tribes in the broader region, such as the Mandan, Pawnee, and Kiowa. Some stories about the place involved a white buffalo, and some featured snakes, but all regional tribes ascribed a degree of importance to pipe ceremonies and to the quarries, and they identified the source of the red carving stone as sacred ground. By the early eighteenth century the Ihanktonwan or Yankton, a Nakota band, attained control of the area and negotiated with the United States, in the Treaty of 1858, to reserve the quarries from settlement. Other tribes that traditionally quarried pipestone agreed that the site needed to be preserved, but they never accepted Yankton claims to the right to negotiate on behalf of the quarries or to represent other tribal interests in them. To varying degrees the Yankton and other regional tribes opposed the sale of pipestone for nonceremonial uses, a practice that became more widespread in the mid-nineteenth century with the creation of popularized imagery about the quarries and then escalated with the founding of Pipestone. Although the establishment of the Pipestone National Monument (PNM) in 1937 strictly regulated pipestone extraction and commercial carving, controversy over the quarries and the use of the stone persists throughout the region, as does tension stemming from European American incursions into tribal spiritual practices, such as pipe ceremonies.[3]

Recognizing the continual presence of tribes at the quarries, this study of Pipestone's relationship to the place includes tribal actions as part of the history of the area. Because of the sensitivity of the issue to tribal members who visit the site as a spiritual practice, the study does not attempt to interpret a cultural viewpoint from the historical tribal members involved at the quarries. Out of respect for the Yankton's ability to speak on their own behalf, this work describes their actions without ascribing meaning to them and shows how tribal people participated in developments at the quarries rather than just responding to events. To presume the authority to give voice to tribal perspectives would, in essence, perpetuate the cultural imperialism that characterized behavior in Pipestone and throughout the United States. Tribal governments represent themselves and their interests in relations with the federal government and American society at large. Tribes and their individual members hold diverse views on the subject of the quarries; their religious and personal perspectives cannot be generalized.

Following the examples of Robert Berkhofer Jr. and Daniel Francis, use of the term *Indian* in this study generally indicates the imagery created and employed by European Americans, whereas the terms *Native* or *tribal* refer to actual indigenous peoples. At places with multiple cultural meanings it is important to recognize the role of human imagination in creating narratives of the past. Questioning accepted heritage can open it to discussion and allow for an appreciation of the diversity of human cultures. Analysis and understanding of the motives that led to the nontribal creation and continued use of images of the pipestone quarries can make genuine cultural exchanges and dialogues more possible and potentially clearer.[4]

In an unpublished 1960 manuscript for his later administrative history of Pipestone National Monument, Robert Murray suggested a possible connection between the popular images of the quarries and the town's sense of itself. He observed that Pipestone's citizenry generated a mass of promotional literature based on the works of Catlin and Longfellow and on their own experiences at the place. Murray did not further analyze the development but commented that "these works have yet to be brought together for study and evaluation. It would seem, though, that they must have had some influence in the formation of local attitudes toward the Quarries."[5] Even though he limited his own work to the study of federal government activity in the area, without further analysis of the images he recognized as important, Murray saw the potential for a scholarly examination of Pipestone's identity.

Because of the preponderance of literary and visual representations of the quarries in the years before Pipestone's founding in 1874, its initial ideological basis developed prior to its actual social and economic growth. Formation of the town's identity, therefore, began before the town existed and continued after its founding in overlapping phases as different European American individuals' and groups' perceptions about and experiences at the place motivated them to act. Their actions provide distinctive themes in Pipestone's history, phases around which to organize an analysis of the process of building on earlier developments and modifying local heritage to address the needs of the time. In all its stages, Pipestone has exemplified common behaviors and beliefs about the tribal past in the United States during the nineteenth and twentieth centuries. Philip Deloria's work on popular uses of Indian imagery to claim cultural authority and to stress Americanness demonstrates a broad pattern of comparable actions by others across the country. Differentiating the expansive, linear narrative of experienced human history from the monolithic symbols and idealized stories of a compressed past that compose heritage, David Glassberg and David Lowenthal's studies show how conceptions about the past and national origin myths can help create collective identity and a sense of belonging to a place, a process that occurred repeatedly in Pipestone's development. With a different perspective on the creation of accepted heritage, Joan W. Scott analyzes historical identity formation and its maintenance through the repetition of representations, both of which she considers strategic and cohesive activities. While heritage is often creatively assembled and can depart from recorded history in its presentation or lack of details, people's experience of heritage is often emotionally charged, very authentic for them, and useful to communal purposes.[6]

In the preliminary stage of Pipestone's layered growth throughout the early nineteenth century, prominent explorers (including Lewis and Clark as well as Henry Rowe Schoolcraft), creative portrayers of Indian themes (such as George Catlin and Henry Wadsworth Longfellow), and scientists (particularly Ferdinand Hayden and John Wesley Powell) extracted culturally appealing images from tribal beliefs about the quarries, published them widely, and collectively created a nationally known site. Part of an evolving American identity that stressed a common national inheritance, their writings established the essential, repeated images of the quarries—a unique place on the vast prairie, sacred ground, site of peace for all Indians, stone quarried since before human memory—that set expectations for the early settlers in the area and served as the foundation for later descriptions and promotions of the place. Attracted by Catlin and Longfellow's popular images, the homogeneous group of town founders—mainly middle-class, white, Protestant merchants from New England and the upper Midwest—saw the quarries as they expected them to be and used their residence at the place authoritatively to promote their town widely. They behaved in ways customary to their time, with the quarries providing a cultural landscape from which they constructed a usable heritage that appealed to the masses but was removed from actual tribal history at the site.

Continually seeking national legitimization of their place, by the 1890s the town leaders were using the site's perceived tribal significance as the grounds for lobbying the federal government to build an Indian boarding school at the quarries. In step with trends in national Indian policy, Pipestone's prominent residents saw themselves as progressive and reform-minded, and they considered the quarries' growing reputation as a place of peace sufficient justification for the establishment of a government boarding school at the site. Toward the turn of the twentieth century, Pipestone's leaders sought to solidify their town by lobbying for federal aid. They continued this pursuit well into the 1900s, a behavior more prominent for economic reasons in the West but useful when seeking national attention in the Midwest—a region already convinced that its geographic location demonstrated its symbolic place in the heart of the country. Full of a sense of American exceptionalism, Pipestone promoters used the quarries to illustrate what made their nation special, often sending carved samples of pipestone to dignitaries abroad and encouraging people within and outside the country to visit "America's only peace shrine."

Participating in a renewed, widespread movement to salvage aspects of tribal traditions that could be used as national historical symbols, local women led the community's preservation movement to seek federal protection of the quarries as part of America's heritage. With the support of others in town, their efforts led to the 1937 establishment of Pipestone National Monument, the first Park Service unit in Minnesota. The general pattern of the citizens' preservation work in Pipestone paralleled the activities of other Americans in an era of increasing interest in identifying and setting aside for posterity important cultural and natural sites, such as efforts to preserve the Indian ruins in the Southwest that were considered part of the same timeless indigenous past as the quarries. Although located in the Midwest, a large region with few Indian sites deemed historically relevant, Pipestone is representative of Americans' intense conflation of local identity and national significance.

By the 1940s and 1950s, the successful establishment of a permanent federal guardian at the quarries led the town's civic and commercial leaders to reassert themselves as cultural custodians of local Indian heritage. Adapting national trends from earlier in the century, an active cross section of residents expressed what they considered their traditional and inherited right to interpret the place's past through the establishment of trading posts and museums and the community's production of the annual *Song of Hiawatha* pageant near the quarries. This phase of Pipestone's identity development resembled that

9

seen with historical reenactments and museums elsewhere in the United States, particularly in the communal sense of custodianship over carefully defined local heritage and identity based on generalized images of American Indians.

Throughout the eighty years covered in this study, Pipestone's population barely exceeded five thousand, and the town has remained a relatively remote farming community on the vast prairie. Yet the same qualities that make it provincial also make it significant and representative of the common experiences that constitute American history. The people who promoted Pipestone and sought to keep the quarries widely known consistently spoke and wrote of the place and themselves as characteristically American. Each successive group of promoters saw the site and their community as contributing to national heritage, as being an important part of larger American culture as they envisioned it. At the grassroots level Pipestone's merchants, journalists, teachers, church groups, fraternal organizations, and women's associations took part in defining for themselves what it meant to be American where they were. Pipestone provides a site-specific example of activities typical within late-nineteenth- and early-twentieth-century American history. It demonstrates the creation, acceptance, and repetition of historical representations central to collective identity, a process that occurs at both local and national levels.

Although they acted in ways typical of proud residents of thousands of other towns across the United States and always stressed what they considered the "American" qualities of their town, the succession of leaders in Pipestone simultaneously maintained that the town was uncommonly significant because of the uniqueness of its setting and its presettlement past. They considered the quarries both a national treasure and a place that made their locality special and unlike any other in the country. This intersection of local and national identity, of being at once singular and part of the whole, *e pluribus unum,* is quintessentially American. From a national perspective, identity requires an impersonal interest in many places, with a broad array of sites contributing to the totality. At any given place, however, people invest themselves in seeing their particular locality not just as part of the whole but as representative of it. They localize the ideological foundation of national identity, interpreting it to fit the world within view and giving the idea of America a familiar form and a place.

The men and women who moved to the quarries built Pipestone from an idea, from images that were of and created by people they had not met. Because of these preformulated perceptions of the area, the site became a known

geographic location before the town existed. But the town of Pipestone became and remained a place—and an interesting one—because of what happened there. Since centuries before Nicollet drew his map, the people who
arrived at the quarries interacted with the natural and cultural landscape and
developed their own meanings for it. Later, Pipestone began as a similarly collective concept. Whether for tribal people or for European Americans, human
relationship to the land personalized the idea of the quarries, and the experiences of individuals there made it a place. Like its name, the history and identity of Pipestone began with the land and continue inseparable from it.

ONE

Creating the National Image
of the Quarries

After visiting the pipestone quarries in 1836, the American artist George Catlin wrote: "Whether it has been an Indian Eden or not, or whether the thunderbolts of Indian Jupiter are actually forged here, it is nevertheless a place renowned in Indian heraldry and tradition, which I hope I may be able to fathom and chronicle, as explanatory of many of my anecdotes and traditionary superstitions of Indian history, which I have given, and *am giving,* to the world."[1] This lengthy single sentence exemplifies the ways in which the American reading public became aware of and fascinated by the pipestone quarries as both a cultural and geological site in southwestern Minnesota. It also set a precedent for the representation by nontribal people of this tribally significant place. Throughout the nineteenth century a series of explorers, self-styled ethnographers, and scientists visited the quarries and described the area in journals and published essays. Like Catlin, who fashioned himself an artist, explorer, and ethnographer, individuals in these three groups wrote from positions of authoritative knowledge. In overlapping, successive phases, first explorers, then amateur ethnographers, and finally scientists consistently employed a kind of descriptive language that reinforced certain images of the quarries and their past. Their writing and illustrations helped to make the tribal site into a nationally known place and influenced how successive generations of European Americans perceived the quarries. Their literary and visual images served as a foundation on which later inhabitants of the area built, using local residence as the basis of authority to adapt and to promote perceptions of the place and to convey its heritage as part of America's developing national identity.

Since the time of early contact with East Coast tribes, European settlers had known of the prevalence of pipe ceremonies in many tribal cultures. Scholarly estimates regarding the time of the quarries' discovery vary from 900 to 1,600 C.E., but most agree that tribes throughout the Great Plains traded pipestone widely and prized it for carving.[2] By the mid-eighteenth century nontribal awareness of this unusual stone and the practices associated with it turned to curiosity about its source. The mysterious site was affiliated with a host of legends about creation and rumored to lie deep in the heart of the continent. The process of exploration and description through which the pipestone quarries became widely known in the United States took its form largely from the persons who told of them, the language and imagery they used, and the national cultural context that gave the site such widespread appeal.[3]

The majority of formative and influential writing about the quarries occurred in the antebellum nineteenth century. Through land acquisitions such as the Louisiana Purchase and conflicts such as the Mexican-American War, the United States expanded to encompass much of the territory west of the Mississippi, including the area that would become Minnesota. In this early national period America's population grew steadily through natural increase and immigration. Urban areas along the Atlantic expanded, and farmers pressed westward in search of unplowed land and the opportunity for agricultural prosperity. The federal government often sponsored exploration of new territory in an effort to support internal development through orderly settlement and the survey of resources. Officially and otherwise, representatives of the United States began to investigate the lands to the west, returning with tales and illustrations of previously uncharted country and extolling the attributes of their continent. In effect this imperialist activity located places within American territory on which to base an emerging national identity, removed from the British past and suffused with faith in an expansive, divinely ordained, prosperous future.[4]

As America's population increased in the early 1800s, the government sought to acquire land for settlement and to do so peacefully, if possible. To avoid the economic and human costs of armed conflict while promoting national growth, the United States negotiated treaties with tribes, exchanging Native ancestral lands in the East for less-populated—but far from empty—areas to the west, initiating the reservation system. Consequently, residents of the states along the Atlantic increasingly had no contact with tribal people and relied more and more on the press and literature for representations of them. With this physical and mental distance, romantically stylized images of the so-called Noble Savage in an unspoiled wilderness helped assuage the ambivalence that whites had long felt toward the tribes. After the forced removal of eastern tribes to territory on the Great Plains in the 1830s, contact between European Americans in the East and tribal people diminished steadily, becoming literary instead of personal. Conceptions of Indians, removed from time and space, reduced real people to caricatures and gained popularity throughout the 1800s. Toward the end of the century Plains tribes in particular began to symbolize "Indian America," perceived as a monolithic culture that was vanishing on the horizon—part of a West both exotic and familiar to those in the East.[5]

EXPLORERS CREATE EARLY IMAGES OF THE PLACE

Within this early-nineteenth-century context, a growing reading public—largely white and urban and predominantly from the middle and upper classes—waited eagerly for reports from those who traveled west of the Mississippi and often published their travel journals. While George Catlin claimed to be the first nontribal person to visit the pipestone quarries, he was not the first to describe them and had been lured there by the tales of others. A series of explorers were the first accepted authorities to write about the site, although they had not actually visited it. Their written accounts assumed credibility from their travels to new territories and from the explorers' own role as eyewitnesses to remote tribal cultures. Following an established tradition of exploration narratives, their writings provided vicarious adventure to those who stayed safely at home. Such early explorers as Father Louis Hennepin in 1680 and Pierre Charles Le Sueur in 1700 had written of pipe ceremonies and tribal customs and identified a branch of the Dakota with the "red-stone quarry" in the territory that became southwestern Minnesota. In the late eighteenth century Jonathan Carver first mentioned the actual quarries with some specific detail in his journal. Published in 1778 in London and distributed widely in both England and America, Carver's narrative told of "a large mountain of red marble where all the neighboring nations resort for stone to make pipes of." Carver set a pattern that later explorers followed. He made note of the physical setting of the quarries on the Côteau des Prairies, southwest of the Minnesota River and northeast of the Missouri River, and he exaggerated the site's attributes. More ethnographically, he also commented on the reputation of the site as a place of peace among tribes. As he put it, "Even those who hold perpetual wars in all other parts meet here in peace."[6] These two descriptive elements situated the quarries in geographic terms and attributed certain values to them.

Influenced by this initial focus on exotic Indian practices in an unusual, distant place, the first U.S. citizens to explore the region officially, Meriwether Lewis and William Clark, included the quarries in their journals. Although they did not actually visit the site on their way up the Missouri in 1804 and 1805, their status as government representatives who interacted with local tribes gave their descriptions unquestioned authority. The growth of public education and literacy meant that excerpts from the Corps of Discovery's journals later reached an audience eager to read about places they would likely never see. Lewis and Clark's travels contributed to the emerging national identity that was tied to expanding across the continent and possessing a new landscape. The language they used defined new territory and also created a lasting impression of the quarries.

The national explorers' journals contained two images essential to establishing the perception of the quarries. Claiming an interpreter for the Dakota as his informational source, Lewis referred to the Côteau area as "remarkable for furnishing a red stone, of which the savages make their most esteemed pipes," a place where "all nations are at peace with each other." Like his contemporaries, Lewis used the term *savages* generically and not necessarily consciously, with an element of violence implied as a tribal attribute that augmented the exceptional status of the neutral quarries. According to the tribe's interpreter on site, Pierre Dorion, the importance of procuring the stone and the spiritual value associated with pipes induced tribes to agree to share access to the site. Such statements stressed the uniqueness of the quarries, in both geological and cultural terms, and set a precedent for regarding the site as exceptional on the continent. To emphasize further the special nature of the place, Lewis continued, "The banks of the creek are sacred; even tribes that are at war meet without hostility at these quarries, which possess a right of asylum. Thus we find even among savages certain principles deemed sacred." After Clark's return to the East, the publication of the journals included a map of the expedition's journey. The notation at the Red Pipestone River read, "Here the different tribes meet in friendship and collect stone for pipes."[7] This official exploration marked the beginning of the quarries' reputation as the sacred site of peace for tribes who used the carved ceremonial pipe. The authoritative combination of geological, cultural, and spiritual descriptions created significant and lasting ways of thinking about the place.

Other explorers with and without government backing elaborated on these themes. Whether they actually saw the quarries, which was a rare occurrence until midcentury, or knew of them only secondhand, travelers such as Stephen Long, Giacomo Beltrami, and Prince Maximilian all considered the place important enough to mention its associated traditions in their journals. These narrative acts bolstered the emerging tradition of European Americans explaining the tribal significance of the quarries to each other, with little or no input from tribal members.[8]

Although his 1820 expedition up the Mississippi River did not bring him near the Côteau, Henry Rowe Schoolcraft yielded to the lure of pipestone and expanded on what he had heard of its source. On his travels Schoolcraft obtained a sample of the stone and reported on its softness and its difference in polish from marble. He was also the first to assert, erroneously, that the stone hardened on exposure to air, a description often repeated by those who had not quarried it. Amid noting the quarries' location on the distant prairie and recording what he had heard about the strata of rock there, Schoolcraft added a significant element to the tales of the site: "The Indians go once a year to procure supplies, and as it has been resorted to for a very long period, the excavations are said to be extensive."[9] Through such imagery he suggested not only that the pipestone quarries were unique within U.S. territory but also that what archaeological evidence was known suggested that tribes had a prehistoric presence at the site. The quarries bore witness to antiquity, in a vague and distant way—something Americans increasingly desired from their continent. The place served as something old and distinct enough to compete with European classical ruins. Its antiquity was sufficiently removed from the national sociopolitical narrative to avoid any suggestion of the societal decay that Americans believed characterized the European nations against which they defined themselves. As Americans continued to construct their national identity, they drew from a perceived timeless Indian past as part of their country's premodern heritage.[10]

Schoolcraft's narrative also reinforced an image of tribes as culturally static—an image that had grown popular in American culture. Seen as having extracted stone from the same place and in the same way since before written accounts, if not before memory, tribes appeared frozen in an indistinct past and removed from linear time as experienced in the eastern United States. This perception of tribes and tribal cultures as outside national history and unchanging since before European contact made images of them a useful, indigenous foil for American measures of social progress. Scholars such as Philip Deloria and Robert Berkhofer Jr. argue that the emerging culture of the United States associated the idea of precontact tribal civilization with traditions uncorrupted by European decay and relegated tribal societies to a different realm, undefined by history. Beliefs about the pipestone quarries conformed to this national pattern in their removal of tribes from known linear time and the association of tribal people with the mythic past of the place.[11]

Following his earlier explorations, Schoolcraft traveled throughout the larger area numerous times before the Civil War. He never visited the quarries, but he believed in their significance. Schoolcraft relied on the journal of independent explorer Philander Prescott for a contribution on pipestone in his own 1852 *Information respecting the History, Condition, and Prospects of the Indian Tribes of the United States;* the last of the government publications to feature exploration narratives regarding the quarries, it appeared in print after both George Catlin and Joseph Nicollet wrote of their trips to the place. Prescott claimed to have visited the pipestone quarries as early as 1830—six years prior to Catlin's trip—which would have made him the first U.S. citizen at the site. Like others of his time, Prescott disregarded Joseph Laframboise as an earlier visitor to the quarries because of ethnicity. A local American Fur Company trader of mixed tribal and European heritage, Laframboise married the daughter of the prominent Dakota leader Sleepy Eye, operated a trading post on the Côteau, and later acted as Nicollet's guide and liaison. Seemingly disgruntled, Prescott contended, "Mr. Catlin claims to be the first man that visited the pipe-stone, but this is not so. In 1830 I found a 6 lb. cannon-ball there." Prescott's journal, discovered after his death, includes an explanation of the cannonball's use in breaking rocks at the quarries and a synopsis of one of the legends of a leaping rock near the ridge. Long a rival and detractor of Catlin's, Schoolcraft may have included Prescott's assertion in an effort to discredit him.[12]

The first government-sponsored visitor to the quarries, the trained cartographer Joseph Nicollet, submitted his initial report to Congress in 1841, five years after his exploratory mapping expedition to the upper Mississippi territory with the company of John Frémont. In his journal Nicollet devoted an entire lengthy section to his trip to the quarries and his enchantment with the

Côteau, a sentiment reflected in his official report. Supplementing his extensive geographic and geological notes about the area's unique features, his report included further additions to pipestone imagery. In reference to George Catlin's self-heralded, unsponsored 1836 trip to the site, Nicollet prefaced his description with the observation that "this locality, having acquired some celebrity, may be specially noticed." He then relayed what he had learned of tribal beliefs about the place. Arriving at the quarries in the midst of a sudden summer thunderstorm, Nicollet commented on the appropriateness of the weather at the location: "The idea of the young Indians, who are very fond of the marvelous, is that it has been opened by the Great Spirit; and that, whenever it is visited by them, they are saluted by lightning and thunder. We may cite, as a coincidence, our own experience in confirmation of this tradition." Fair weather favored the remainder of their days at the site, but Nicollet's writing emphasized the belief that a Great Spirit had given the stone to local tribes, making the site spiritually charged. Having a good rapport with local elders, Nicollet heard a different story from older tribal members, who explained that the annual pursuit of migrating bison led to the unearthing of the quarries. He commented, "It may be well imagined how interesting such a discovery must have been to a people who attach so much importance to the pipe, and who were thus furnished with a material bearing their favorite red color."[13] Nicollet considered it a particularly fortuitous find in a place otherwise consisting of exceedingly hard quartzite.

Like other explorers and being of a romantic bent, Nicollet found that the area, set in a treeless, low valley on the rolling prairie, had a "very picturesque appearance" that would "deserve a special description if this were the place to do so." By no means was it a spectacular landscape that would draw attention to itself. Rather, the attraction of the pipestone quarries came from the imagery they abundantly provided, allowing the site to become mystified in American culture, regardless of its actual uses to regional tribes. Nicollet noted in his journal that "the Indians have no superstitions about the red rock that do not also pertain to other circumstances of their lives when they look for a plant, an animal, or an enemy." Again he commented on Catlin's writing, noting, "There have been stories written recently on this subject that, when we tell them, greatly amuse the Indians and those who have lived a long time among them." Nicollet achieved better relations with the tribes in the area than American explorers and informal ethnographers had done, but he became ill in 1841 and was unable to revise his report before his death two years later. His experiences and authority might have affected public opinion to a greater extent had his personality inclined him to capitalize publicly on his achievements. Nicollet did not live long enough to see his journals published or to comment on the popularized stories of the quarries, with which he may have disagreed. Instead, he left only a short government report that contributed to images of the place and a detailed map of how to find it.[14]

CREATIVE REPRESENTATIONS OF THE QUARRIES ON PAPER AND CANVAS

Published too late to make any difference in the public eye, descriptions by Nicollet and Prescott could not match the popularity of George Catlin's writing and paintings. One of the most popular artists of the nineteenth century and a prolific writer, Catlin gained notoriety as the self-described "first white" visitor to the sacred quarries. His 1836 visit testified to the site's significance and established a lasting foundation for descriptive pipestone imagery. Catlin and his colleagues—essayists, artists, and poets—drew on some of the themes and information provided by earlier explorers, but they wrote more extensively and in accessible prose directed at a larger audience. Although still interested in tribal practices, these writers focused more on what they perceived as the site's romantic past and generated more elaborate images to influence their readers. Brian Dippie, a scholar of Catlin and popular Indian imagery, has noted that they considered tribes "the most intrinsically American of themes: nothing could be more native than the natives, and those who wrote about them or painted them . . . had a special claim upon the nation."[15] By their hands the pipestone quarries became less a geographic site with its own human and temporal history and more a setting for an epic, timeless Indian drama that predated the grand national narrative.

The son of Connecticut Yankees and a native of Pennsylvania, George Catlin was both typical and atypical of the amateur ethnographers and aspired to be a contributor to popular culture. Exceptional in the extent of his travels in the mid-1830s among tribes along the Missouri River, he used his unusual role as an experienced eyewitness to promote himself and to bolster his credibility. In addition to the almost five hundred paintings in his touring Indian Gallery, Catlin's extensively illustrated two-volume *Letters and Notes on the Manners, Customs, and Conditions of the North American Indians,* a compilation of some of his earlier articles for the *New York Commercial Advertiser* and other writings, was published in 1841 and contained a combination of self-promotion and what has been called *salvage ethnography.* The phrase denotes a determination to preserve on paper and canvas what Catlin and other European Americans in the East considered vanishing Native cultures; their power to define and to preserve what they interpreted as indigenous traditions was vital to the nineteenth-century creation of a national heritage.

This sense of purpose mingled freely with Catlin's romantic preconceptions about tribal beliefs and his desire to be the expert who would interpret them to the rest of the country, as demonstrated in his professed hope of being the one to give "traditionary superstitions of Indian history" to the world. He and his peers saw contemporary, evolving society as a contaminant for the perceived pure Indian cultures, grounded in a safer, timeless, unchanging past central to American identity, something he hoped to capture for posterity. Intending to boost sales, he created "certificates of authenticity" to accompany his paintings, and the claim of expert, authoritative knowledge infused his writings. His widely circulated self-portrait, in which he stands at an easel painting a tribal group assembled before him, visually reinforced his chosen identity and gave the larger public an image with which to associate him. Whether or not he intended to do so, Catlin became the first individual to appropriate and to begin marketing tribal lore about the pipestone quarries. This use of aspects of tribal culture for personal or communal gain was typically American, as shown in Philip Deloria's work on white uses of "Indianness," and it was the first instance in a long tradition of commodification of the place. Catlin and his colleagues clearly possessed the cultural power, ability, and opportunity required to appropriate and redefine other cultures' beliefs for their own benefit or advancement.[16]

Early in his two chapters on his trip to the quarries, Catlin claimed to have met in St. Louis with Gen. William Clark, who showed him a collection of carved stone pipes. He asserted that Clark provided information about the quarries as the source of the pipestone and authorized him to tell the world about this regionally important place. Catlin consciously crafted his own image as an expert, then freely embellished on the main descriptive themes established by previous explorers—that the quarries were unique and had been sacred to many tribes for countless generations. He concentrated his writings about the quarries on timeless tribal tales of creation, using phrases such as "Indian Eden," "sacred fountain of the pipe," and "on the mystic horizon" that made the site seem both familiar and yet shrouded in Native mysticism. In a romantic search for an "Indian Muse," Catlin rhapsodized, "Thus far have

I strolled . . . for the purpose of reaching *classic ground.* . . . This place is great (not in history, for there is none of it, but) in traditions, and stories, of which this Western world is full and rich." This theme of timelessness and a place outside recorded history would be repeated later and become central to ideas about the quarries. Catlin described the ground itself as majestic and inspiring awe, possessing "a sublime grandeur" that "without the aid of traditionary fame, would be appropriately denominated a paradise." Making clear the importance of his visit, he hastened to note that he was "encamped on, and writing from, the very rock where the Great Spirit stood when he consecrated the *pipe of peace,*" and a tone of authority permeated both of his lengthy letters about his experiences on the Côteau.[17]

Catlin described the landscape around him, often in exaggerated terms. To his eyes the quartzite bluff overlooking the quarries was "the summit of a precipice thirty feet high, extending two miles in length and much of the way polished" and "a perpendicular wall of close-grained, compact quartz . . . running nearly North and South with its face to the West." From this advantageous perch, he had a clear view of the "far-famed quarry or fountain of the Red Pipe." There he claimed to witness "the poor Indian . . . humbly propitiating the guardian spirits of the place" before digging stone for a pipe. Emphasizing the timelessness of this supposedly pantribal activity, he explained that the place had been "visited for centuries past by all the neighboring tribes . . . that such has been the custom, there is not a shadow of doubt." Catlin stressed his authority in the matter derived from travels that were "witnessed by hundreds and thousands of Indians of different tribes, now living," from whom he had "personally drawn the information" that he eagerly sought to paint and to publish.[18]

Catlin's work provided images of an exotic and mysterious but peaceful and natural Eden—"an anomaly in nature" that appealed particularly to East Coast urban residents who had never traveled west. Reinforcing his written descriptions, he sketched and later painted the pipestone quarries. Completed in 1837, his painting *Pipestone Quarry, on the Côteau des Prairies* provided the first visual representation of both the place and the tribal activity there, intimately associating landscape and human tradition. In it, the expanse of green prairie contrasts with the intense red tones of both the quartzite bluff that establishes the horizon and a dark red open-pit quarry being worked by scantily clad Indians in the foreground, as well as outcrops of stone running in parallel veins across the canvas. On the far right edge of the painting Catlin included "a group of five stupendous boulders" where "the guardian spirits of the place reside," as well as a tiny figure making an offering in supplication before digging pipestone. The vivid painting made the quarries appear as a dramatic landscape, and it toured with his Indian Gallery in the mid-nineteenth century throughout the United States and Europe before becoming part of the Smithsonian Institution's collection in the late 1870s, shortly after his death.[19]

To enhance his influence on the subject of the quarries, Catlin sent samples of pipestone to a geologist in the East to have it analyzed. Others, such as Lewis and Clark and Schoolcraft, had obtained carved stone earlier, but they had never submitted it for analysis. When geologist Charles Jackson identified the sample as a "new" stone and published his findings, he reinforced the perception of the quarries as uniquely American, with prehistoric associations. That the stone soon became known in scientific circles as "catlinite" only heightened Catlin's reputation. With his prolific art and writing Catlin hoped to receive official recognition and to become the congressionally favored Indian expert, backing that would provide both funding and stability. However, an ability to offend powerful men in the territories and a decided lack of political acumen in Washington combined to deny him the official sponsorship he desired. Nonetheless, the upper- and middle-class literate public embraced his works as authentic and based their impressions of tribal cultures on his representations.[20]

Somewhat a rival of Catlin's, Henry Rowe Schoolcraft acquired the coveted government sponsorship for his ethnographic work. Married to an Ojibwe woman, Schoolcraft served as an Indian agent in the upper Great Lakes region throughout the 1820s and 1830s, and he claimed credibility from both his sources and his local experiences. By the 1840s his writings (particularly the *Algic Researches* of 1839), his personal connections, and his ability to garner political favor earned him the reputation of an expert on tribal cultures, particularly on the legends that he found most fascinating. Federal backing for his multivolume *History, Condition, and Prospect of the Indian Tribes,* his previous explorations, and the artistic assistance of Seth Eastman compensated for his lack of extensive travels west of the Mississippi. Although more a self-professed realist than the romantic Catlin, Schoolcraft exhibited a typical antebellum fascination with Indian legends in his works. A tendency to adapt folktales to his audience's cultural references and to dehistoricize tribal people and their experiences marked much of his writing and made his work representative of the American view of the nation's Indian heritage. More significantly for the future reputation of the pipestone quarries, Schoolcraft wrote at length on the Algonquin tale of the historical Hiawatha, the peacemaker of the Iroquois League in northern New York. In the process, he failed to distinguish the Hiawatha tale from the Onondaga and Ojibwe myths of the trickster characters Nana'b'oozo and Manabozho and thereby imposed cultural homogeneity on Great Lakes tribes.[21]

In the 1850s Catlin's view of the quarries as the site of creation and Schoolcraft's tamed, mythic hero of the Great Lakes converged in the poetic mind of Henry Wadsworth Longfellow. Influenced by a summer spent in northern Michigan and accepting both popular ethnographic writers as sufficiently accurate sources of cultural and historical information, Longfellow relied on their writing for the inspiration for his lengthy poem *The Song of Hiawatha*. Longfellow joined James Fenimore Cooper, Edgar Allan Poe, Nathaniel Hawthorne, and others as key figures in the mid-nineteenth-century development of a distinctly American literary tradition that drew variously on indigenous themes. Longfellow was the first poet to attempt to create an American epic. His writing emphasized the imagery of the mythic past and the peaceful nature of the archetypal Noble Savage, fading westward before the arrival of European civilization.

Longfellow's poem followed the established tradition of repeating exaggerated descriptions of the pipestone quarries (the "mountain of red marble") and of their reputation as a sacred site associated with tribal origin myths. Part 1 of *The Song of Hiawatha* opened with these lines:

> On the Mountains of the Prairie,
> On the great Red Pipe-stone Quarry,
> Gitche Manito, the Mighty,
> He the Master of Life, descending,
> On the red crags of the Quarry,
> Stood erect and called the nations,
> Called the tribes of men together.

After creating a river that flowed over the bluffs, Gitche Manito established the sacred pipe ceremony for all tribes:

> From the red stone of the quarry
> With his hand he broke a fragment,

> Moulded it into a pipe-head . . .
> And erect upon the mountains,
> Gitche Manito, the mighty,
> Smoked the calumet, the Peace-Pipe,
> As a signal to the nations.

As the smoke drifted across the continent, leaders of twelve major tribes—Delaware, Mohawk, Choctaw, Comanche, Blackfeet, Pawnee, Huron, Dakota, and others—interpreted the summons and convened at the quarries:

> All the warriors drawn together
> By the signal of the Peace-Pipe,
> To the Mountains of the Prairie,
> To the great Red Pipe-stone Quarry,
> And they stood there on the meadow,
> With their weapons and their war-gear.

In his great compassion, Gitche Manito told them of all the gifts of the land he had created for them and asked why they were not content with the bounties of the earth and why they waged war on each other. The Spirit instructed them to learn the pipe ceremony from him and to find strength in unity:

> Bury your war-clubs and your weapons,
> Break the red stone from this quarry,
> Mould and make it into Peace-Pipes . . .
> Smoke the calumet together,
> And as brothers live henceforward!

The attending tribes did as instructed, letting the waters of the stream wash the blood from their hands before digging the stone and crafting pipes that they took back to their people, forever thereafter following the lessons of the Great Spirit at the pipestone quarries. Longfellow's romantic depiction of warring tribes pacified through spiritual practice complemented national Indian policy with its prominent belief in the "civilizing" effect of religion. In an era of increasing sectional tensions, imagery of a peaceful prehistory may have ameliorated anxiety about the country's future, and Longfellow's depiction of Gitche Manito as a Christlike figure presenting twelve tribes, akin to disciples, with a commemorative ceremony made Native beliefs seem familiar to his audience.[22]

Throughout *Hiawatha*, Longfellow freely confused and conflated Ojibwe and Dakota cultures. He based his writing on popularly accepted authorities and provided a saga with enormous appeal for a reading society that continued to grow with the spread of public education. The regular, lilting meter of his work was suitable for recitation and made the lines easy to memorize, and his poem quickly gained popularity, selling over eleven thousand copies in its first month and becoming a national literary phenomenon.[23]

Far from noting any fallacies in the poem and perhaps flattered by references to his earlier work, Schoolcraft dedicated his 1856 *The Myth of Hiawatha and other Oral Legends* to Longfellow, whom he claimed "demonstrated . . . that the theme of the nature lore reveals one of the true sources of our literary independence." Longfellow, like Schoolcraft and others, associated tribal cultures with the continent's natural history and considered indigenous people part of the American landscape. Other public figures of the time complimented Longfellow on his ability to capture the spirit of "genuine Indian life" before it vanished forever. One of his contemporaries, the Reverend Benjamin Franklin DeCosta, considered Longfellow's poem beautiful but criticized him for not making the main character even more positive, which DeCosta would have considered more historically accurate.[24]

Longfellow's work was, as Robert Berkhofer Jr. has noted, "the culmination of the tendency to romanticize the dead Indian at the expense of living ones." Like Catlin and Schoolcraft, the poet paternalistically considered tribes part of the American past; for these individuals, sites such as the quarries were appealing scenes of antiquity, and both Native people and places were considered resources to be used by the larger national culture, which the writers and ethnographers believed they themselves actively represented. Before the town of Pipestone was settled near the quarries, it had become publicly acceptable to extract images from the place and its perceived tribal past—a standard activity in creating a usable American heritage. As the common perception of tribes pictured them steadily vanishing onto the western horizon, Longfellow and other writers waxed nostalgic for a preindustrial lost time of natural innocence, and they promoted themselves as the keepers of memory and salvagers of the continent's cultural past. Literary ethnographers envisioned a nonexistent, nonthreatening mythical Indian, detached from any living individuals, who could be invested with qualities that supported eastern American longings for a golden age, even if a borrowed one, on their continent. Alluding to Longfellow, Richard Rodriguez defines this cultural tendency as "Gitchegoomeism—the habit of placing the Indian outside history . . . a white sentimentality that relegates the Indian to death." Longfellow's poem satisfied a cultural need for a classical Native past and quickly became accepted as historical poetry and mandatory reading and recitation for generations of schoolchildren across the country.[25]

Closer to the site and with less literary purpose, more casual historians and incidental ethnographers of the era encouraged settlement in the upper Midwest and on the northern Great Plains and contributed to the quarries' reputation. In his 1856 *The States and Territories of the Great West,* Jacob Ferris devoted a paragraph to the "celebrated red pipe-stone quarry," which, he claimed, "tribes all believe . . . to be consecrated ground, and never chip off a bit of the rock without many superstitious observances." Moses Armstrong wrote from Dakota Territory in 1866 and described the area's past and added to widespread perceptions of the quarries. With the authority of a resident and a traveler in the West, Armstrong expanded on previous narratives about the pipestone quarries as the site of creation. A trip home from the East took him "within the holy atmosphere of the great red pipestone quarry [and] celebrated spot." In such phrases as "the sacred birthplace of all the red people" and "tradition points us back to the period of Adam and Eve, and the days of the flood," Armstrong furthered the trend of making the quarries' legends seem familiar by comparing them to biblical stories and making references to common cultural images. While intending to write a history of the region, Armstrong reemphasized a conception of the quarries as part of a mythical past apart from recorded history. Tribal traditions remained exotic, but this "place of peace," like Catlin's "Indian Eden," could also be considered safe, as well as singularly American in its heritage.[26]

SCIENTISTS CONFIRM IMAGES OF THE QUARRIES

The final group that contributed to popular images of the quarries as a national place in the nineteenth century were scientists, mainly geologists who wrote authoritatively and gave public lectures as learned men. By the 1830s geology was becoming a legitimate, empirically based science in the United States, as theories of organic changes in the earth over vast periods of time supplanted beliefs based on biblical interpretations of nature. Scientists were part of the professionalization of disciplines in the nineteenth century; they published in scholarly journals and often had government backing for their research. Although scientific writing found a more limited audience than the works of Catlin or Longfellow, the attention given to pipestone and its source seemed to justify public interest in the site and acknowledged the quarries' reputation. When Charles Jackson's analysis of pipestone, or catlinite, as a "new compound" appeared in the *American Journal of Science* in 1839, his report about the stone immediately enhanced Catlin's reputation as "the celebrated traveler in the West and the successful painter of Indians," and it confirmed assertions about the quarries' uniqueness on the North American continent. The popularization of scientific inquiry ensured that Jackson's findings and successive reports about the pipestone quarries carried authority.[27]

No scientist visited the quarries until Ferdinand Hayden made a trip through the region in 1866. His narrative—subtitled "with a notice of a short visit to the celebrated Pipestone Quarry"—was published the following year in the *American Journal of Science and Arts,* and it displayed qualities typical of most of the scientific writing on the site. As a geologist Hayden primarily noted the setting and special qualities of the stone. He found the place itself so inconspicuous amid the expansive prairie that he remarked, "Had I not known of the existence of a rock in this locality so celebrated in this region, I should have passed it by almost unnoticed." By the 1860s the term *celebrated* almost always preceded any reference to the quarries, although it alternated with *famous* and *legendary.* Hayden cited Catlin as the first visitor to draw attention to the stone. Perhaps being more accurate in his cultural analysis than he intended, he acknowledged that "nearly all of our writers on Indian history have invested this place with a number of legends or myths," a line that others would quote repeatedly long after Hayden's visit. Despite popular belief in the site's ancient past, he continued to assert his skepticism about the antiquity of excavation there. Like other scientists, Hayden readily stressed the uniqueness of pipestone and the quarries, but lacking the romantic bent of an artist or an ethnographer, he found no material evidence to support the popularized myths.[28]

Similarly, Charles White, the Iowa state geologist who wrote of his trip to the "Great Red Pipestone Quarry" two years later in *American Naturalist,* combined scientific curiosity with reserved cultural interest. White's group marched across the monotonous prairie, with "nothing above us but the open sky," until their guide stopped. "He merely says 'Pipestone' as he points forward, and there, three miles away in the distance, is the famous spot," White noted. He then expressed his disappointment at the inconspicuous nature of the place, so unlike its poetic reputation of being "on the mountains of the prairie," although he became somewhat more impressed as he drew near. Once at the site, White, more generously than Hayden, stated that tribes "from time immemorial" had visited the site, which had become "almost as famous among those who speak the English language as among the aborigines themselves, who, to some extent at least, regard it as a sacred place." He attributed this notoriety to Catlin and others and acknowledged the importance of popular perception and interest. After quoting them at length he went on to say that his purpose lay in "correcting the fallacies of the Indian legends" but without the wish of "diminishing popular interest in them."[29] Indeed, this seems to be the effect that he and his colleagues had. Their efforts to debunk some of the popular perceptions of the place or to ground them in scientific realism went unnoticed, while their attention to the newly named stone and its source affirmed the quarries' uniquely American qualities.

Later in the century two federally employed scientists, Charles Rau and John Wesley Powell, added to the quarries' mystique and acclaim by providing an anthropological view of past activity at the site. In an 1872 Smithsonian report for Congress, Rau devoted a long section to "the celebrated red pipestone," its source in "classical ground," and the "many legends that lend a romantic interest to that region." He cited Hayden's doubts about the site's antiquity but held vaguely that "many succeeding generations" had traded the stone extracted there.[30] In 1898 Powell conveyed his thoughts on the quarries to the commissioner of the Bureau of Indian Affairs. Contrary to some earlier writings, Powell asserted with an ethnographer's zeal that "it is not too much to say that the great Pipestone Quarry was the most important single locality in aboriginal geography and lore," a place at which extraction "continued through uncounted generations."[31] His statement confirmed many previous descriptive themes and carried professional authority because of his explorations on the Colorado River and his work for the Bureau of Ethnology. The scientists' unanimity on the exceptional nature of the quarries outweighed any skepticism expressed about the site's significance in tribal cultures. Their attention reinforced public perceptions of the place as unique and mysterious, and it possibly hastened later vandalism at the quarries by people seeking samples of the unusual stone.

Minnesota government officials also did their part in popularizing the quarries. In the 1870s the state geologist, Newton H. Winchell, surveyed the geology and natural history of Minnesota and devoted a lengthy section of his extensive report to the attributes of the Côteau. His overview of earlier written accounts of the quarries began as follows: "This locality has become somewhat famous on account of the extensive use made of the red pipestone by the Indians, and the difference of opinions expressed by scientists as to its origin and age." Winchell provided no specific opinion of his own about scientific estimates or tribal legends, except to note that the area was "sacred ground" associated with various stories and marked by hieroglyphics (petroglyphs), unlike other rock outcrops in the vicinity, which would signify the site's cultural significance.[32]

Years before Winchell submitted his report, territorial governor Henry Sibley successfully offered a half-ton slab of pipestone to represent Minnesota in the 1849 building of the Washington Monument. Sibley considered pipestone symbolic of Minnesota, "peculiar to our Territory," and useful for promotion. He opposed naming the stone after Catlin, whom he considered a fraud, arguing, "It is notorious that many whites had been there and examined the quarry long before he came to the country." Regarding the use of the term *catlinite* as "improper and injust," Sibley instead proposed classifying it by the Dakota term, *eyanskah* or *inya sa,* which would be consistent with the territory's Dakota-derived name and would identify the stone with its source, rather than with a man from Pennsylvania. Sibley's animosity toward Catlin undoubtedly influenced his recommendation more than any sense of propriety or justice toward the Dakota. In his readiness to use pipestone imagery to further his and his territory's national promotion, Sibley differed little from Catlin. His actions also marked the beginning of what later became extensive white extraction of the stone for purposes unrelated to tribal practices. Once nontribal people began to appropriate and commodify cultural images of the quarries, public claim to the pipestone itself and its source followed without hesitation.[33]

TRIBAL RELATIONS AND THE QUARRIES

Even while tribes consistently resisted settlers' interference with their practices and beliefs and sought to preserve the quarries as a tribal place, some of their actions in the mid-nineteenth century supported the formation of pipestone imagery. Although Sibley took vigorous exception to the story, Catlin claimed to have been forcibly and dramatically detained at Traverse des Sioux on the

Minnesota River by the Dakota, who would not let him, a white man, near the quarries because of the site's sacred nature.[34] No other explorers reported such difficulties, and some, among them Nicollet, readily made allies among the local tribes, but they lacked Catlin's popularity and were no counter to his assertions. European Americans who lived in the area or who had substantial interactions with Native peoples recognized differences in tribal lore and cultural practices, particularly between the Ojibwe in the northern woods and the Dakota bands across the prairies and plains. But because the use of pipes for ceremonies extended across much of the continent, popular perception recognized only a singular, static Indian culture, centered on the quarries as the sacred site of creation.[35]

One of seven bands in the highly decentralized Lakota/Dakota/Nakota cultural confederation, the Yankton (Ihanktonwan) maintained the closest residence to the quarries and consistently enjoyed peaceful but proactive relations with the United States. According to tribal oral history, Yankton leader Struck-by-the-Ree was born shortly before Lewis and Clark visited the area in 1804, and his parents presented him to Clark as a sign of goodwill. In response Clark purportedly wrapped the baby in an American flag and predicted that the two nations would always live in peace. Faithful to this famed meeting, Struck-by-the-Ree—later known as Old Strike—grew into the expected role, urging harmonious relations with the United States and assimilation whenever practical. The Yankton participated in the negotiations for the 1815 Portage des Sioux treaty and the 1851 Fort Laramie treaty, agreeing in both to avoid hostilities with American citizens and immigrants. But unlike other Dakota bands in Minnesota Territory, they refused to sign the 1851 Traverse des Sioux treaty that ceded substantial tracts of tribal land in exchange for scattered reservations, choosing instead to negotiate later with the United States.[36]

Subsequently, in the Washington Treaty of 1858, Old Strike and other Yankton leaders ceded their land in Minnesota and accepted relocation to a reservation along the Missouri River in Dakota Territory because of a singular goal. Through article 8 of the treaty the Yankton successfully gained what the other Dakota bands had not considered in previous treaties—a federal guarantee of "free and unrestricted use of the red pipe-stone quarry," on a 648.2-acre reserved section of land.[37] Because the 1851 treaty had not stipulated protection of the stone or the site, the Yankton had chosen to act on their own to secure the assistance of the U.S. government in preserving the quarries as a tribal site. Their insistence on finding nonviolent, legal means to reserve the increasingly famous quarries supported popular images of the sacred place of peace.

Behavior on the part of other tribes continued to complement larger cultural perceptions of them and their traditions. In 1855 a small group of Wahpekute Dakota, led by Inkpaduta, countered settler encroachments at Lake Okoboji in northwestern Iowa with violence in the so-called Spirit Lake Massacre. After taking three white hostages, the group headed for Dakota Territory, stopping briefly at the quarries for a short ceremony of pipestone extraction and pipe carving. The Yankton and other bands refused to support the Wahpekute men's actions and instead helped to track them.[38] Seven years later, in 1862, the Dakota located along the Minnesota River attempted to prevent starvation by securing food outside their reservation, an act leading to a violent conflict that received national attention. All but a few of the Yankton remained neutral and unwilling to break their peace with the United States. The conflict marked the culmination of tense relations between the eastern Dakota bands and newer Minnesotans; the degree of violence and animosity deterred the settlement of the southwestern corner of the state until years after the Civil War. As tensions and confrontations moved west onto the Plains with the more archetypal Lakota bands, the Yankton continued their life of adapting to their reservation and making annual trips to quarry pipestone.[39]

The quarries remained an active tribal place in the late nineteenth century, by which point the site had become enveloped within American geography and culture through decades of description and the repeated use of appealing phrases and imagery. The place served two sets of separate interests. For the tribes who used the pipestone, it provided material with which to continue spiritual traditions and practices. For an expanding American population, it provided less tangible historical and figurative material from which to shape a useful, celebrated past. Shortly after the Civil War the quarries attracted the first permanent nontribal settlers. The founding of the town of Pipestone built on the national images created during the nineteenth century and began a new local tradition of representation and commodification of the quarries.

TWO

Building on the Image

Fascinated by the quarries after his exposure to Catlin, Longfellow, and others, Charles H. Bennett, a druggist from LeMars, Iowa, a town just south of the Minnesota border, took his interest a step further than most readers of the quarries' legends. Bennett determined to visit the site and, if he found it suitable, to establish a town there, to be called Pipestone. Taking an overland route north across the prairie, he arrived at the quarries in fall 1873, the year of the region's grasshopper plague and a national economic panic. Neither circumstance daunted Bennett, who envisioned capitalizing on the lure of the legendary place. With seemingly little effort he convinced acquaintances from nearby Rock Rapids, Iowa—Daniel Sweet, John Lowry, and Job and D. C. Whitehead—to travel there with him the following spring and to take claims on land near the quarries, over forty miles from the nearest rail line. For the first two years a few other people arrived in the summers to establish additional claims to property. Until 1876, however, Sweet and his family qualified as the only real residents, staying alone during the long winters in the prototown's only building, a small shanty. In that year Bennett and Lowry began constructing small business buildings, demonstrating their investment and intent to stay at Pipestone and their commitment to the quarries' perceived national significance.[1]

The establishment of local stability and identity characterized the twenty years following the town's inception. Drawn to the place by the romanticized tales of Catlin and Longfellow, Bennett and his fellow town founders arrived with preconceived images and expectations of the quarries and the Côteau. They saw what they anticipated finding, and they echoed and elaborated on previous eyewitness accounts. Using their new residential status as a basis for an authoritative interpretation of the past, they augmented the attraction that the site had held for middle-class Americans like themselves. In a country still recovering psychologically from the Civil War and redefining itself culturally as a unified nation, the quarries' mythic past and reputation as a place of peace proved appealing and useful.[2] Throughout the first two decades of Pipestone's existence the quarries and the legends associated with them served as the main extractable resource for much of the town's promotion and promise of economic growth. In these years Pipestone as an idea mixed freely with the material development of the place.

Bennett, Sweet, and other early settlers who boosted the area did not consider the quarries solely as a source of profit, nor did they ever treat the site as such. An equally consistent and frequently harmonious theme accompanied the blatant efforts to market the town in the age of enterprise. Pipestone's creators had a vision of the quarries as important nationally because of what they perceived as its valuable heritage, and they persistently sought to have the place included in America's picture of itself. They took the images of the quarries initially created by others in response to historical circumstances, adapted them to suit their current needs, and projected them outward, thereby participating actively in the shaping of national identity. In an age of ambivalence, Pipestone's residents found themselves, not entirely consciously or intentionally, in a dualistic relationship with their country. Although they considered themselves wholly American—made more so, if possible, by residing at a place of purported national significance—they also recognized and emphasized the special quality of living near the unique quarries. This dualism, being both different and typical at the same time, characterized pluralistic American culture from its earliest period and made Pipestone representative of countless other small towns whose inhabitants experienced life in the United States on a local level. Residents of isolated areas across the country sought meaning in the landscape surrounding them and a connection to their place, as well as ties to the larger society. They localized American heritage and redefined the past in order to create a communal sense of identity.[3] Pipestone was an unusual place settled by average people. The continued interrelation of local and national perspectives served as the bedrock for building the town at the quarries.

EARLY SETTLEMENT

Although interest in the area's sites and sagas grew in the mid-nineteenth century, the rocky southwestern corner of the state remained relatively unsettled, with Pipestone County mapped but unorganized until almost twenty years after Minnesota achieved statehood in 1858. Outcrops of hard Sioux quartzite and a limited water supply made tracts of the prairie unappealing to farmers. During the 1850s and 1860s struggles with tribes in the region delayed extensive settlement, and popular perception resulted in the area and contiguous parts of Iowa and Dakota Territory being labeled "Siouxland." A history published in 1911 observed that "the very name of the county suggested Indians" and led to "a mistaken idea that the region was infested with savages attracted by the wealth of pipestone." This association both lent the area a hint of the Wild West and ensured that it could only be attractive to large numbers of homesteaders once actual tribes resided safely further west, a recurring pattern in American settlement. Gratia Ferris, whose family moved to Pipestone in 1878, remembered not feeling safe as a child on a farm located along the Minnesota River to the north during the 1860s' conflict; as a result, the family temporarily moved into the town of Belle Plaine. After the Civil War railroads extended lines throughout the state and skirted its border with Iowa. Without the population necessary for a market, no rail lines reached onto the Côteau until the late 1870s, which made the area less accessible and delayed the development of commerce and communities.[4]

The relatively late arrival of rail lines to the southwest corner of the state did not, however, entirely hinder settlement. Increasing prosperity, immigration, and internal migration, encouraged by the federal government through the 1862 Homestead Act and land grants to railroads, hastened the desired national development and caused rapid postwar expansion west of the Mississippi. Newer states such as Minnesota experienced a dramatic population influx, particularly from other northern-tier states, and settlers soon pushed out onto the vast prairie. Although Pipestone had few permanent residents in its early years, the ones who lived there immediately began creating a sense of community and civic commitment. In spring 1876 Charles Bennett, Daniel Sweet, and three other residents held the first town meeting and elected each other to administrative positions. As secretary, Bennett recorded their early priority as committed citizens to build a courthouse, an act that would demonstrate the settlers' belief in a solid communal future. Unlike others of their time who sought access to tribal lands, they promised to "respect and enforce to the best of our ability the rights of the Indians to the Indian reservation."[5] This resolve was less a philanthropic act than an acknowledgment of the site's value for their future. From the beginning their commitment to the quarries stemmed from their interpretation of and investment in the place rather than from local tribal interests.

The area held unusual resources, but the town's development proved customary. As a step toward preparing for future prosperity, Bennett and Sweet spent part of the summer of 1876 as voluntary surveyors platting the town, located south of the quarries and the quartzite bluff depicted by Catlin, and planning wide streets in anticipation of growth. This action put Pipestone officially on a map, if not a map immediately seen by many. Fifty-two more claims added to the sense of the community's potential that season, though not until the following summer did most settlers make improvements on their land and prepare to reside there. By 1878 state promotional literature, newspapers, and correspondence spread the word that a viable settlement was growing on the prairie near the famed quarries and that farmers could find land throughout the county, drawing hundreds of people to the area. The state's initial refusal to acknowledge an insubstantial population at Pipestone in 1877 briefly halted efforts to establish the county seat, but renewed petitions met with success two years later, and Pipestone's public life began in earnest.[6]

ACTIVE SETTLERS

Pipestone followed a development pattern typical of urban settlement in remote rural areas, particularly in what was then the Great Northwest. Merchants with means of investment founded towns, merged business and politics by establishing themselves in governing positions, and shortly thereafter established a local press to help advertise their community. Five years after Pipestone's tentative beginnings with Daniel Sweet as its first settler and only a few months after the county's official organization in early summer 1879, the inaugural edition of the city's primary newspaper, the *Pipestone County Star,* appeared for sale and subscription. Founded by Isaac L. Hart, who moved west from New York, the paper represented the spirit of the first residents, who, from the initial conception of a city near the pipestone quarries, energetically attempted to persuade those near and far of the locale's significance. Descriptions of the quarries and associated tribal legends were featured prominently on the front page and throughout almost every issue of the paper, which often included in its title banner a picture of Winnewissa Falls cascading over the quartzite ridge at the quarries. The first edition asserted that "Pipe-Stone City is located adjoining the most celebrated quarry of the same name in the world. . . . What has seemed to be the foundation for value, strife and profit to the red, has also proven the same to the whites."[7] This statement proved more prescient than Hart might ever have anticipated, as he joined Bennett, Sweet, and others in building on the foundation that quarry imagery laid for local and national importance as well as for continuing contention.

Many of the farms and towns founded later in Pipestone County drew populations of immigrants from Germany, Scandinavia, Ireland, Belgium, and the Netherlands. Pipestone itself, like parts of Minnesota settled earlier, attracted predominantly Protestants of New England, or Yankee, stock from the Northeast and Great Lakes states. This literate, middle-class group most likely read Catlin and Longfellow as part of the emerging canon of American literature. As they moved west across the northern tier of states, the Yankees brought with them both the conviction of a prosperous new existence and a sense of American identity and values that overlooked any differences among them. These northerners believed in private enterprise, economic prosperity, education, and civic participation and pride. Yankee town founders readily established businesses, churches, schools, and fraternal organizations. Many were Civil War veterans who belonged to the Grand Army of the Republic and shared a sense of American brotherhood as they fulfilled their new civic duties as volunteers in city government.[8]

Pipestone's founding residents were a homogeneous group who typified this settlement pattern, and that homogeneity enabled them to craft a unifying local identity. They were entrepreneurial, optimistic, Republican, northern Anglo-Americans who immediately became active in local politics and community life. Prior to setting up shop in northwestern Iowa, Charles Bennett spent his early boyhood in Michigan, then attended school in Philadelphia and served the Union in the war. In Pipestone he not only operated his drug store but also acted as town clerk, justice of the peace, a city councilman, and a county commissioner. Daniel Sweet, who had lived in Pennsylvania, Wisconsin, and Iowa, filled roles as Pipestone's postmaster and probate judge. The Whiteheads hailed from Ohio originally, before living in Illinois and Iowa. The publisher of the *Pipestone County Star*, Isaac Hart, moved to Minnesota from New York. One of the early settlers and the county auditor, John Pearson, believed Pipestone offered more building opportunities than his home state of Ohio, and one of the town's mayors, Vermont native James Carson, left Wisconsin to claim land near the town. Arriving in 1874, just after Bennett and Sweet, the first Pipestone physician, Methodist Episcopal William J. Taylor, hailed from New York, and one of his successors, Ezra M. Carr, moved from Canada and became involved in civic life as the village recorder, registrar of deeds, probate judge, and a county commissioner. Active roles in communal life created bonds among them and a sense of participation in the larger process of building America. Their actions to establish their community developed in concert with the conscious creation of their place-based identity.[9]

Within this mainly Anglo-American community in the late 1870s, another group of settlers began to find themselves readily at home. As in other small pockets of northern Iowa and southern Minnesota, Pipestone had an influx of British settlers. One of the first immigrants from England, E. W. Davies, moved to the county in 1876 and soon joined the county bank, through which he developed the financial status necessary to help establish the nearby town of Jasper and own part of its newspaper. Into the 1880s the bank remained under the direction of British residents, as Charles Mylius and Henry Briggs left England and joined Scottish immigrant Fraser Mackay in working with Davies.[10] This early British presence in Pipestone complemented the local Yankee character and prepared the way for a more organized British influx in the 1880s that proved crucial to increasing the town's renown.

Prior to the arrival of British promoters, Pipestone's founders busied themselves solidifying the romantic imagery of the quarries and the place's generalized tribal past. The town's original plat preceded any planned promotional efforts other than shipping stone samples eastward, but it included streets named Catlin, Hiawatha, and Longfellow. In Victorian fashion, other streets received women's names in honor of the town's early wives and daughters. Charles Bennett's new life in Pipestone embodied another version of middle-class romance based on the quarries' presence and widespread sense of mystique. In 1877 he married Adelaide George, whose name soon graced a street. George, an aspiring poet and Longfellow devotee who lived in New Hampshire before her marriage, had memorized much of *The Song of Hiawatha* and learned of the existence of a town "on the mountains of the prairie" near the "great red pipestone quarry." With interest piqued, she wrote to the town postmaster, requesting a piece of the stone. Daniel Sweet—who, being Pipestone's first full-time resident, was the postmaster at the time—passed the letter on to Bennett, who eagerly complied with the request. The *Star* later referred to the stone as "that specimen of pipestone which secured a wife for our friend Bennett." A lively correspondence and long-distance courtship ensued, culminating in marriage.[11]

Consistent with the theme of their courtship, the couple sent invitations for the ceremony carved on slabs of pipestone and included Longfellow on the guest list, the first in a series of invitations to visit the town that the poet declined. For their honeymoon the couple toured the East and included a visit to Longfellow's home in Cambridge, Massachusetts, to thank him personally for inspiring their romance. In the *Star* Hart commented on behalf of the community that the Bennetts' courtship and marriage gave "a wide notoriety to the parties as well as to the pipestone itself. Among the Indians this red stone was always considered sacred and now it has become romantic. We should not be surprised to hear that the whole quarry had been purchased by the bachelors of Pipestone City." Doubtless Bennett did not send Adelaide George the stone intending to "secure a wife," but he found in his new spouse an eager companion in advertising the town.[12]

In the following years Adelaide Bennett devoted herself to celebrating and promoting the quarries through her poetry, which she published both locally and nationally. One of her published poems, "The Peace-Pipe Quarry," approximates Longfellow's meter and begins with romantic scenery:

> Outward swell the rolling prairies,
> like the waves of ocean deep; . . .
> 'On the mountains of the prairie,'
> on the wind-swept emerald sea."

Although she created poems for many occasions, the quarries and their associated legends provided the primary source of inspiration for her muse.[13]

THE YANKTON ACT ON RIGHTS TO THE QUARRIES

Use of the quarries and pipestone for nontribal cultural purposes, such as the Bennetts' wedding invitations, began in earnest in the 1870s and flourished in the following decade. Amid periodic encroachment by settlers and curious visitors, the Yankton—and occasionally other tribal members—continued to visit the quarries annually and to protect their interests and rights whenever necessary. In the early 1870s tribal leaders called on the federal government for action in what developed into a long-term issue.

Although the earliest residents of Pipestone resolved to respect tribal rights to the section reserved by the 1858 treaty and containing the quarries, others from the area made no such promises and freely encroached on tribal land. In 1871, prior to Bennett and Sweet's arrival at the townsite, the government had the area surveyed, but it neglected to mark the reservation boundaries at the time. In the interim, August Claussen took advantage of the delayed settlement of the state's southwestern corner, claimed land within the reserved section, and filed his claim with the General Land Office, which noticed no discrepancy. Claussen made no improvements on the property and sold it indirectly to Herbert Carpenter, a Minneapolis resident. As it became clear that Carpenter meant to hold the claim, the Yankton pressed their agent, John W. Douglas, for legal action. The case went before the U.S. circuit court in spring 1880, which ruled in favor of Carpenter's claim, then moved on appeal to the Supreme Court four years later. The Court upheld the validity of the 1858 treaty and the right of the United States to reserve land from settlement, a right land offices could not usurp or ignore.[14] While waiting for the Court's ruling, the Yankton gained valuable legal experience that would prepare them for the next conflict.

Between the court rulings, the tribe members used federal support to continue their annual quarrying. Before their summer visit in 1879, which was Old Strike's last trip, Yankton leaders known as Poor Bull, Jumping Thunder, and White Swan secured letters from their agent, Robert S. Gardner, as well as a letter from the reservation missionary, John P. Williamson, introducing the main tribal members, reiterating the treaty right to quarry, and requesting "kind consideration" for the tribal presence near and in town. Poor Bull, the tribal police officer, carried with him an additional letter of introduction from the agent, which identified him as a U.S. officer and urged respect for him and the tribe members. Under the headline "Our Red Guests," the *Star* published the letters and anticipated hospitable treatment from townspeople, who had no direct involvement in the land dispute and who continued to consider the Yankton as "a kind and peaceable class," particularly under Old Strike's leadership.[15]

The newspaper readily acknowledged a primary reason for the town's interest in having the tribes quarry peacefully and annually. After a brief review of the 1858 treaty, Hart, the paper's editor, expressed the hope that it would "never be extinguished, as the Quarry and Reservation which surrounds it is a charming spot and the annual visitation of the Indians in the summer lends interest and attractions to our town which could be had in no other way." In addition to providing town businesses with trinkets and ornaments made from stone unsuitable for carving pipes, quarrying activities and the working tribal members provided a spectacle, a free tourist attraction that was an early form of the living history exhibits that would become popular in the twentieth century. With the arrival of a railway line in 1879 travelers could more readily visit the town to observe the Indian novelty. That year the *Star* raved that "visitors to the number of hundreds look in upon the Indian camps near town every day." Locals also turned out to observe the digging and occasionally received free entertainment in the form of dancing or singing.[16]

Although town businesses profited from the annual visits, Hart's paper sometimes revealed underlying ambivalence about Native visitors as Pipestone's boosters tried to reconcile living tribal people with cherished beliefs about the mythic Indian past. In the same edition in which the *Star* editors expressed hopes for treaty rights in perpetuity, an article with the heading "Heap Big Injun" revealed some conflicting sentiments and the extent to which Catlin and Longfellow had conditioned European American expectations of activity at the quarries. Describing two Yankton visitors who had ridden horses into town from "their favorite and consecrated resort," the paper complained about the men's appearance, which was "somewhat similar to the Anglo-Saxon style" but "ridiculously demoralized by the addition of their own piebald 'toggery.'" The commentary continued, "One remarkable and grotesque feature of their costume was the blessed union of the American flag and their own famous symbol—a turkey feather about two feet in length. Although of very fine stature, stately and towering in appearance we could not call them very desirable representatives of so fine a country."[17] Expecting "real" Indians to embody the noble qualities associated with the quarries' mythic past, Hart and others sometimes experienced disappointment in their encounters with living tribesmen, whose dress did not always project the kind of image that would attract tourists and meet visitors' expectations. Like other European Americans, Pipestone's citizens often had difficulty reconciling the Indians they envisioned after reading Catlin and Longfellow with the real tribal people they seldom met and did not know as persons. The dissonance between the imagery on which Pipestone residents based local identity and the reality of human experience intensified whenever tensions over the quarries heightened, reflecting a common experience across the nation whenever groups with differing interests disputed Indian lands. Beliefs about the timeless past were occasionally disrupted by present realities, a recurring problem with identities created from historically based imagery derived from someone else's traditions.[18]

BUILDING A ROCK-SOLID TOWN

After its initial boom in 1878 Pipestone gained momentum, and in the 1880s it experienced a surge in growth. During this decade Minnesota's population expanded rapidly with immigration from northern Europe and the development of railway lines, the milling industry, and improvements in agricultural technology. The importance of the railroads was absolute: towns required these vital market connections and died rapidly without them. Part of the initial influx of settlers to Pipestone resulted from the announcement by the Southern Minnesota Railroad Company that it planned an extension line to Pipestone from the southeast in nearby Jackson County. In 1878 the company began the surveying and grading necessary for laying track. Town leaders invited Longfellow, "the great poet . . . to witness the advent of the railroad into the heart of the red pipestone quarries" and asked him to speak at the celebration, but he again declined. In the absence of Longfellow, Adelaide Bennett wrote a poem for the occasion, once more using his characteristic cadence where she could. She gave it the title "A Thanksgiving Song" because the first train arrived in late November. Early verses proclaimed: "See the looked for train advancing o'er the classic plain / Shout your notes of glad thanksgiving in one loud refrain." Bennett's allusion to Catlin's "classic ground" would have been familiar to many gathered for the occasion.[19]

Railroads expanded throughout Minnesota as settlers claimed farms and markets expanded. Pipestone's location in the state's southwestern corner, located en route from Minneapolis and St. Paul to market centers such as Sioux Falls and Omaha, combined with Pipestone's reputation to make the town attractive to rail companies. The Chicago, Milwaukee and St. Paul Railway purchased majority stocks in the company with the provision that by 1883 the Milwaukee Road would fully acquire the Southern Minnesota. News of the extension sparked competition. In spring 1879, as the first tracks neared Pipestone County, the St. Paul and Sioux City Railway made public its plans to extend a line to Pipestone from adjacent Murray County and on westward to the Black Hills. Eager for town growth, the entrepreneurial Bennett granted rights-of-way and depot land from his extensive holdings. With the arrival of the Southern Minnesota in November 1879 and the completion of the St. Paul and Sioux City extension in 1881, Pipestone residents found themselves in greater command of a hinterland and connected to the Twin Cities, Chicago, and the larger country beyond the region. The lines also provided access to those seeking land in the area. By the time of the 1880 census the town population already exceeded two hundred, a sufficient number for city incorporation in the following year.[20]

One year before official incorporation, Bennett, Sweet, Hart, and other prominent citizens, self-appointed guardians of the history of the place, decided that the growth of the town sufficed to form the Old Settlers Society. They believed in the universal significance of the quarries' past, and they also sought to chronicle their experiences in the area as participation in what they perceived as the great, unfolding national drama. Like other Americans, they experienced both history and nation at the local level. Bennett, Sweet, and other founders celebrated their role in the town's development because they believed that Pipestone would exist far into the future and that later residents would commemorate its beginnings. Approximately forty townspeople attended the society's first meeting, agreed to meet annually in March, and limited membership to anyone living in the county prior to or at the time of the first meeting, thereby reaffirming the Old Settlers as an exclusive core group. Elected unanimously to give the address at the next annual meeting, Adelaide Bennett found plenty in the town's short history to inspire one of her lengthy poems, with its theme of a settler "by fast train bount to Pipestone's promised land." In her poem and her address she pointed out the importance of the quarries in Pipestone's existence and growing reputation. Bennett urged her neighbors to "take considerable pride and satisfaction in reflecting that we have helped to build up a town which now has a name and a prestige abroad as well as a place on the map." Her husband, the society's official historian, echoed this sentiment by rereading a proclamation he had presented about the quarries three years earlier at the first town gathering.[21]

During Pipestone's first decade of incorporated growth the quarries assumed an increasingly material importance, in addition to their symbolic significance. Although the catlinite deposits were limited and seemingly unique to the relatively small quarry area, extensive deposits of Sioux quartzite lay across much of the prairie of southwestern Minnesota and the larger drainage area of the Big Sioux River. An exceedingly hard metamorphic stone in varying hues of reds, pinks, and warm grays, quartzite lent itself to buildings, pavement, and ornamental uses. Particularly in the 1880s and into the 1890s, quartzite suited Richardsonian Romanesque, the popular architectural style of Henry H. Richardson and his followers that marked the beginning of truly American architecture. Characterized by massive, roughly hewn stone masonry, sturdy arches, and unpolished rock facing, Richardson's style utilized indigenous materials and gained popularity particularly in the upper Midwest, an area rich in quartzite, granite, and sandstone. During this period of rapid urban growth and industrial expansion, hundreds of public and private buildings in the style—courthouses, churches, residences, schools, warehouses, and department stores—dominated the streets of cities such as Chicago, Minneapolis, and Sioux Falls and smaller towns as well, including Pipestone and many of the county seats in the Siouxland area.[22]

Surrounding the pipestone quarries, a vast bedrock of reddish quartzite provided an extractable and useful resource for Pipestone's builders. The arrival of the railroad and a substantial number of settlers made it seem that the town promised a future to those willing to invest, and by 1880 some residents began to agitate to open quartzite quarries outside town. The *Star* summarized local opinion by noting that "the development of our stone quarries is a matter of the deepest concern to the future prosperity of the village." Deposits of quartzite on reservation land remained off-limits, but another large outcrop north of town attracted attention and speculation. The earliest quartzite extraction began in 1880, with a merchant named Phelps shipping stone to neighboring towns for building. Despite hopes that the railroad would initiate investment in the quarries and despite continual urging by the *Star,* no serious business developed for another three years.[23]

As in other matters, Charles Bennett assumed the leading role. A landowner who worried that Pipestone could be losing its place in potential markets, he rallied others to invest or to consider selling land to companies that might open the quarries. In spring 1883 he sold half of the interest in his land north of town to Leon H. Moore, a talented mason, and a Mr. Walbridge, who agreed to develop the quarries as Bennett and Company. Moore and Walbridge soon sold half of their interest to Herbert Corbett, an English immigrant with additional resources, and quarrying began in earnest. The quarries undercut competition from Sioux Falls, Dakota Territory, forty-five miles to the west, and provided Pipestone quartzite by the trainload to Chicago and other urban areas that were growing rapidly and required building stone.[24]

In addition to shipping stone for buildings and pavement elsewhere, Pipestone businessmen, such as Bennett and Moore, realized its applicability to construction purposes at home, and not solely in a literal sense. The year 1883 marked the beginning of a building boom encompassing business blocks, smaller shops, churches, and residences. Clustered together along the town's main street, several business blocks made of dark red quartzite slowly grew up from the ground. As in many other small towns in the region, a vernacular version of Richardsonian Romanesque characterized the buildings—large, heavy sections of stone in sturdy two-story buildings that seemed both at one with the ground and impervious to the elements. Built by enterprising members of the community, among them Bennett and Moore, the early business blocks spoke of investment in a "substantial, thriving and prosperous town." The durable structures reflected a community that was dependable and rooted in place. Although the buildings varied in the degree to which they followed the Richardsonian style, most incorporated its main elements, particularly the hefty effects of solidity and permanence. They also communicated values important to the residents' sense of their town and their era—progress, success, confidence, and growth. The style conveyed to those who saw the blocks a sense of permanence, solidity, and faith in the future of the town. Isaac Hart acknowledged this effect in his newpaper. In comments about the new buildings and the town's growth he asserted, "Towns that show faith in their advantages by putting money into improvements and building up generally make large cities. . . . Our belief has grounded itself upon a rock as firm as was that on which the Mayflower band stood on that wintry December day so long ago." The paper continued to praise the "substantial character" and "architectural beauty" of the buildings and the civic confidence that they displayed in a future "as solid as the hills of rock north of town." Gratia Ferris recalled that her husband, the Honorable Allen D. Ferris, later built a "large stone block" as the Opera House because "he had great faith in the future of the city."[25] Later, builders of the Syndicate Block incorporated not only native stone but also Indian symbols of a bow and a peace pipe in its facade. The quartzite blocks gave local residents a symbol of their association with their place and a source of security in an age of rapid change.

As Hart and others observed, architecture served more than its obvious utilitarian function; it also conveyed the values and goals of those residents who constructed the buildings. Quartzite buildings translated ideas about place into physical form, and Pipestone gained much of its visual appeal through the symbolism they embodied. When Bennett christened the town, he emphasized the presence of catlinite and the town's tribal past, rather than the abundant quartzite that contributed equally to the town's success. The choice of name gave Pipestone an immediate association with valuable stone and a connection to its surroundings. Present-day observers can still recognize the importance of the red stone structures that combined natural and cultural heritage and enhanced the early settlers' tangible place-based identity.[26]

To anyone passing through town, the buildings announced Pipestone as not only a prosperous but also a distinctive place. While neighboring towns contained buildings of pink and gray stone, Pipestone's quartzite approximated the deep red shade of the substance from which the town took its name, connecting it directly with the heralded quarries and their assorted legends. Given the intention of the founders to associate the town inextricably with the romanticized past of the locality, the similarity in color and the antiquity and durability of the stone supported efforts to construct Pipestone's place-based identity. Most local people understood the difference between quartzite and catlinite, but they frequently neglected to distinguish the common building stone from the mythologized one suited only for carving. In an article about quartzite extraction, the *Star* referred generically to "the celebrated stone from our quarry." When visitors from St. Paul took home quantities of both catlinite and quartzite, the paper gleefully reported that "almost every man had his pockets and arms full of the stone when they left here, and some in their zealousness to obtain pipestone, filled their pockets with building stone, not knowing the difference." Similarly, promotional literature often blurred the distinction between the two stones, referring to the quarries (of which there were several) without clearer specifications about the two very different types of mineral deposits found in them. One state brochure used the language of earlier explorers in the area, touting, "At Pipestone are to be found the celebrated Pipestone Quarries. These quarries are now being developed, and the best building stone take therefrom. . . . The supply is inexhaustible and no better quality can be found in the State." Thus, the dark red quartzite advertised the quarries and the image of Pipestone, whether through buildings in town or shipments of the stone for use throughout the region. The stone, like the town's name, spoke of a peaceful, mythic past on a sacred plot of land.[27]

Although undeniably important economically, the quarries yielded more than quantifiable profit; they also provided the literal and figurative bedrock for the town's identity, the foundation for the residents' sense of self and their future. Rising out of the prairie in imitation of the nearby quartzite ledge, the rugged buildings reinforced the town's connection to the landscape and its past. In the eyes of the townspeople, the land's prehistory and resources made Pipestone necessary—as inevitable as the national march of progress in which they believed. The land provided hope in abundance in the tangible form of both catlinite and quartzite. Pipestone's buildings created civic confidence in a solid future and the belief that they would stand permanently on the prairie.

Pipestone's development demonstrates the ability of buildings to stand as dual constructions, functioning both physically and symbolically. Similarly, quartzite served as both a material and a cultural resource that helped to promote economic viability, to reinforce visually the town's purpose, and to create and sustain its local identity tied to the stone not suitable for building. By use of a popular national and regional architectural style, Pipestone participated in larger American trends and consciously belonged to a developing common culture. But the massive quartzite buildings also expressed the celebration of a specific place. This interplay of commonality and belonging with an emphasis on the uniqueness of locality paralleled the promotion of the place's mythic Indian past and gave the town added American character. Although Pipestone looked outward and depended on railway connections to the rest of the country and used a nationally popular architectural style, it was, from its inception and throughout its development, grounded in its place, tied intimately to the land around it. The town's founders built business blocks, homes, and churches with permanence and promotion in mind, and their actions contributed to the construction of communal identity.

ENGLISH PROMOTERS ARRIVE

Another development of the early 1880s fueled the building and settlement boom and contributed significantly to the promotion of Pipestone and the quarries. Taking advantage of land sales in the Siouxland area, an English familial real estate company known as Close Brothers—formed by William, Frederick, John, and James Close—bought large tracts of land first in northwestern Iowa and then, after prospering there, in southwestern Minnesota. In April 1883 the brothers initiated their purchase of twenty-seven hundred acres in Pipestone County. Close Brothers and Company signed a contract with town leaders in the county seat, agreeing to locate its headquarters in Pipestone, to secure additional railroad lines, and to improve lands surrounding the town. Not long after their arrival, the brothers erected the Calumet Hotel to accommodate visitors who came to Pipestone by rail. That such a large land company would relocate to Pipestone promised great things to those with the town's future in mind.[28]

Limited by inheritance laws in their homeland and attracted to the Siouxland area by romantic travel literature and the American promise of possibilities, the Close brothers brought with them Victorian ideals of respect for tradition and enterprise that melded well with Pipestone's image and interests. In their entrepreneurial spirit and gentility, the English brothers complemented Pipestone's homogeneity; their intense interest in the legends of the quarries helped blur any incongruities between old European heritage and the new American community. The land company's arrival and immediate success in the area drew other Englishpeople, such as Henry Briggs, who became Pipestone's leading banker and a committed investor, to the area. British settlers on the prairie continued their lively country traditions, including steeplechases, foxhunts, and polo, which entertained other residents. More important, however, they also wrote letters, journals, and articles about their experiences on the Côteau, an informal but crucial form of promotion.[29]

With land to sell for a profit, Close Brothers advertised much more intentionally, widely, and vigorously than the town could have done through its own resources. Although its holdings directly around Pipestone consisted of under three thousand acres, the company's promotions for the "Great Pipestone Region" claimed over two hundred thousand acres of wild land, improved farms, and town lots. This approach to advertising exemplified the way that Pipestone promotion differed from that for land in other places. Close Brothers used typical means to draw attention to its lands, including railway banners and excursion trains "bound for the great Pipestone Country," but it joined the townspeople in promoting a familiar image of the place as part of selling land. The town newspaper saw the obvious result, noting that "the advertising done by these trains in the country through which they have passed must be largely beneficial to Pipestone as well as to the Close Brothers." Excursion trains from as far away as Chicago lured potential settlers to town and not only showed them lands available for purchase but also took them to the quarries, particularly in the spring and fall months when tribal members were most likely to be extracting pipestone. The *Star* eagerly supported Close Brothers' efforts and hoped tribal representatives from Flandreau,

Dakota Territory, fourteen miles west, would come over, in order to have "the quarries alive with them digging pipestone when the excursion train arrives."[30] Using tribes as attractions fit both the town's tourism needs and the landowners' search for sales.

For those who might not be able to make the visit by train, the company found another approach. Having experienced firsthand the attraction of the romantic tales of the quarries, the brothers mailed tons of promotional material specific to Pipestone across the country and abroad. This material included a brochure entitled "Legends of the Pipestone Quarries" and often a sample of catlinite from the heralded source. Similar to a publication by the *Star*, the front of this lengthy pamphlet featured an etching of Winnewissa, or Pipestone, Falls and Longfellow's oft-repeated lines, "On the mountains of the prairie / On the Great Red Pipestone Quarry." Inside the back cover Close Brothers again claimed there were over two hundred thousand acres for sale in the "Celebrated Pipestone Region" and stated that "information regarding land or quarries will be cheerfully given upon application." An advertisement for Bennett's store on the outside cover promised that "the tourist will find here one of the most interesting spots on the continent." Between these pages an enticed reader found several poems. In addition to the appropriate excerpt from *The Song of Hiawatha*, the brochure included a more specific poem in the familiar meter entitled "A Legend of Pipestone," with lines such as "On the plains of Minnesota in the days of long ago" and

> Indians yearly pay a visit where the stone so precious lies
> Guard it closely as they dig it for 'tis sacred in their eyes
> Make their pipes and tokens from it in their crude artistic way
> Pipestone is the name they gave it which it bears unto this day.

The promotional piece also featured two similarly themed poems by D. Ivan Downs. One, called "Chon-oopa-sa," told the legends of the quarries, supposedly relayed by Old Strike. In Longfellow's style, Downs began, "In the mystic land of legend, told in Indian song and story" and went on to tell of the "land of red men's home and story, land of legend, strange tradition; lies a peaceful, dual valley, vale of marvel, vale of myst'ry." Even without the inclusion of excerpts from Longfellow's poem, readers would have recognized the allusions to *Hiawatha* and accepted as authentic the rhyming representations of the place.[31]

As part of their initial agreement with the town, Close Brothers acted to attract additional railroad service to Pipestone. The town's first two rail lines already served the area well, but two more sets of tracks soon crossed the county at its center. Interested in extending a line north from Iowa, the Burlington, Cedar Rapids and Northern Railroad negotiated for a right-of-way that cut across the county at an angle, surveying first in 1883 and laying track the following year. By 1886 James J. Hill's Great Northern Railway located the office of the Willmar and Sioux Falls branch line at Pipestone. Local men responded by voting on a bond that brought the new railroad through town from the northeast within three years, providing direct connections to the largest cities in the region. In 1889 Pipestone had an unrivaled four railroad lines, with over thirty passenger trains each day that brought more settlers and tourists to the county and connected its residents to the rest of the country.[32] The unusual number of companies willing to invest testified to the success of promotion efforts and the extent of interest in the place, not just as an agricultural market center but also as a culturally appealing location.

Railroad companies serving the town employed Pipestone imagery to attract business much as Close Brothers did. In an advertisement for the "Great Pipestone Country" the Milwaukee Road featured the familiar etching of Winnewissa Falls, set against a bucolic background and trimmed by collections of farm implements. This image represented local aspirations to benefit from the past and to prosper as an agricultural market town. A pamphlet for another rail line highlighted the town, named for the "Great Red Pipestone Quarries that are mentioned by Longfellow in his 'Hiawatha,' and that are quite close to this city." Others mentioned the "celebrated quarry of red stone" and the source of the "Peace-Pipe." The railways hastened to run excursion trains to the area, promoting their services, Close Brothers' lands, and the town with banners along the side of trains on "The Great Pipestone Route." The 1884 meeting of the Old Settlers Society honored the rails with a Glee Club song, part of which claimed, "There's a name of magic import, and 'tis known the world throughout, 'tis a mighty corporation called the great Pipestone route." In a booster poem for the occasion, Adelaide Bennett wrote of the local welcome extended to the British settlers, claiming "We join our hands, across the waters / With England's cordial sons and daughters / And welcome all of every race / Who make this their abiding place."[33] Although not formally affiliated and seeking, first and foremost, their own financial gain, the three interest groups cooperated loosely toward a similar, profitable goal.

WIDESPREAD PROMOTION OF PIPESTONE

In addition to constructing quartzite buildings and luring businesses to town, Pipestone's leaders worked ceaselessly to promote the town and to make its image known as extensively as possible. Prior to the arrival of the Close brothers the *Star* published and distributed a version of the "Legends of the Pipestone Quarries,"—touted as "the genuine Indian story of the blood red stone"—initially with only Longfellow's poetry, then adding new selections and printing additional pamphlets as demand required. Weekly editions of the paper included portions of the poems and a steady stream of references to writings about the quarries. Longfellow's work proved useful for maintaining the romantic imagery and also boosted the surrounding countryside, where, he was quoted as rhapsodizing, "the fields are most fair and fertile" and the land of "streams to fish in, all full of trout and beaver and fowl." Obviously aware of other national writings about the quarries, the newspaper's editor repeatedly (and incorrectly) borrowed from geologist Ferdinand Hayden, stating that "nearly all of our writers of Indian history have investigated"—rather than "invested"—"this place with a number of legends and myths." An issue rarely appeared without some reference to pipestone itself, and frequently, particularly in special editions, the *Star* devoted long columns of print to summaries of the legends or to describing the town as associated with the quarries. As public culture became increasingly focused on the moral resources of the past as an antidote to the excesses of the Gilded Age, Pipestone's citizens told and retold themselves and others about the importance of the "sacred heritage" of the "land of tradition" and the timeless values of peace and mystery invested in it. They joined others in the postwar era who helped a common American experience coalesce by identifying unifying sites of national significance, including shrines placed outside recorded history.[34]

Town businesses advertised their services using familiar images. The Lincoln Photograph Gallery did so literally, offering "views of the falls and the famous pipestone quarries" for sale. The quarrying firm of Walbridge and Moore printed ten thousand copies of Longfellow's "Peace Pipe" section from *Hiawatha* for use in advertising the red quartzite. In addition to printed promotions, many of the merchants in town sold "trinkets and ornaments" carved from catlinite, something Bennett had been doing since opening his drugstore. The newspaper also operated a bookstore, from which it supplied pipestone samples for a nominal fee to all those requesting some of the stone. As knowledge of the town spread through copies of the "Legends" mailed to papers in other towns and cities, such as Chicago and New York, and through the efforts of Bennett and others to make the town a familiar name by correspondence and paid advertisements, the demand for pipestone samples from across the country and abroad increased.[35]

THE YANKTON RENEW LEGAL EFFORTS TO PROTECT THE QUARRIES

The growth in Pipestone's promotion and use of the stone caused a new phase of legal tensions with the Yankton. Members of the tribe continued to have a role in the town's identity development by being present and actively quarrying on a regular basis. Because they usually visited annually and spent the remainder of the year on their reservation in Dakota Territory, the tribe members maintained only a limited control over the quarries. Representatives from other tribes in the region, such as the Flandreau Santee, also received permits to quarry. But most of the time the quarries lay unattended on the outskirts of town, open to the wide prairie sky and to profit seekers with no tribal affiliation. The *Star*'s first issue reported that unidentified tribal men would "get out a few wagon loads of Pipe-Stone [and] dispose of it to the whites, who readily buy it to work up into all kinds of ornaments," as well as selling carved items.[36] Much of the stone extracted was not of the quality required for pipe carving, which left a substantial portion of the removed stone unusable and thus "disposable." Pipestone's boosters apparently noticed no conflict between their images of stoic Indians worshiping at the ancient sacred site from which they had tried to deny Catlin access and existing tribal members marketing low-grade stone for profit.

If this exchange troubled Old Strike and other Yankton leaders, they voiced no public opposition but rather saved their protest for obvious trespassers. In January 1881 the town newspaper published a notice from the Pipestone County Bank. It read: "Having been appointed agents by the owners of the Pipestone Quarry, all persons are forbidden from removing any stone therefrom. Persons desiring to purchase stone in any quantity will be accommodated upon the most reasonable terms." The notice proved ineffectual. Some enterprising types took advantage of the Carpenter land dispute, then lingering in the court system, to remove pipestone for their own uses. Within six months of the notice in the paper the Yankton agent, W. D. Andrus, appeared in town to serve notice to locals who had been quarrying illegally. Although supported by a representative of the federal government in their efforts to reserve the quarries, the tribe members also acted on their own. Several Yankton visited the following month, in July, to open a new quarry and to assert their rights. During the winter months of 1882 the *Star* reported that "Yankton Jim" planned to "stand guard over the 'sacred quarry' of the red men." The sentry did not stay long, however, and the paper soon observed that "the 'pale face' diggeth stone there as usual." By summer a letter from Old Strike to Daniel Sweet appeared in print. The aging Yankton explained that the Carpenter case troubled him but that he had been in contact with government officials in Washington, D.C., and had their assurances that the treaty conditions remained inviolate.[37] The mood in town, interpreted by the *Star,* took on an increasingly neutral tone, distant from early promises to support tribal rights on the reserved land.

By the time the Supreme Court issued its ruling upholding government treaty law, the Yankton had worked through federal agents on another case. During the first four years of the 1880s, while the Carpenter case awaited decision, the former New Ulm, Minnesota, land office registrar who acted on behalf of Carpenter, Charles C. Goodnow, moved to Pipestone. An ambitious man, Goodnow soon became mayor and moved onto the reserved section, where he built a house and began quarrying. Anticipating a ruling to uphold land law over treaty rights, other locals squatted on the section, and the town continued to spread north on Bennett's lots toward the quarries and the falls.[38] Isaac Hart and particularly Daniel Sweet publicly opposed Goodnow's actions, but removing squatters required more than social pressure.

As before, the Yankton mobilized their current agent, William Ridpath, a U.S. Army major, to act on their behalf. With the support of the commissioner of Indian Affairs, Hiram Price, Ridpath visited Pipestone to assess the scope of the problem. The squatters produced no proof of title, yet they refused to move when requested to do so. Ridpath's recommendation to use force for eviction met with resistance from the secretary of the interior, Henry Teller, who believed that the treaty provided the Yankton solely with quarrying rights, which he did not consider disturbed by the squatters. The 1884 election of Grover Cleveland as president brought a more supportive cabinet into office. An Indian reformer and advocate of the developing Dawes Allotment Act, the new Bureau of Indian Affairs commissioner, J. D. C. Atkins, secured the political and administrative backing necessary to address the situation but was still slow to act. Despite the change in personnel and the decision of the Supreme Court later in the year, nothing changed—other than more squatters moving onto the section, to the continued dismay of the Yankton.[39] The tribe members had done their best to abide by the expectations of Indian reformers and expected more than noncommittal goodwill in return for their cooperation.

After a formal petition in late 1886, the Yankton finally received active assistance from federal officers. The new agent, J. F. Kinney, served final written notices to the squatters. When none had moved by the deadline in mid-1887, Capt. J. W. Bean and ten enlisted men from Fort Randall in Dakota Territory moved into Pipestone in October. Facing U.S. Army men with a mission, Goodnow and the others finally agreed to remove their residences within six months. The incident was a rare reversal of the standard American narrative of government troops forcing tribes onto reservations and off "public" land, but it was consistent with the exceptional behavior of the United States in protecting, to some degree, tribal interests at the quarries. After securing the squatters' agreement to move, the Fort Randall contingent surveyed and marked the reservation boundaries to prevent any future argument about the extent of government-controlled property.[40] Mostly, these actions established that future disagreements would manifest themselves in other forms.

RESURFACING AMBIVALENCE

During the course of these events rival newspapers in other towns, such as Sioux Falls and New Ulm, used the squatters' episode to criticize Pipestone, even though their readers likely would have behaved with similar greed. Bennett, Davies, and other promoters particularly disliked negative articles in the regional presses that accused all Pipestone residents of disregarding federal laws. The *Star* defended its citizenry, but it also recorded an ambivalent atmosphere in town. Although Hart openly disliked Goodnow, he admitted to admiring the squatters' pluck. In November 1883 the newspaper printed a rebuttal to an article that had appeared in Sioux Falls, arguing that the Dakota Territory press had sensationalized the issue. From the perspective of the *Star*'s editor, the townspeople had "no interest in the reservation whatever" and their respectful behavior warranted no association with the actions of a few men who chose to disregard the law. The paper stressed that the town "does not now and never has encroached upon the reservation," which its citizens would rather see reserved as "a grand park of Indian curiosities." In the end,

Hart, Bennett, Sweet, and the other town leaders who opposed Goodnow's actions preferred to consider the problem a government matter and hoped it would not reflect badly on them; clearly, it did not spark the kind of national attention that the Land of Hiawatha sought. Instead, the town boasted that "the truth about Pipestone has the color of romance."[41] Promoters such as Bennett, who were invested in the town financially and psychologically, refused to allow their contemporary contested ground to taint the legendary peaceful past of the quarries or to deter tourism and interest in the quarries.

Like Secretary Teller and others of their era, many locals believed that the treaty reserved land for the federal government, which then granted tribes quarrying rights. Even this limited interpretation of the legal position of the Yankton implied that only tribal members could use stone from the quarries, to the exclusion of all others. But the obvious interpretation of use bore little resemblance to the daily reality. During the 1880s Charles Bennett reportedly had "a number of Indians, as well as white men employed in the manufacture of . . . pipestone articles," through which he could "supply trade at all times." Others were less organized but equally industrious. Apart from Daniel Sweet, few residents appeared moved to voice opposition to the illegal quarrying or use of pipestone, which did not, from their perspective, interfere with tribal use of the quarries as protected by the treaty. Sweet wrote repeatedly to the Yankton agent and to his representatives in Congress, requesting more of a federal presence on the reserved section. Perhaps tiring of conflict or merely in need of a change, Sweet and his family relocated in 1887 to Louisiana, where he later operated a steamboat company.[42]

During the 1880s, when armed conflicts with tribes in the West made national headlines and tensions over squatting at the quarries intensified, local racial tension rarely surfaced in print. Much of the time references to the living Yankton and the Flandreau Santee took common colloquial forms, such as the paternalistic "Poor Lo" or the jovially degrading "red skins," "old bucks," "squaws," and "papooses" or, rarely, the more derogatory "savages." During the early dispute over the land claims, the *Star* uncharacteristically reprinted a negative article from the *Jackson Republic* in southern Minnesota. The reporter, Burt Day, wrote of his visit to the quarries—"huge pits" in a "genuine Indian desert." Citing Longfellow's verse of Gitche Manito calling the tribes of men together, Day improvised, claiming that the Spirit called the "dirty, greasy, skulking, rat-eating, flea-breeding, scalp-lifting human failures" together. But apart from disparaging the quarrying men, who intruded on the historical imagery he expected of the place, he expressed admiration for the area: "The country north of Pipestone City is entrancing to the eye. A rugged cliff of red—deep red—granite rises majestically from the Valley. At the highest point—about 20 feet—the water pours over the rocks, forming very pretty falls."[43] Day provided a none too subtle example of the common tendency to contrast romantic, literary images of tribes relegated to the American past with equally unrealistic but passionately held views of contemporary Native people.

The article marked a conspicuous departure from the *Star*'s usual reprints of complimentary reviews of the area and its neutral language about the tribes. In the hundreds of routine booster articles describing the quarries and legends, even those that included the 1858 treaty, the paper rarely maligned the tribes who had lived there. Later in 1882, however, the *Star* included an atypical paragraph in its promotional Harvest Edition. Boasting that the town developed rapidly in what was previously tribal land, the paper assured readers that "the savage has folded his tent and the blight of his presence has gone forever. The shadow of his dusky face no longer falls . . . his war whoop is no more heard in the rich valley of tradition. . . . The curse of his presence has become a memory of the past." In printing these lines, the editor evidently saw no incongruity in lauding the removal of tribes while using their local traditions to promote Pipestone's development. Other than a reference to the angered Yankton as "bloodthirsty," future articles resumed the language of the "sacred land of tradition" and the "historical pipestone quarries."[44] Like other Americans of their era, Hart and his neighbors preferred to keep tribes safely ensconced in the past and the quarries a part of the sweeping national epic; they were able to separate their views of living tribal people from the popular Indian images they embraced.

CELEBRATING THE HISTORIC QUARRIES AND THE GENERIC INDIAN

For the early residents of Pipestone, then, it was only logical to observe the quintessential American holiday—the Fourth of July—at the quarries. During 1878, the first year of sustained habitation in the town, Sweet, the Bennetts, and a few others gathered on the quartzite ledge by the waterfall to celebrate the nation's past. In a typical blend of national ritual and developing local tradition, Charles Bennett read both the Declaration of Independence and part of Longfellow's *Song of Hiawatha,* then retold some of the site's legends as popularly perceived and received. Festivities in the following years featured fireworks, then more subdued picnics, and then livelier parades, as Bennett and the other founders tried to entertain themselves on the sparsely populated prairie and to solidify Pipestone's identity. Like their peers in other small towns across the country, they took pride in their role within the larger pageant of America and considered their place's celebrated past an important part of national heritage.[45]

Variations in celebrations of the Fourth of July embodied elements of national trends while remaining distinctly local. Pipestone's first community holiday at the quarries featured a performance in which the town's men dressed up and enacted a dramatic encounter between Uncle Sam and Sitting Bull, with his interpreter, complete with "a band of improvised savages fantastically painted and attired." The theatrical piece culminated in the ratification of a treaty that allowed residential Pipestone to remain peacefully near the quarries. Pipestone residents perched on the quartzite cliffs and dressed as tribesmen fit Philip Deloria's analysis of American notions of "ruin/rock formation Indians" and the popular act of playing Indian to express nostalgia and ambivalence. When not working out their communal connection to the place by staging imaginary Indian dramas, Bennett, Sweet, Ferris, and other leaders in the town's public life occasionally invited actual tribal members to participate in their celebrations and paid their travel expenses. Plans for the 1883 Fourth festivities featured a separate "grand Indian parade" that consisted of representatives from several regional tribes, followed by a "peace or grass dance" later in the day.[46] Committed to the idea of the quarries as intrinsic to national heritage and important for their symbolism of peace, the residents of Pipestone could not observe the essential American holiday without also celebrating the cultural significance of the site.

National literature of the late nineteenth century buttressed their beliefs by helping to keep the quarries popularly known. In 1883 another long, epic poem about the place's tribal legends appeared in print—*The Calumet of the Coteau,* by Philetus W. Norris, a former superintendent at Yellowstone National Park. Norris may have encountered Pipestone promotional brochures and obviously had read and seen Catlin's work; the frontispiece of his book featured an etching of the quartzite bluff and quarries very similar to Catlin's painting. Published in Philadelphia, Norris's work encompassed a sweeping overview of regional history, from the mythic Manito's creation of all "stalwart red men" after a flood at the quarries and its designation as a place of peace, to the spread of the "artless child of nature" into various Plains and Woodland tribes, to the arrival of European explorers, the "bold, thrifty yeoman [seeking] wealth in the West," and the bloodletting at Little Bighorn, complete with a map of the battle. After the carnage on the Plains, the warring tribes yielded to their fate, fading with the setting sun, leaving the new occupants of the Côteau to live peacefully in the sacred area that they had rightfully inherited. In endnotes almost as long as the poem itself, Norris provided a detailed account of the European exploration and knowledge of the site and a description of its topography. A shorter poem, "The Tattooed Artist," added to local lore and continued the conflation of history and hearsay. The poem told the story of Catlin's visit to the quarries and supposed arrest and detainment by tribesmen at Traverse des Sioux on the Minnesota River. In his introduction, perpetuating the coarser sentiments of salvage ethnography, Norris explained his intent to have "rescued from impending oblivion a few of the thrilling scenes of unknown actors of this momentous era, and thereby encouraged others to fill future poetic volumes of authentic history." Throughout the work Norris held in tension the romanticism of the legendary Indian and the lauded heroism of the intrepid European descendants who fought contemporary tribal people.[47]

Other forms of national attention tended to concentrate on either the noble or the savage aspect of the popular Indian image. Also in 1883 *Harper's* published "The Home of Hiawatha," an article about Minneapolis and St. Paul that provided a brief history of the area. The piece mentioned neither Longfellow nor the Iroquois hero, assuming that Hiawatha's name was by then synonymous with Minnesota in the popular mind. Elsewhere, literate people freely associated the poet with the quarries he had never visited. In 1881 managers of a booth dedicated to Longfellow at a fair in Cleveland, Ohio, telegraphed Charles Bennett to request pipestone samples. Bad winter weather, however, blocked the railroads and prevented Bennett from taking advantage of the advertising potential of the fair. Throughout the 1880s and 1890s Abigail Gardner-Sharp lectured in the Midwest and lured tourists to her cabin in Iowa, capitalizing on her captivity and forced visit to the quarries in the 1850s during the Inkpaduta incident near Spirit Lake. Her visits to Pipestone drew crowds, and her talks across the region always mentioned the mystique of the place to tribes, whom few of her listeners had ever encountered and whose images were becoming increasingly fictionalized and generic.[48]

Toward the end of the century other writers continued to show an interest in the stories associated with the quarries. In his 1896 *Myths and Legends of*

Our Own Land, a work more creative than geologically accurate, Charles Skinner included a section on pipestone. A stranger to the site, Skinner described the stone as "a smooth, hard, even-textured clay, of lively color, from which thousands of red men cut their pipe-bowls." Mistaking soft catlinite for hard quartzite, he claimed pipestone formed a wall two miles long and thirty feet high. He also offered yet another variation on the legend of the quarries, stating that the Great Spirit visited the place to kill buffalo whose blood reddened the stone, out of which the Manito then shaped humans. In a different vein, Henry Inman, a retired army colonel, reminisced about his visit to the area before the town existed and how tribes traded the stone across the Plains and into the Southwest. Referring to the site as "from time immemorial . . . visited for untold centuries by *all* the Indian nations," Inman offered only a brief mention of the general creation story to accompany his description of the landscape and explanation of the relevance of the pipe. Although his work was geographically sound, Inman seemed less legally informed, contending that "the quarry has long since passed out of the control and jurisdiction of the Indians and is not included in any of their reservations."[49] Skinner and Inman continued the century's tradition of weaving myth and memory, making the quarries attractive while firmly placing generic Indians in the site's timeless past.

SOLIDIFYING LOCAL IDENTITY

By the mid-1890s Pipestone had existed for almost a generation, and its residents enmeshed their own memories with the place's presettlement past. Despite national economic slumps, the town continued to grow, and its leaders persisted in their promotional efforts. The English banker E. W. Davies formed a real estate company to continue the work begun by the Close brothers. In the "safety valve" language popular in western booster literature of the age, Davies advertised lands in the county as a solution to eastern problems: "Cities congested, towns overdone, urban speculation gone to seed . . . half the mills and factories shut down . . . all trades and professions crowded to suffocation." Davies also extolled the special virtues of Pipestone, located in "famed Indian country, around which so many historic memories cluster . . . upon these prairies, where not so many moons ago the red man roamed at will, now school houses and churches are to be found." Like most other promotional pamphlets for the place, the Davies brochure included pages about the tribal tales and excerpts from Longfellow, complete with illustrations of "peace-pipes" carved from the "sacred pipestone" and the boulders near the quarries juxtaposed with engravings of quartzite buildings in town.[50] The lure of the legends continued to differentiate Pipestone from other localities.

Beginning with the Old Settlers Society, townspeople mingled their identities with the perceived past of the quarries in more organized ways. Davies concluded his promotion of the town with a list of its voluntary groups, observing that "Pipestone has a full quota of secret societies and they are in a most flourishing condition." Like other Yankee settlers in the area and across the northern part of the country, Pipestone's founders expressed much of their civic spirit in fraternal organizations and identified their social participation with their particular locale. The Masons formed the Quarry Lodge, while their female counterparts in the Order of the Eastern Star met in the Calumet Chapter, which did not overlap with the Calumet Lodge of the Independent Order of Good Templars. In the Odd Fellows, the men gathered on the Gitche Manito Encampment and the women in the Lodge of Winnewissa. Before long, the Modern Woodmen of America organized the Catlin Camp and the Knights of Pythias settled into their Hiawatha Lodge. One of the final groups to form in town, at the turn of the century, was the inevitable Wasta Tribe of the Improved Order of Redmen. In small towns membership tended to be inclusive, and residents often belonged to several groups in addition to a particular church congregation. Such organizations nurtured communal cohesion by providing a forum for social interaction, education, and support in times of trouble.[51] The groups' names and proliferation revealed the extent to which the residents of Pipestone associated their public lives with the imagery of their location and adapted common American behaviors to their particular place.

In 1893 Bennett and his neighbors joined many other Americans in a nationally popular effort to promote their localities widely. They sought to have Pipestone included at the Columbian Exposition in Chicago. Fortunately, government officials in St. Paul had long considered the quarries a state asset, and the Fair Board admitted several entries from townspeople. The board had hoped to send an Ojibwe group from northern Minnesota as a living cultural exhibit but found the idea too expensive to pursue. In Pipestone the bank donated $220 to defray costs, and the quarry owners contributed stone for a hearth made of quartzite from their quarries and those at nearby Jasper. The women's auxiliary group participated in the creation of a large pipestone mantel that featured the carved cameo of an iconographic Indian head.[52]

When approximately a hundred thousand Minnesota residents visited the World's Fair, they saw not only the Pipestone County Fair Club's mantel and hearth but also award-winning exhibits from individuals in town. Charles Bennett's carved catlinite pieces and core samples from the quarries that revealed the strata of quartzite and pipestone received recognition among the mining displays. Mrs. L. O. Pease garnered a women's award for a miniature engine made of catlinite. Samples of carvings, including pipes, also appeared in the North American Indian exhibits.[53] Pipestone had found yet another venue for successfully attracting public attention on a national level.

After the exposition, the U.S. Bureau of Ethnology purchased one of Bennett's larger pieces for the Smithsonian's collections. The bureau's policies and pursuits complemented some of Bennett's activities. Although no one mentioned the source of the pipestone for his carved "monuments," Bennett made no effort to disguise his continued use of stone removed from the quarries. His actions in this period typified the pattern of nontribal behavior at the site. Alarmed that tourists had begun to carve their initials and other graffiti on some of the rocks in the area, Bennett removed larger stones that featured the only tribally created petroglyphs near the quarries. This effort to "salvage" objects of ethnological importance removed them from their original context, resulting in the loss of clues to their significance.[54] Beginning with Catlin, non-Native people at the quarries had consistently extracted images from the human history of the site and removed their original meanings from them, all in the name of preserving the nation's Indian heritage.

Bennett's actions, however contradictory they may have seemed, marked the beginning of a new phase in Pipestone's development, which built on Catlin's legacy of cultural salvage. Although Daniel Sweet had urged the Yankton agents and the Bureau of Indian Affairs commissioners to protect the quarries, he had done so on behalf of tribal interests and rights. When Bennett and others in town began to express a desire to have the federal government manage the site, they believed they were safeguarding their investment in the source of the imagery that gave the town its identity and its future potential. They also considered a national presence at the site as a legitimization of the quarries' importance to the entire country.

Some sentiment for involving the federal government in preservation of the quarries existed from the town's earliest days, but in the late 1880s it began to take organized form and then to gain momentum. No one in Pipestone doubted the significance of the place to tribes throughout the region, nor did anyone dispute the prevalent logic that called for "civilizing" tribal children through education. With successful land companies, railroads, and assorted businesses all prospering in Pipestone and contributing to its growth, local attention turned to securing a federal presence in the form of an Indian boarding school at the quarries.

THREE

Institutionalizing the Place

Early in 1893, the year that Charles Bennett and other Pipestone citizens prepared to display the quarries' acclaimed bounty at the World's Fair in Chicago, the town gained attention across the country through the opening of the Pipestone Indian Training School. Located on the northeastern edge of the reserved section, the school added a new element to ongoing efforts to identify Pipestone and the quarries as nationally significant. Not located near any residential reservations, the federal institution appeared to legitimize the town promoters' continued claims about the uniqueness and cultural relevance of the place and its heralded Indian heritage. In addition, the school bolstered Pipestone's reputation as a vibrant community, important because of its pre-settlement past but also relevant to contemporary issues and worthy of external investment.

In the late-nineteenth-century era of economic growth and emerging social reform sentiment, Pipestone's residents identified themselves as representative Americans. They sought an active part in developments in culture, politics, and Indian policy, particularly when the perceived progress of the country benefited the town directly. More immediately, Minnesota grew rapidly in the 1880s, reaping the economic rewards of agricultural and industrial developments to emerge as a major market center for the Great Northwest.[1] A thriving commercial and rail hub in its intensely agricultural corner of the state, Pipestone profited from regional prosperity as much as from local promotional efforts. Sustained growth provided town developers with a firm sense of security and confidence. Believing Pipestone's economic future was ensured, Charles Bennett and other boosters could continue their pursuit of national recognition and support for their locality.

Pipestone's efforts to acquire a federal Indian boarding school near the quarries followed the town's familiar pattern of broad self-promotion through popular Indian imagery. Charles Bennett, Isaac Hart, Allen Ferris, and other local businessmen trumpeted the site's legendary tribal past and its significance on a national scale while embracing and adapting for further use any outside authoritative interpretations of the place. As they had from the town's beginnings, Pipestone's merchants subscribed to prevailing beliefs in the societal benefits of commerce and, with some ambivalence, the existence of a more innocent past prior to the increasing excesses of industrialization. They promoted the town accordingly. Pipestone's founders repeatedly proclaimed their place's contemporary and historical importance within the context of America's heritage, and specifically, they began to tout its relevance to the federal government. When possible, they attempted to shape the response from outsiders or to adjust its effects as necessary for enhancing Pipestone's reputation. Once the boarding school opened, Bennett and his neighbors found that the national government had its own interests, as it had with the earlier land disputes on the reservation, and that these federal priorities did not always agree with local expectations or wishes at the quarries. As town residents sought to benefit from the school's presence, the process of promotion and adaptation continued into the twentieth century.

PIPESTONE PARTICIPATES IN NATIONAL POLICY TRENDS

In 1879 the Carlisle Indian Industrial School, the first major off-reservation federal boarding school for tribal children, opened in Pennsylvania. A testament to the growing support for reform and assimilation in American Indian policy, Carlisle drew immediate attention across the United States. The school garnered hopeful praise from reform-minded American citizens convinced that the reservation policy had outlived its usefulness. Boarding schools seemed to be the long-awaited solution to government difficulties in finding supposedly fair relations with tribes while incorporating a country that spanned a continent. In a period of wars and skirmishes among tribes, federal troops, and land-hungry settlers west of the Mississippi, many in the United States considered the treaty and reservation systems failures. Reformers looked instead to the cultural transformation of the youngest generations of Indians as the primary means of creating a more peaceful, modern nation. Education seemed the most promising and philanthropic reform option, and its development as a policy took on the sense of a drama fueled by national conscience.[2] Pipestone's residents, touting the values of the quarries as a sacred site of peace for all tribes, eagerly seized on the moral spirit of Indian education and tried to associate the town with the progressive and potentially lucrative cause.

Pipestone's public view of Indians typified popular beliefs of the time. Clinging to a literary and artistic image of a pure and noble Native archetype who existed "authentically" in a past before European arrival on the continent, people on the Côteau and throughout the nation considered contemporary tribes to be corrupted and in need of "civilizing." In Pipestone the press generally presented positive images but sometimes differentiated between "good" Indians, who fit expectations for the "traditional" tribal visitor to the quarries, and "bad" ones, who displayed characteristics less attractive than the supposedly universal reverence for the red stone. An edition of the *Pipestone Farmers' Leader* ran a lengthy front-page treatise entitled "Indians Real and Ideal: Romance Has Given Poor Lo a Halo which the Truth Causes to Vanish"; the article claimed that Catlin and Schoolcraft would not recognize the tribal people of the late nineteenth century. Partial to the Yankton, who had assimilated more readily than many tribal groups, the *Pipestone County Star* compared them favorably to Indians visiting from Nebraska. The paper ignored tribal cultural differences and economic circumstances, claiming both groups shared the "invariable Indian reverence for the sacred pipestone," but noted that "the Nebraska Indians have retained more of their savage characteristics, their love of gaudy colors, etc." In comparison, the paper observed of the Yankton and the Flandreau Santee that "the rising generation among them are making rapid strides toward civilization," in large part because of their schooling.[3] With their Yankee belief in self-improvement and hard work, Bennett, Hart, and the other town leaders valued education highly. The concentrated exposure of tribal children to the principles of American civilization offered a means to close the cultural gap. Schools promised to bring all succeeding generations into some segment of the larger society, if only at its margins.

From its earliest days Pipestone manifested a local vision projected nationally. In founding the town, Charles Bennett and Daniel Sweet dreamed of capitalizing on the widespread popularity of the quarries in art and literature and of centralizing the distribution of the place's legends and image. Pipestone organized formally in 1879, the same year that Carlisle opened in the East, and town leaders lost no time in discussing the possibility of acquiring an "Indian seminary." For the next decade, a school remained the subject of talk. But disputes over the title to the reservation delayed any action, and rapid growth temporarily distracted many local businessmen.[4]

Hope for an Indian boarding school near the quarries was incorporated in larger aspirations for the town. As more railroads built lines through Pipestone, Bennett, Sweet, and the Whiteheads wanted to attract some sort of institution that would attract national attention and provide a stable economic asset. Discussion turned briefly to the possible establishment of a Presbyterian college, an idea that appealed to Bennett and other members of one of the town's main churches. But an Indian school had the most consistent support. Pipestone's leaders remained cognizant that the town relied on the quarries and their reputation for its prosperity. They persisted in their romantic belief in the site's significance within American heritage, and they wanted to see it simultaneously preserved and further advertised, preferably by some larger entity such as the federal government. Benefiting from land grants in the form of homesteads and railroad routes, the first generation of Pipestone settlers lived in an age in which American citizens considered the national government a public servant rather than a large bureaucracy. Their young state was steadily developing a tradition of highly participatory, representative politics. These Minnesota Republicans foresaw only positive, noninterfering, economically enabling federal actions rather than any negative potential for externally imposed control.

From the local perspective, all the seemingly obvious factors pointed to the probability that an Indian school would be established at Pipestone. Widespread interest in the quarries and their popularized legends continued to grow. Tribal members made their annual visits to extract stone, lending credibility to assertions about the site's relevance but not staying long enough to be perceived as troublesome. Following Carlisle's lead, federal Indian policy and American sentiment in the 1880s and 1890s favored off-reservation boarding schools. Pipestone itself offered modern urban amenities and accessibility through rail transportation that was exceptional for a rural region. Also important was the fact that town residents, like other American citizens, assumed, if somewhat naively, that their elected officials served the needs of the constituents, responded to requests from the electorate, and supported the continued development and prosperity of the country.[5]

ACTIONS TO SECURE A FEDERAL PRESENCE AT THE QUARRIES

With the selection of Pipestone as the site for a school only a matter of time in the minds of the citizens, men and women in the town organized and decided on the best means to make their expectation a reality. A decade of boosterism and steady growth provided experience and success in the self-promotion required to garner public interest. In addition to favorable popular sentiment, they needed to ensure they would have congressional sponsorship and influence in the Bureau of Indian Affairs (BIA). This dual approach quickly became standard in Pipestone's development plans in regard to the quarries.

General promotion proceeded, with town merchants and land marketers such as the Close brothers continuing their efforts to inundate the reading public with literature and imagery, including new editions of the "Legends of the Pipestone Quarries." The *Pipestone County Star*'s June 1889 tenth anniversary issue featured a "new legend" by D. Ivan Downs, whose poems provided much of the content of the widely circulated "Legends" pamphlet. After the opening of Carlisle, others, such as Isaac Hart, the editor of the *Star,* began to encourage a focused discussion of an Indian school. At an "Indian seminary" youths might be "taught more fully the way of peace." Stressing the town's unique qualifications for the institution, Hart claimed that the quarries' "associations themselves are of such a character that all the Indians would favor" a school at the site. The retelling of some of the legends, the mention of "the immortal Longfellow" and "other noted writers from one end of the land to the other," and the emphasis on the romance of annual tribal visits all bolstered assertions of the quarries' significance.[6]

In winter 1889–90 developments in Washington, D.C., spurred more organized action. Expanding its education program, the Indian Office made public its plans to build an Indian industrial school at Flandreau, South Dakota, fourteen miles west of Pipestone and home to a settlement of Santee, some of whom frequented the quarries. Alarmed that the federal government might build a school close enough to eclipse Pipestone's chances and to limit opportunities for continued growth, Bennett, Davies, and other prominent residents met in February. With no further delay they drafted a petition to circulate for signatures and to send to Rep. John Lind.

Convinced that the "worshipping place for the tribes of all nations" was "no less valued by the white race," the petition's creators ambitiously called for both a school and a "National Indian Park" for all Americans to visit. On behalf of a school, they argued that "peace, industry, education and enlightenment" held the solution to perceived problems in Indian policy and that Pipestone offered a unique "common meeting ground" for people from all parts of the nation. At the quarries the federal government already held title to the reserved land, simplifying property issues. The quartzite deposits provided sturdy building stone, and the four railroad lines could transport other necessary supplies cheaply and efficiently. Apart from pragmatic considerations, the petition touted the less tangible but equally valuable benefits of Pipestone over those at Flandreau. With no small tinge of self-interest, it read: "This being a spot where Historic Interest draws large numbers of tourists from among the scientific and educated class of our people, the establishment of the proposed school here would enable a more appreciative class, as well as all who come, to observe the practical workings of the munificent endowment of our Government on behalf of the Indians, than if located in some place around which cluster no historic associations connected with the race, or at a location more obscure, or less accessible." Continuing the line of reasoning that a federal presence at the site would prove a national asset, the petition concluded with a plea for funds to establish, improve, and care for the "National Indian Pipestone Park."[7] Local interest in acquiring some form of "public enterprise" for the town eclipsed any perceived contradiction between assimilating tribal children and maintaining a site associated with traditional tribal practices.

Throughout winter and spring 1890, hundreds of copies of the petition circulated in the region, reaching cities, towns, and reservations. Boards of trade and chambers of commerce in Minnesota's urban areas endorsed the proposal, and almost three hundred tribal members, as well as almost everyone in the county, signed the petition. Pipestone also summoned the support of the regional press, such as the *St. Paul Daily Globe*, which saw in the proposed school a "singular appropriateness," a place in which tribal children could be "schooled in the arts of peace," and an "opportunity for interweaving aboriginal history into American civilization."[8] The proposal combined familiar romantic images of the quarries' past with a national sense of urgency in funding a practical Indian policy that satisfied reformers.

Although they believed that their elected officials would yield to reason, the Pipestone group augmented the influence of popular support with persuasive artifacts. When the petition arrived at Rep. John Lind's office, he also found himself in possession of an ornately carved pipe, and in March other members of Congress received pipestone ornaments. The gifts served the dual cultural and economic purposes of familiarizing the representatives with the product of the quarries and demonstrating what pupils at the school could manufacture for profit. Before the end of May, Lind introduced a bill requesting Indian schools at both Flandreau and Pipestone but omitting mention of a national park.[9]

Significant to its success, the proposal carried the support of the commissioner of Indian Affairs, Thomas Jefferson Morgan. A staunch advocate of Indian education as a means for assimilation, Morgan particularly favored off-reservation schools that separated children from the tribal influences of family and community and immersed them in an English-speaking, non-Indian environment. In office for only four years, he proved influential in securing congressional appropriations for boarding schools and federal commitments to places such as Pipestone. Once the government had invested in such institutions, the schools became less susceptible than smaller programs to changes in the political climate. When the Pipestone school bill passed in Congress and obtained President Benjamin Harrison's signature in winter 1891, the town received a substantial and enduring new asset.[10]

GIVING A FEDERAL INSTITUTION LOCAL CHARACTER

During the remaining months of 1891 a jubilant atmosphere pervaded Pipestone. To those who lived there, the success of the petition confirmed all that the town claimed about itself, and the school manifested national recognition of the importance of the quarries. In addition, as the *Star* hastened to comment, the U.S. government would be investing directly in Pipestone's improvement. The Indian Office requested samples of quartzite to determine its suitability for planned buildings and sent the superintendent of Indian schools, Daniel Dorchester, to visit Pipestone. With a sense of justification, town residents believed in the validity of their continued assertions about the place's historical and cultural importance. Government officials and elected representatives appeared to agree that the quarries had always been "irresistibly attractive to not only all the tribes of the Great Sioux Nation, but to every Indian in all of Uncle Sam's vast possessions."[11] In their view of all tribes as generic Indians in need of assimilation into a perceived homogeneous national society, the people of Pipestone were indeed the average American citizens they proclaimed themselves to be. If the federal government sought a nontribal community with a typical outlook on national issues as the setting for the school, Pipestone could rightly recommend itself.

Town leaders such as Bennett and Hart readily presumed that Congress planned to follow the school bill with legislation to establish a national park. Before long, however, they learned that the government acted according to its own priorities and provided assistance for town improvement only as a by-product of larger pursuits. Other than the use of quartzite for buildings, the development of the school proceeded with little regard for its local setting. At the end of the nineteenth century the pursuance of conformity characterized Indian policy, particularly in education. Government officials and reformers believed that uniformity in curriculum and environment would result in consistent and desirable outcomes among the tribal children, regardless of their specific needs or a school's particular surroundings.

When the Pipestone Indian Training School opened in 1893, it served a dual educational and administrative role as a school and as the central agency office for the Dakota communities in southwestern Minnesota. Otherwise, it differed little from any other institution in the system. Like Carlisle, Haskell, and a dozen other off-reservation boarding schools, including that in nearby Flandreau, its curriculum for grades one through eight focused on basic academic courses combined with training to develop manual, or "industrial," skills along recognized gender divisions. Indian reformers believed instruction in farming, woodworking, laundering, and useful crafts provided the most practical means of helping integrate Indian youth into American society. Local popular opinion supported the reformers, believing that industrial education was "the best possible compensation . . . for the loss of ancestral territorial holdings" and a solution to the perceived problem of "a large population of uneducated and nonproductive Indians." An emphasis on self-reliance and individual ability complemented the standard courses in English and U.S. history in an effort to detribalize children.[12] In this regard the school at Pipestone, despite its touted unique location, proved virtually indistinguishable from its peers.

Despite the government efforts to attain uniformity, the school could not avoid reflecting its setting or absorbing some of the local character. Town promoters claimed the quarries drew tribes from across the continent, but the Pipestone Indian School concentrated on recruiting pupils from Minnesota and the contiguous states. Early on, government officials and local residents anticipated that having a school at the site would appeal to the tribes, but contrary to expectations, few parents volunteered to send their children to the institution for months at a time. Consequently, the superintendents at both the Pipestone and Flandreau schools resorted to bribery in their first years and competed to some degree until they established reputations for their facilities. The enrollment at Pipestone Indian School rapidly settled into a demographic pattern that reflected Minnesota's tribal population and Longfellow's vision of Native America, attracting mostly Dakota and Ojibwe pupils from reservations throughout the area. Over the years the school also hired tribal members from the region for manual work. Some of these workers quarried pipestone and carved objects to sell to tourists for added income and later stayed on to establish a small Dakota community in Pipestone.[13]

In planning the school compound, the Indian Office followed some of the advice of town leaders. On receipt of the requested samples of quartzite from deposits on the reservation, the federal government issued a contract to John M. Poorbaugh, a local quarry owner, for construction of a large stone building. Poorbaugh completed the three-story structure by fall 1892, which allowed the school to open during the winter. The single building contained both classrooms and residential space until dormitories could be erected the next summer. A steady succession of buildings followed, lauded by a St. Paul paper as "splendid stone structures which would grace the campus of the proudest university of our country."[14]

Made of the dark red quartzite in Richardson's prevailing style featuring massive blocks, the first buildings resembled those in town. Because of their proximity to the bluffs at the quarries, the structures seemed a natural outgrowth of the landscape around them. Activities inside the school followed the dictates of a distant bureaucracy, but externally the buildings appeared related to their surroundings as they rose from the prairie. In an effort to limit expenses, the government had created an institution that was indigenous to its location and out of place anywhere else.

With a long-awaited Indian school that looked similar to the town, many in Pipestone considered the institution an extension of the community and eagerly anticipated its benefits. Few trees broke the prairie horizon, which added to the impression that the two clusters of buildings existed as parts of a settled whole. Pipestone residents already possessed a sense of claim to the quarries; this proprietary perspective widened easily to include the school that they had worked hard to acquire.

Like the quarries, the Indian school served as "a credit to the town." The federal institution legitimized the quarries' supposed historical aspects, and beyond that, it added new significance to the site. Town promoters wasted no time incorporating the school into publications designed to lure tourists to the area. Hart readily included the school in the *Star*'s special editions highlighting the town's assets, and almost every regular issue featured a column or two on developments, such as new buildings, or relevant articles from papers elsewhere in the country. The *Star*'s editor and others in Pipestone expected the entire area to benefit from "the national reputation this school will give us." In the 1890s editions of his promotional brochure, realtor E. W. Davies gave the new attraction a prominent place. Intending to demonstrate the "enterprising and progressive" nature of Pipestone, Davies placed a large-scale drawing of the school, with no description, in the middle of the first page of a section summarizing some of the quarries' Indian legends.[15] This juxtaposition struck no one in town as incongruous but rather typified the collective attitude about local assets and Pipestone's character.

INCREASED NATIONAL CONNECTIONS AND REPUTATION

The hopes of the townspeople were realized to some extent as the school augmented the national attention that the quarries received. Once the 1891 school bill passed into law, Congress dealt annually with issues of appropriation and policy review. The superintendent of the school traveled to Washington, D.C., for business, and Indian Affairs officials, such as Daniel Dorchester, visited Pipestone with regularity and proclaimed that "no finer location for a government school could have been found." Others, including U.S. Sen. W. D. Washburn and BIA commissioner Morgan, made site visits and wrote of the school, keeping its name and that of the town recognizable across the country. When Washburn visited, he received a reception at the Calumet Hotel in town and reported to Congress that he was "highly pleased with the surroundings" of the institution. Women's church groups from the East Coast added the school to their preferred charities, sending books and other goods. The presses of Minneapolis, St. Paul, and Chicago featured articles about the petition, the buildings, the visits of bureaucrats, the pupils' activities, and stories of interest regionally. When any other paper mentioned Pipestone, the *Star* readily reprinted the piece.[16]

Pipestone also enjoyed the anticipated direct economic advantages derived from the proximity of the Indian school. Through its choice of quartzite for construction material, the federal government aided the development of stone resources and sustained the building boom in town that began in the 1880s and carried the momentum into the 1890s and 1900s, which otherwise might not have slowed with the financial depression at the end of the century. A new city hall and other substantial public structures of local quartzite arose in the center of town. In addition to its impressive county courthouse, its Presbyterian church, and its distinctive Carnegie library, Pipestone also solidified its sense of itself in the massive, deep red buildings. Through the use of indigenous stone and the sturdy Richardsonian Romanesque style favored in the region at the end of the century, the town demonstrated both its connection to its surroundings and its intent to remain as a permanent part of the landscape.[17]

The town reaped more routine benefits through other institutional needs and contracts. Although the federal government supply system operated by taking bids on supplies that could be shipped by rail from Chicago or Omaha, the school supported the local economy through the purchase of smaller orders of items such as flour, paint, and soap from town merchants. On their days off staff members, occasionally accompanied by pupils, spent time and money in Pipestone, where they shopped for personal necessities. The town also supplied essential services such as deliveries, repairs by carpenters and plumbers, and the constant availability of physicians, police, and firefighters in case of emergencies. For some, the new presence of the federal government provided a more direct livelihood. The first school superintendent, Clinton J. Crandall, resigned his position as county education superintendent to assume leadership at the Indian school. Others acquired jobs in the laundry or kitchen, but teachers interested in employment faced the standard examination required for civil service positions and a system that transferred employees from other schools.[18]

In less tangible and more long-term ways, the people of Pipestone hoped that the school at the quarries would enhance the image of the site as historically important and draw a larger and steadier stream of tourists to town. But the presence of the government did not lull promoters into complacency. They actively continued to advertise the town and to adapt imagery of the quarries for a changing national audience.

After his success with pipestone displays at the Columbian Exposition in Chicago, Charles Bennett sent some of his personal collection and items from his store on touring shows and also took his exhibits on the road. He donated a pipe to tour worldwide with the Liberty Bell model from the fair. Accompanying it was a placard signed by Ulysses S. Grant, the former president, stating, "The American Indian Pipe of Peace—Made from the typical stone of America from the Great Red Pipestone Quarry, near Pipestone City, Pipestone County, Minnesota, USA." Following a successful appearance at the Buffalo Exposition, Bennett traveled in 1904 to the Louisiana Purchase World's Fair in St. Louis. Once again he took the mantel carved from catlinite and set on a quartzite hearth, as well as assorted trinkets, stone samples, and the collection of petroglyphs that he had taken from the quarries with the intent to safeguard them from souvenir hunters. A fellow townsman, Frank Raymond, took his "Winnewissa cutlery" with carved pipestone handles to the fair as well. Bennett's award-winning displays drew more acclaim at St. Louis, and he brought home to Pipestone a silver medal for the "pictographic or hieroglyphic carvings by Prehistoric Dakota Sioux" and a bronze medal for the mantel. Like many of the items, the mantel later retired from touring and went into permanent display in the courthouse.[19] More important than the awards, Bennett's exhibits offered thousands of Americans from all parts of the country the opportunity to see samples of pipestone and to listen to a recitation of the legends of the quarries.

At home, Bennett and his neighbors hosted tourists and various groups that visited the town. Just before the World's Fair in 1904, Pipestone was the site for the state's Firemen's Convention. For the occasion, dignitaries received "a huge key [to the city] made of the sacred red pipestone," and the groups took tours of the quarries, falls, Indian school, and other points of interest. For the firemen, an excursion train ran to the quarries every twenty minutes, where members of another visiting group—"an Indian camp"—conducted their annual dig, serving as a spectacle and "a novel sight for many visitors to the city." Bennett entertained the firemen at the bluffs with a speech about the legends. At the federal school, a group of pupils sang "This is the Indians' Home" to the tune of "The Battle Hymn of the Republic." Between choruses of "Glory Glory Halleluja," the children praised their school for changing "savage" tribal customs into civilized behavior that united the people of America.[20] The firemen left Pipestone having enjoyed an unusual experience that blended local and national culture.

Other groups visited with less fanfare. Before the school held its first classes, the regional posts of the Grand Army of the Republic chose the Pipestone area for their annual encampment. As members of the Simon Mix Post #95, locally prominent men and Civil War veterans, such as Charles Bennett and Leon

Moore, viewed their town, with the nearby quarries, as a natural place for their Grand Army of the Republic brothers to gather. Close to ten thousand veterans visited Camp Fremont—so named to honor John "the Pathfinder" Frémont's visit to the site with the Nicollet expedition sixty years before— below the quartzite bluffs, to which a special rail track ran. Not one to miss an opportunity to promote Pipestone, Bennett wrote to Gen. Frémont; mixing religious imagery, Bennett asked him to attend the encampment at the "Mecca of all tribes of Red men," but Frémont declined the invitation. Later, groups of Methodists at a conference in Sioux Falls took excursion trains across the state line to visit the quarries. After the St. Louis fair, Presbyterian missionaries convened in Pipestone. The federal government provided additional guests by selecting the Indian school as the location for the regional teachers' summer meeting.[21] Periodic visits by members of such varied organizations supplemented the steady stream of summer tourists and helped spread word of Pipestone through personal recommendation and testimony to people town promoters might not otherwise reach.

Especially after Bennett's displays at prominent expositions, individuals with regional and national reputations visited, wrote, and spoke of Pipestone in popular venues. The *Star* noted enthusiastically that the area was "attracting increasing interest and attention as the years pass." Into the 1890s Abigail Gardner-Sharp continued to make pilgrimages to the quarries to retell the story of her abduction at Spirit Lake. She dedicated her life to self-promotion and Indian reform and used the site of her infamous captivity as a platform to speak to a sympathetic local audience on behalf of both themes. To the southeast in 1904 Professor Samuel Calvin from the University of Iowa lectured at Davenport on the quarries and their legends. Superintendents of Indian education, including Charles Rakstraw and W. N. Haliman, stopped in town when touring the school, as did members of Congress, such as Minnesota's Rep. James McCleary. Part of the Republican establishment, Col. Louis Ayme of Chicago granted an interview to the *Minneapolis Tribune* after his visit to Pipestone. Invoking language worthy of Catlin, he said he had hoped for years to see the "Great Peace Plain" and found it a "resting spot for traveler and artist, for historian and poet."[22] Such external affirmation of Pipestone's promoted image reinforced the efforts of local boosters such as Bennett and reflected back the images they projected.

Though not always at the pen of historians or poets, news about Pipestone and the quarries continued to appear in print across the country. The site even inspired a Minnesota physician to express himself in verse. A. D. Hard's poem captured the ambivalent modernism of the early twentieth century, beginning with "We went touring in our auto to that spot to Red Men dear / To the sacred Pipestone quarries." After crossing the prairie roads Hard found romance and joy in a tour "coupling ancient savage customs, in this age when science lives." Transferred by the Indian Office from Pipestone to the boarding school in Santa Fe, New Mexico, Clinton Crandall represented the quarries' legends in the Southwest, giving talks on Indian education and geology and writing for *Frontier Monthly.* Amid dry reports of legal issues involving the quarries, the *Chicago Daily Tribune* and the *New York Daily Sun* elaborated on the "legendary lore" of the "famous red pipestone reservation."[23]

Other national publications continued the growing tradition of including the quarries in works about tribal culture. Mary Catherine Judd compiled *Wigwam Stories,* which would not have been complete without the tales of Hiawatha and a retelling of the legend of "Leaping Rock in the Pipestone Valley." Judd cited Schoolcraft as her main source for the Hiawatha sections, but she did not mention if she had been to the "Valley of Peace." In a more scientific work written for the Smithsonian, Frederick Webb Hodge's *Handbook of the American Indians North of Mexico* featured a lengthy section by William H. Holmes on catlinite. Holmes relied extensively on Catlin and Pipestone-produced interpretive materials for his descriptions of the area and for ethnographic information, possibly obtained during an earlier visit to the town. He referred to letters to and from Charles Bennett and reproduced a photo from Bennett's collection featuring an "Indian quarryman" at work in the rocks. Although a work about Native Americans, Holmes's essay on catlinite and the quarries barely mentioned tribes.[24] Imagery of the place projected by Bennett and others was increasingly accepted and reproduced across the country. In the work by Holmes, the Yankton appeared briefly and more as the kind of cultural curiosity that Pipestone promoters represented them to be than as historical and contemporary people making decisions and acting on behalf of their own interests.

YANKTON CONTINUE LEGAL ACTIONS FOR USE OF THE QUARRIES

Indeed, the 1890s and early 1900s were difficult years for the Yankton. Like many tribal groups, they believed their best option was to accommodate federal policies and assimilate in their corner of eastern South Dakota. As elderly

leaders from the prereservation era died, a new generation of Yankton continued their tradition of cooperation despite the government division of their
reservation for sale to outsiders following the 1887 General Allotment Act,
known as the Dawes Act. Even as circumstances changed, the Yankton persisted in their disputes with the United States about rights to land around the
quarries.[25] The successful resolution of the squatter problem of the 1880s led
to new issues for the tribe. In the midst of the tension over squatting on reservation land, the Burlington, Cedar Rapids and Northern Railroad laid track
into town across one corner of the section set aside by the 1858 treaty. At that
time the railroad company saw no need to secure a right-of-way, and others
presumed the tracks crossed public property. The government survey of the
section that followed the eviction of the squatters in 1887 revealed the railway's
trespass. The Yankton took immediate action, protesting the encroachment,
and the commissioner of Indian Affairs sent the matter to Congress.

The ensuing act of Congress strengthened the positions of both the tribe
and the government while maintaining Pipestone's interest in the land. At the
urging of the town's voters, Rep. John Lind drafted a bill that created a board
of appraisers for reservation land, including the corridor used by the railroad,
and that gave the townspeople first choice should the tribe decide to sell. The
bill, which was passed, also granted the Yankton the right to dispose of the
land by majority vote, imposing U.S. political standards on the tribe. In 1889
members of the tribe met with a government commission to settle the issue.
Although they accepted the $1,740 compensation payment by the railroad,
they refused to consider selling any of the reserved land.[26]

The calm that came after the settlement lasted only a few short years. In
Pipestone, those who drafted the Indian school petition believed strongly that
tribes would support a school at the reservation and feel themselves drawn to
it. Certainly, some tribal representatives perceived advantages in having a government school in Pipestone and signed the petition, but this group did not
include the Yankton, whose opinion differed greatly. As soon as they learned
of passage of the school bill in 1892, the tribe lodged a formal protest with their
agent, E. W. Foster, and generated a petition of their own, with 167 signatures
in opposition to the construction of a federal institution on the reservation.
While publicly returning to its earlier evaluation of the section as reserved by
the United States for tribal use of the quarries, the government renewed negotiations with the Yankton.[27] Both sides settled into a familiar pattern of legal
posturing, neither anticipating the thirty-year dispute that ensued.

From the Yankton perspective, the government had repeatedly acknowledged tribal possession of the land and had upheld treaty rights. Although a continuous federal presence at the quarries might reduce the amount of illegal quarrying, the school did not directly benefit the tribe, which had already yielded plenty in land and rights over the years. A Yankton man who grew up visiting the quarries during the 1890s later recalled, "That school operated there for a good many years; we never got a dime out of it."[28] At the time, the government offered the Yankton little that could be deemed adequate compensation for land that was invaluable.

Congress and successive BIA commissioners tried several tactics to appease the Yankton, but they never hesitated in the construction and operation of the school. In 1892 Congress passed an Indian appropriation act that allowed the federal government to buy allotted lands deemed surplus. The Yankton refused to accept that the section surrounding the quarries qualified for sale under those conditions, and many in Washington questioned whether the government could buy what it already claimed to own. Against the advice of the attorney general, Congress and the Department of the Interior then opted to present the matter to the Supreme Court, which in turn saw no reason to consider the matter. In response to the Yankton request for clarification of the title to the reservation, a second appropriation act in 1897 authorized further negotiations. For the next two years, James McLaughlin, familiar with general Dakota culture after more than two decades in the Indian Service, met with the Yankton and tried to reach an acceptable solution.[29]

At the end of 1899 the two sides concluded discussions. By a narrow margin the Yankton approved a settlement for the reservation. The government agreed to compensate the tribe in cash and cattle, to guarantee quarrying rights, and to preserve forever the reservation as an unsettled section. The Yankton ability to act as shrewd negotiators met with resentment in Washington. Despite repeated efforts to ratify the long-awaited agreement, many members of Congress refused to accept that the Yankton held title to the land and expressed dismay that government representatives had negotiated with the tribe as an equal. A series of four bills died before leaving committee, and the Yankton entered the twentieth century with uncertain title.[30]

This legal limbo rarely affected the activities of the tribe at the quarries. As they had for almost fifty years, the Yankton made regular visits, usually carrying letters of authorization from their agent. The new presence of a government representative at the school caused the tribe to negotiate the timing of their quarrying. Although the townspeople preferred to have Yankton individuals camped on the reservation at all peak tourist times, the tribe yielded to the preference of the superintendent to visit during summer recess. This cooperation proved to be reciprocal. Prior to establishment of the school, the Yankton had to rely on requests from their agent to the people of Pipestone to guard the reservation and to uphold tribal rights. Although Bennett and others had promised to do so, they usually ignored quarrying by nontribal individuals and profited from the illegal sale of pipestone carvings. With the superintendent in residence near the quarries, trespassers faced greater risks, and the tribe occasionally received compensation, though begrudgingly, from Pipestone for the use of reservation land to graze cattle or to celebrate the county fair.[31]

STUDENT ACTIONS AND LOCAL RESPONSES

Creating an authoritative presence and developing congenial relationships with tribes and townspeople constituted a substantial part of the government's activities at Pipestone. Establishing an Indian boarding school proved more routine. Despite its location, the school's daily functions closely followed the standardized institutional plan for off-reservation education. With a definite degree of self-interest, Pipestone petitioners had eagerly recommended teaching pupils to carve catlinite for marketable crafts. The BIA, however, considered the activity pointless and did not encourage it. Ignoring the proximity of the quarries, the bureau's assistant commissioner, E. B. Meritt, advised that "lace making is an industry in which the Office is much interested, because it believes that industry can be made a profitable one, and the work itself will have an influence for good upon the Indians." Reading material in the classroom also revealed no appreciation for location. Pupils joined thousands of others in American schools who read *Robinson Crusoe, Some Merry Adventures of Robin Hood, Ivanhoe, Rip Van Winkle,* and *An American Book of Golden Deeds.*[32] Although books on Minnesota history appeared on the list of curricular requests, pupils at the Indian school received a more generic, displaced national education than did their peers at the Pipestone public school less than a mile to the south.

With their standardized curriculum, Indian boarding schools across the country contributed to the development of pantribalism. Children from different tribes and cultures lived in close quarters with each other, bonding through shared experiences in a new environment and a second language. Daily life at the Pipestone school fostered a pantribal perspective both on and off the grounds. In the classroom pupils could also read books that encouraged the perception of a common Indian culture, such as *Old Indian Legends* and *Eskimo Stories*—books that could also be found in nontribal schools. With some recognition of the local legend said to pertain to all tribes, facility officials chose the name *The Peace Pipe* for the short-lived school paper.[33]

Outside the classroom school-directed activities also reinforced the kind of pantribal or general view that the residents of Pipestone had held since before the establishment of the town. In the most direct way, the children enacted white images and expectations of tribal people. The school held an annual play for an audience of townspeople. In 1908 the children's ensemble presented *Ten Little Indians*. Two years later they performed *Half-Breed,* a play set on an Arizona reservation. Its main character, Arizona Jack, described as a Dakota graduate from Carlisle, shared the stage with a colorful western ensemble of trappers, cattle thieves, renegades, and cavalrymen. Pipestone's press cheered the "Indian thespians" and saw nothing unusual in the entertainment. One year before, the town had hosted Wah-ta-waso, an Iroquois actress, at the Ferris Opera House. During her visit she made a special guest appearance at the Indian school to encourage the young actors.[34] Decades later, productions of Longfellow's *Song of Hiawatha* as a school play would meet with enthusiasm and inspire a new chapter in Pipestone promotion.

Some of the pupils' behaviors outside the school unwittingly affirmed popular stereotypes of tribal children. When in the company of Superintendent Crandall en route from their homes, children who had never been off their reservations energetically explored their new surroundings in a St. Paul hotel. The *Pioneer Press* reported that they played loudly and "chattered away in their guttural language." To St. Paul journalists, such behavior constituted a spectacle in the lobby and solidified the image of "wild Indians" in need of the school's civilizing influences. One of Crandall's successors, James Balmer, received a letter from a teacher in Woodstock, a farming community ten miles east of Pipestone. Her pupils, the children of Dutch immigrants, had never encountered any tribal people and wanted to visit the school to observe their Indian peers at work and play.[35] Balmer did not report whether his pupils shared a similar curiosity about Dutch American children.

As individuals, some children engaged in other behaviors that the press deemed worthy of local headlines. Their actions confirmed both positive and negative Indian stereotypes and often affected the relationship between the school authorities and the townspeople. From his childhood in Pipestone in the 1910s, Charles B. Howard remembered the Indian school and its almost two hundred pupils as the main tribal presence on the reservation. When he and his friends swam at the quarries, they occasionally encountered Dakota and Ojibwe boys from the school who tried to chase them home, reportedly in an effort to protect the area.[36] Such encounters supported local beliefs about the quarries' pantribal importance.

Like children at boarding schools anywhere, many tribal pupils at Pipestone decided that they wanted to be home and ran away in order to get there. With only a limited staff, the superintendent called on the city police and occasional volunteers to track runaways and return them to the school. Local presses noted each escape as a natural occurrence, expecting the "wild" children to resist the "uplifting" efforts of the government on their behalf, efforts that were designed to bring them into the fold of American civilization.[37] Neither school nor town officials demonstrated an attempt to understand the children's wishes and needs, but they cooperated to enforce the federal plan for Indian education.

Prior to and during the Prohibition period, national and state laws criminalized the sale of alcohol to minors and to Native Americans, but enforcement of the statutes varied with time and place. Local vendors periodically ignored the restrictions. In one of the more flagrant violations, two saloons in Pipestone sold alcohol to over a dozen pupils from the Indian school in 1908. The youths became intoxicated and rowdy, assaulting the police chief, Luke Brown, and damaging property. This "old time Indian uprising" made sensational front-page news that played up familiar images of drunken "red-skinned rioters," again resisting assimilation efforts at the school. During Prohibition the school superintendent, F. T. Mann, urged pupils to sign temperance pledges, while bootleggers plied their trade in Pipestone and kept alcohol available. The quarries became a popular spot for secluded imbibing. In fall 1916 two pupils from the school discovered an unattended car filled with whiskey and beer near the falls and served themselves, becoming the talk of the town.[38] The situation mandated cooperation between local authorities and Superintendent Mann in curtailing the actions of the bootleggers and in supervising Indian pupils.

Other actions by the children created more positive impressions and demonstrated possibilities for the changes sought by Indian policymakers.

The *Chippeway Herald,* a newspaper on the White Earth Reservation in northern Minnesota with the masthead "Education, Civilization and Citizenship," regularly reported on the schools where Ojibwe children boarded. In 1902 the paper noted that the older pupils at Pipestone had access to the public library in town and spent spare hours there reading. This pastime suited the press's theme, and the paper applauded townspeople who supported the school's policies for transforming tribal children.[39] Although library policies did not directly affect the town, such publicity enhanced Pipestone's image and encouraged continued cooperation with the school.

Popular thought of the time conflated Christianity and American civilization. As part of the perceived great moral effort to assist the federal government in "uplifting" tribes, Pipestone's churches welcomed Indian children and sought to convert them. Shortly after the school opened, in 1893, they celebrated their first success: Charity May Palmer chose to be baptized as a Presbyterian and became the first Native church member in town. In ways that blurred the line separating church and state, the school's children could exercise little choice in regard to religious observations. Christmas was an annual ritual in town and in the school, sometimes characterized by an odd syncretism such as an "Indian Santa" in "full Indian regalia." Spring commencement featured a sermon by the Presbyterian minister. The school choir performed Christian music in both government buildings and the Baptist church.[40] Pipestone's residents, who petitioned for federal protection of a tribal sacred landscape and expected school authorities to be responsive to their requests, certainly saw nothing unconstitutional or even unconventional in such activities.

FEDERAL FRUSTRATIONS WITH PIPESTONE'S PRIORITIES

The BIA cooperated with the town when their interests overlapped, as they often did in the form of education provided at the school. In some ways, however, federal management of the reserved section diverged from Pipestone's expectations, as government representatives addressed policy matters concerning the unusual place and the tribes who visited it. With dual duties as educational administrators and agency officials, the school superintendents had to balance institutional needs and reservation issues, on the one hand, and local expectations, on the other.

Despite continuing legal questions about the title to the land, the United States consistently assumed responsibility for protecting the quarries where possible, in somewhat atypical governmental behavior in regard to tribal interests. Superintendents sought to coordinate school schedules and tribal visits, but they also attempted to prevent interference with approved quarrying. During James McLaughlin's negotiations with the Yankton in 1899, DeWitt Harris advised ceding the portion of the reservation encompassing the quarries to the tribe, with perpetual government oversight, and purchasing private land to the north for school use.[41] Although the school generally operated without reference to the quarries, the superintendent oversaw both and on occasion needed to act to protect treaty rights.

Harris's successors dealt with both the tribal visitors at the quarries and the residents of the area who trespassed on government property. When necessary, F. T. Mann took an active stance. He contacted the Yankton agent, A. W. Leech, about a tribal disagreement regarding bailing water out of the flooded quarries. Without hesitation, Mann billed a local farmer who had taken hay from the reservation without permission. When approached in 1915 by a minister from South Dakota who wished to procure a large amount of pipestone, the school superintendent issued an unequivocal refusal. Referring to the 1858 treaty, Mann stated that he would not "permit white men to come on the reservation and take this stone . . . I would not permit even an Indian to make a practice of digging this stone and shipping it out in large quantities." Following Mann, superintendent Ora Padgett also assumed a directly active stance. Padgett mediated during a dispute among Santee quarrymen from Flandreau. Through a series of written and verbal statements, he warned nontribal visitors that the federal government would prosecute anyone vandalizing the rocks, removing stone, or starting illegal fires in the vicinity. When he placed signs and notices around the perimeter of the reservation, he found them shot to shreds within days, typically by teenage vandals.[42] Mann's and Padgett's exercise of authority occasionally frustrated local entrepreneurial efforts to continue the commodification of the quarries.

Frustrations frequently came by direct order from the commissioner of Indian Affairs. Unlike the school superintendents, distant federal authorities had little knowledge of or interest in local practices or sentiment regarding the quarries, and they dictated policy accordingly. Pipestone residents enjoyed swimming at the pond near the quarries—referred to as either Lake Hiawatha or Lake Manito—and picnicking near the falls, two recreational activities sanctioned by the Indian Office. Prior to the establishment of the school on the reservation, townspeople followed a path or roadway across the section and to the quarries that the earliest settlers had created. With the construction of the Indian school, federal officials decided to eliminate the road in order to minimize access to the reserved land and to prevent interference with the school's separate environment. The commissioner and his staff experienced no direct consequences from this decision, which upset local residents. DeWitt Harris found himself in a difficult position, trying to uphold BIA policy while placating angry townspeople and discouraging another popular petition to members of Congress that might adversely affect the school's appropriations.[43]

Unknowingly, through its standard policies, the federal government's presence began undercutting local interests. Pipestone profited not only from sales of carved catlinite crafts but also from the spectacle offered by tribes visiting the quarries. Although they never considered providing entertainment their first priority, Yankton and Santee groups camped at the quarries sometimes invited local residents and tourists to watch them celebrate after a day's quarrying. In 1923, toward the end of another period of pressuring tribes to assimilate into national culture, Commissioner Charles Burke issued a statement nationwide urging tribes to cease dancing entirely but particularly "at public gatherings held by the whites." Burke considered customs associated with these "useless and harmful performances" (such as giving away property) a waste and a distraction from work and the progress of acculturation.[44] For the people of Pipestone this move diminished the site's attraction for guests who paid to visit the place, an aspect of no consideration in Burke's cultural crusade.

As the school continued year after year and became more widely known nationally, it slowly assumed some of Pipestone's professed authority on the quarries' stone and legends. Increasingly, people from across the country associated the school with its location. Although interest in Pipestone never diminished, a growing number of Americans, as well as people from abroad, directed their inquiries about the quarries and the site's perceived past to the school superintendent. Many wanted to acquire objects carved from catlinite, such as napkin rings and ashtrays, while others sought information about the tribal use of the site and related customs. In response to requests for carved goods, the superintendents generously referred people to merchants in town. When the Indian Office provided pipestone objects for an exhibit at the 1922 Travel Club meeting in New York, Assistant Commissioner Meritt instructed Superintendent Padgett to send the materials with brochures from the appropriate merchants, in case tourists visiting the meeting might be interested in the future. To requests for information, the superintendents provided the sanctioned *federal management* [handwritten annotation]

government interpretation of the tribal past and the legal status of the quarries, without the poems and town promotion included with Pipestone's descriptions of the site.[45] In this way, federal management of the quarries' human history slowly expanded its scope and authority.

FEDERAL AND LOCAL RELATIONS ON A PERSONAL LEVEL

local – Crandell oversaw institution for two years [handwritten annotation in left margin]

Throughout the first three decades of the school's operation, the townspeople adjusted to the proximity of U.S. government officials and the immediacy of federal policy. In the early years, more tension marked the relationship between town and school than the petitioners had anticipated. The success of their popular effort with Congress and the appointment of their own county education commissioner, Clinton Crandall, as the institution's first superintendent bolstered the town's desire for close relations with the school. Crandall served only two years at Pipestone before his transfer to New Mexico. After his departure, townspeople began to realize that the responsiveness they expected from the federal government did not apply to the Indian Office.

Although school personnel generally maintained congenial relations with people in Pipestone, Indian Affairs officials demonstrated that the school's mission did not include acceding to the town's wishes. Crandall worked closely with associates and contractors in town to construct the buildings and to begin operations. Transferred from BIA institutions elsewhere in the country, his successors arrived with no connections to Pipestone's residents, and they concentrated on their professional duties at the school. Contact between school staff and townspeople ebbed under the superintendencies of DeWitt Harris and F. T. Mann. During their tenures—1894 to 1904 and 1912 to 1919, respectively—tensions increased, as the government employees became increasingly frustrated by the town's proprietary attitude toward the quarries and the school.

Assuming leadership of the boarding school after Crandall's departure, Harris sought to separate the institution from its neighbors. In a pointed letter to BIA commissioner William Jones in 1902, Harris requested bluntly that no teachers from Pipestone be transferred to fill vacancies at his school. He presumed Jones understood his reasoning but emphasized that he wished "to keep *entirely* free from local influence." To stress his position further, he observed that "the citizens of the town take great pride in the school, but only as an institution connected with their town" and, he contended, as a source of gossip.

When townspeople began drafting another petition to pressure the Indian Office to reopen a road to the quarries, Harris expressed his frustrations to Rep. James McLeary. He feared appropriations might be cut and considered the locals "very short sighted when they attempt to antagonize the interests of the government in this way." Caught between duties and town pressure, he lamented being "accused of antagonizing the interests of the town."[46] Pipestone's efforts to enhance its reputation by extending its cultural claim to all activities near the quarries, including those of the government, met with frequent resistance from Harris, who had an Indian training school to run and an agency to manage.

In the interim years of 1905 to 1911, after Harris was transferred to a Cherokee school in North Carolina, Willard S. Campbell served as superintendent. He encountered seemingly fewer tensions but more spectacle involving the school. The episodes with drunken pupils occurred during his tenure. Although seen as somewhat of a setback in the educational program's progress, the incidents did not keep Campbell from asserting to the *Cleveland Plain Dealer* that Indian children would soon assimilate fully. Perhaps to counter lingering public doubts, he also commented that his pupils had great senses of humor and learned readily. In 1906 the school received a different kind of publicity when a "sensational shooting" happened there. A former teacher, Alex Hart, had been fired for beating a pupil. He returned to the school with a gun and attempted to shoot Campbell in the dining hall. Hart hanged himself in jail. The following year his widow, Mina Cook Hart, married William Madison, a former student, and resigned from her teaching position.[47] Minor incidents such as the gossip that irritated Harris perhaps paled in comparison to the dramas Campbell experienced.

After Campbell, F. T. Mann faced issues and attitudes similar to those Harris encountered. He limited contact with the town by authorizing staff and pupils to go to Pipestone only on Saturday afternoons and only if necessary for business purposes. The town responded to the superintendent's snub in its new city charter by defining town boundaries as commencing at the southeast corner of "the so-called Indian reservation." When the school closed early in spring 1917 after federal funds were reallocated to War Department needs, Mann became aware of local rumors that the government planned to give the school to the town. He wrote to the other superintendents in the Indian Service that such an assertion was "a lie, pure and simple," generated by "some person or persons of this locality, whose regard for the truth is entirely overshadowed by their desire to create a sensation." In the same year, an unidentified incident at a patriotic rally in town caused tension that was acknowledged by both Mann and Pipestone's residents, after which both parties expressed the wish for improved relations.[48]

A self-professed "real American" town, Pipestone's patriotic enthusiasm during World War I drew responses from government officials of higher rank than Superintendent Mann. Local nationalism expanded beyond rallies and loyalty speeches into the kind of zealous Americanization efforts that occurred across the country. In 1918 the town's Public Safety Commission ordered the Evangelical Lutheran congregation, St. Paul's, to omit their traditional German-language services and use only English. The parish protested with a letter to President Woodrow Wilson. In June the Oval Office responded with assurances that no federal law prohibited the use of German and that the government did not support actions to suppress the language. Having always considered themselves part of the national drama, practically everyone in town participated in the war effort. Pipestone County ranked first in the country in per capita purchases of fourth-issue Liberty Bonds, reflecting a pattern of behavior that was consistent with local attempts to be involved in the government school's operations.[49]

After the war, strident Americanization spirits waned and the school administrative staff changed. Superintendent Ora Padgett took charge for the first five years of the 1920s and developed a more harmonious relationship with Pipestone's citizens than that of his predecessors. In 1924 the Indian Office transferred Padgett and replaced him with James W. Balmer from the school at Lac du Flambeau in northern Wisconsin.

As superintendent at Pipestone for an unprecedented twenty-two years, Balmer presided over significant changes in terms of the role of the government in managing the reservation and interacting with the town. He had relocated willingly, leaving the isolated woods of Wisconsin and settling near a community that offered better educational opportunities for his own children. In his first few months at Pipestone, he described the town in letters as a "very neat place" and a "buzzling little city," home to "the only Pipestone quarry in the World." He touted the sixteen miles of paving and observed that "everyone in town is a booster for their little city." In addition to sending his children to public school, he joined civic organizations, including the Masons' Quarry Lodge.[50] Balmer's eagerness to move to Pipestone and to become involved in the community on a personal level directly affected the federal-local relationship.

During Balmer's lengthy tenure, from 1924 to 1946, his hands-on approach to administration and interpersonal affairs changed the nature of the government presence at the quarries. The school's reputation had never suffered, but Balmer's supervision secured the school's place among the most respected government educational institutions. A 1931 publication that was otherwise critical of BIA policies labeled it "undoubtedly the best school in the Indian Service" and described Balmer as "kind, jovial, patient, and constructive" and "a singular breeze of fresh air in a stagnant desert of disappointments." In contrast to previous superintendents, he routinely visited reservations in the region and introduced himself to his pupils' parents.[51] With a typically limited budget in an era of decreasing numbers of off-reservation schools, Balmer maintained a clean, comfortable facility with a healthy environment and a waiting list for admission.

The cooperative spirit and openness to change that characterized Balmer's work at the school also typified his relations with people in Pipestone. Postponed during legal maneuverings between the Yankton and the United States, Pipestone's wishes for a national park or other official form of federal preservation of the quarries never diminished. In Balmer's twenty-two years at the site the townspeople reorganized and acted to attain their long-awaited goal, with the support of the Indian school superintendent. Balmer assisted town efforts and represented the kind of responsive government that local residents expected. During his term, the role of the U.S. government on the reservation experienced a major transition in terms of the nature of the site's management, a change effected by new leaders in Washington and in Pipestone. Through the 1920s and 1930s, the sacred past of the site became officially enshrined.

FOUR

Enshrining the Quarries

Since the time of Pipestone's founding in the 1870s, its residents identified the town with the quarries and maintained both a conviction of their national importance and a proprietary sense toward them. In regard to this unusual geological and cultural place, they hoped consistently, if not always formally, to achieve three interconnected goals, none of them atypical for Americans of their era. As women across the country took the lead in historic preservation, women in Pipestone strove to preserve the quarries, both as a place of perceived national significance and as the town's raison d'être. No less important, town civic leaders and merchants also wanted the public to be able to use the quarries' scenic assets for recreation, and they sought to commodify the site's cultural attributes for profit. Increased economic prosperity, particularly for the expanding middle class, and the growth of the automotive industry in the 1920s resulted in a surge of tourism in the United States, a development on which Pipestone's merchants hoped to capitalize. Through persistence and a variety of community efforts, active Pipestone residents, led by Winifred Bartlett, finally secured federal preservation of the quarries during the Depression years of government programs and subsidies. As a result of attaining that goal, however, they experienced unanticipated, federally imposed limitations on activities related to the quarries. Consequently, they adapted their strategies for marketing the place, adjusting to national conditions, as they always had, and continuing the local tradition of promoting the quarries to as wide an external audience as possible.

The most substantial changes in the town's relation to the quarries developed during the 1920s and into the years of the Depression and World War II, as Pipestone residents built on the community's past. Town merchants, civic leaders, fraternal organizations, and women's groups continued to augment local traditions regarding the quarries, particularly in efforts to preserve them and to popularize further their associated legends. Almost a century after their highly publicized visits to the Côteau, George Catlin and Joseph Nicollet still occupied a central place in the story of the quarries. Like other explorers, they helped to situate American landscapes in a national context and to ground them in the country's past, perpetuating a European-oriented historical narrative tendency that located tribal experiences and occupancy of the land outside recorded history and therefore within a timeless realm. Both Philip Deloria and David Lowenthal have noted this tendency to equate Native Americans with nature, as part of antiquity and the landscape rather than within the national historical narrative.[1] By the 1920s people in Pipestone wanted the quarries protected almost as much because of the celebrated European American affiliations of the site with explorers and writers as for the place's mythic tribal associations.

This accretion of another layer of meaning for the quarries prompted renewed preservation efforts after World War I. Inspired by conservation activity elsewhere in the country, interested local people relied on proven techniques, such as government petitions, and also formed new organizations for the purpose of obtaining the kind of federal or state custodial presence that the Indian school superintendent alone could not provide. As happened with the arrival of Bureau of Indian Affairs (BIA) officials near town, Pipestone's citizens discovered that successful preservation of the quarries included changing relationships with government representatives. Only a few years after the United States and the Yankton settled the reservation title issue in 1928, the National Park Service (NPS) became Pipestone's newest federal neighbor.[2] Preservation did not develop in the anticipated form, and throughout the 1930s and 1940s the Pipestone community continued to adapt its uses of the quarries' imagery and heralded Indian heritage.

REVIVING CATLIN'S VISION OF A NATIONAL INDIAN PARK

The local preservation movement began in earnest in the 1890s, with the earliest interest in establishing some form of park, preferably a federally protected one, at the quarries. When Charles Bennett, Isaac Hart, and other businessmen organized and circulated a petition in favor of an Indian boarding school on the reservation, they included a plea for a "National Indian Park" as no less a priority. They appealed to what they considered the site's established place within American culture. Because of the quarries' "rich traditions and charming landscape—rendered classic by the immortal Longfellow and others in story and song," the petition claimed that the land was "no less valued by the white race" than by tribes. They considered it a "common meeting ground," already under federal jurisdiction and easily accessible by Pipestone's railroad lines.[3] Unlike towns near large Indian reservations throughout the West, Pipestone would benefit more from continued federal presence in the area than from dissolution of the nonresidential reserved acreage. Containing quartzite expanses and drainage areas, the section held virtually no agricultural potential. The lasting worth of its uncommon mineral deposits relied on its continued existence as a cultural site. These attributes made the quarries more similar to early national parks with unusual landscape imagery, such as Yellowstone, than to western reservations rich in ores or grasses for grazing.

Basing their images of the quarries on the *Letters and Notes* of George Catlin, with its two chapters detailing his 1836 visit to the place and providing his interpretation of Dakota legends about the site, Bennett and the residents of Pipestone drew an additional vision from him. Catlin, at his romantic "salvage ethnographer" best, proposed a "nation's Park" to preserve attractive aspects of tribal cultures that he believed were vanishing. Within this park, "the world could see for ages to come the native Indian in his classic attire," preserved in a natural and cultural landscape well stocked with bison. Catlin considered the Great Plains the most appropriate location for such a park, with its "finest specimens of the Indian race."[4] Less than forty years later the idea of a "National Indian Park" seemed reasonable and imminent in Pipestone.

Borrowed from Catlin and Longfellow, a belief in the cultural and historical significance of the quarries formed the basis of continued preservation efforts in the late nineteenth and early twentieth centuries. At the same time, however, the popularization of pipestone imagery threatened the site's integrity, as seasonal groups of tourists—and mischievous local teens—not only left their marks on the rocks in the form of graffiti but also took souvenirs, including petroglyphs, from the quarries. Concerned citizens in Pipestone by no means wished to limit tourist interest in their area, but they sought to preserve the quarries within a controlled environment that would attract even more visitors.[5] Had the quarries not been neither private property nor in the public domain, local organizations might have been able to provide their own interpretive and custodial presence. Because this option for action did not exist, Bennett and other Pipestone merchants petitioned the federal government for assistance.

After the creation of Yellowstone National Park in 1872 and the growth of the conservation movement, led by highly visible persons such as Theodore Roosevelt, the U.S. government, through the aegis of the Department of the Interior, emerged as the protector of lands and landscapes deemed nationally important. Since 1849 the same administrative agency had represented itself as guardian of Native American interests. Minnesotans—including railroad baron James J. Hill and his son, Louis—successfully urged the creation of Glacier National Park, using its dramatic landscape and images of the Blackfeet tribe to promote the Great Northern Railway. Because the pipestone quarries also combined unusual geology and tribal traditions, the people of Pipestone expected the federal government to act as conservator of the site, preserving it for tourists who benefited the town economically and confirmed the quarries' place within American identity.

The success of the educational component of the 1890s' two-part petition and the ensuing establishment of the Indian boarding school on the reserved land in 1893 temporarily reduced talk of a national park for the area. As employees of the BIA, superintendents at the school served as de facto custodians for the quarries but only to the extent that doing so did not interfere with their educational responsibilities. With the quarries located on the other side of the reservation, close to a mile away from the school compound, geography limited the effectiveness of the school officials as guardians. At the turn of the twentieth century Pipestone's residents waited to see how the new federal presence at the quarries would manifest itself and how local relationships with government representatives would develop.

While the title to the reserved section of land remained unclarified until 1928 and the responsibility for protection of the quarries settled on the BIA official at the school, families, church groups, and free-roaming youths from Pipestone continued to use portions of the reservation for recreation. The prairie meadows above and below Winnewissa Falls offered bucolic settings for picnics and baseball games. In summer months Lake Manito provided an escape from the heat in the form of a natural swimming pool with shade created by trees planted along the quartzite cliffs. The construction of a dam by pupils at the Indian school enlarged the lake, as did the channeling of Pipestone

Creek above the falls, and townspeople considered creating a small beach on one of the shores. Local residents thought of themselves as entitled to enjoy the scenery and wished to keep the area accessible to tourists, provided that recreation did no obvious harm to the quarries themselves. Although leisure activities took place separately from any tribal quarrying, published descriptions of natural attractions on the reservation—such as the "historic falls" and the "legendary ledge"—ensured that visitors remained mindful of the mythic context of their outings.[6]

Little chance existed that they could forget. Few tourists would have ventured to a remote location on Minnesota's western prairie had it not been for the popularized imagery and constant promotion of the site. Building its identity—and its tourist business—on the quarries and their associated legends, Pipestone attracted people because of the place's unusual cultural assets. Beliefs about the uniqueness of the quarries drew the first settlers to the area in the 1870s, and their descendants perpetuated the perception of the place as significant and worth visiting through the repetition of inherited imagery. Into the early twentieth century, Americans lost none of their interest in Indian culture represented as antiquity or timeless tradition but continued to view it as part of their country's heritage. National tastes tended toward simplified myths about the continent's past that reassured and entertained without intruding on daily life in the present. Among middle- and upper-class urban European Americans, a fascination with dehistoricized and depopulated tribal sites, including cliff dwellings in the Southwest or, less dramatically, the pipestone quarries, created a thriving market for relics from and visits to such cultural landscapes.[7] Residents of Pipestone in the early 1900s continued their efforts to capitalize on this trend through the promotion of their local American attraction.

Like middle-class European Americans across the country, townspeople viewed tribes as unable to preserve important or at least interesting and usable aspects of their own traditions. At Pipestone fewer Yankton and other Dakota came to quarry each year; instead, they concentrated their energies on adjusting first to their reservations and then to allotment life in South Dakota. The limited number of tribal members who did come to quarry often sold their rough stone to local, nontribal entrepreneurs to carve and to sell. By the turn · of the century, members of regional tribes accounted for less than 10 percent of people carving catlinite, with some estimates ranging as low as 1 percent. Although this decline resulted directly from the assimilation and acculturation policies that had widespread support in the nineteenth century, white Americans responded with characteristic ambivalence and lamented some of the unintended outcomes of the efficacious policies. Perceiving selective tribal traditions as authentic antidotes to the artifice of modernity and motivated by a sense of nostalgia about the cultures they had helped to dismantle, members of fraternal and women's groups in Pipestone, like others throughout America, assumed roles as guardians of what they interpreted as significant aspects of Indian prehistory. With perception shaped by local identity and common American beliefs about Native traditions as static and uniform, they could not appreciate tribal cultures as adaptive or view a landscape such as the quarries and accept that its meaning could change with new generations.[8] Convictions about the virtues of a timeless past led them to fear damage to important cultural sites in the present and motivated them to act to preserve what they saw as an unchanging legacy.

More than a decade after the establishment of the Indian boarding school on the reservation, concerned citizens in Pipestone realized that the superintendent alone was not sufficient protection for the quarries. While the school served as a curiosity and a symbol of the town's progressive nature, it did not substantially enhance local attractions in promoting the area. By 1910 renewed interest in the idea of protecting the quarries officially in the form of a park gained strength as townspeople joined in the groundswell of national conservation and preservation sentiment, spurred in part by anxiety about modernity. The desire to set aside spectacular or unusual tracts of land for the enjoyment of successive generations had grown and spread since the mid-nineteenth century. By the early 1900s, when the United States had changed dramatically through technology and territorial consolidation, the interest in preservation had broadened and taken root among the middle class. In the new century, designated American heritage sites embodied national values and cultural reference points distinct from Europe, and places such as the quarries enshrined common myths on which to continue building communal identity.[9]

Efforts to preserve wilderness and historically significant sites converged in Progressive-era legislation. Passed in 1906, the Antiquities Act provided for the creation of national monuments by executive order. The loose terms and liberal interpretation of the act made it applicable to a wide variety of preservation causes. Originally designed to protect Indian ruins in the Southwest, the act contained provisions that allowed for federal preservation of public lands with broadly defined "prehistoric, historic, or natural features." Nothing in the act distinguished clearly between human cultural landscapes and natural ones, reflecting common perceptions of historic tribal sites as part of the natural world. Rather than wait for Congress to pass legislation establishing national parks, U.S. presidents frequently used their authority under the act to set aside significant areas as national monuments, ensuring their protection until Congress granted park status. This tactic, which blurred the distinction between monuments and parks, remained popular long after the passage of the 1916 act that created the NPS.[10]

People in Pipestone considered the Antiquities Act propitious. At last other like-minded Americans had organized to preserve what they considered nationally significant sites of tribal prehistory, and a responsive government supported their efforts. After 1906 members of civic and church groups in Pipestone formed to promote the national park idea, as well as other uses for the reservation land. Although no proposals could succeed while the title remained unclear, local activities increased throughout the 1910s and into the 1920s, laying the foundation for later organized attempts and gaining wider attention for efforts to preserve the quarries.

PETITIONS FOR A PIPESTONE PEACE PARK

Interest in a "National Indian Pipestone Park" had not gone dormant after construction of the boarding school. During an 1895 visit from Rep. James McCleary, Charles Bennett and others in town called for a park with "perpetual maintenance by the government." Until 1912, however, no organized group met to act toward the desired goal. That winter, members of the local Inter-Church Federation convened, discussed the theme, and stated their reasons for believing it "eminently fitting and proper that the site be preserved forever as a national park preserve." Not only were the quarries considered geologically unique and sacred to tribes, but both history and sentiment also characterized the site, similar to tribal ruins being preserved in the Southwest. Noting that Longfellow had portrayed these qualities in his work, the group wove his writing into the popular history that formed the rationale for their activities. No local effort to preserve the quarries limited itself solely to obtaining protection. The *Pipestone County Star*'s editor, Ralph G. Hart, summarized local opinion and acknowledged that a park would be "a decided advantage" to the town. It would provide "a suitable pleasure ground" and "promote the fame of Pipestone far and near."[11] No one in town separated preservation from the wish for a recreational area and a tourist attraction. Although the Inter-Church Federation's plans did not advance, their goals persisted and spawned new efforts.

Tourist attractions could draw more visitors with pleasant scenery, an unusual object of interest, and amenities. The reservation offered the first two elements, but the land surrounding the quarries and the falls remained fairly rustic prairie, almost a mile from the graded streets of town. In 1916 Ralph J. Boomer drafted a report recommending plans for park development along the lake and creek. In training as a civil engineer, Boomer saw great recreational potential in the area and proposed a series of "improvements" to make the land more accessible and usable for both townspeople and tourists. He summarized local interest by noting that Pipestone's residents sought to turn part of the reserved section into a "National Indian Pipestone or Peace park, as will not interfere with the treaty rights of the Indians to dig pipestone, nor interfere with the Indian Industrial Institute." In addition to improving the dam to make a larger lake and building a bridge across the creek below the falls, he proposed several other changes. After the creation of a beach along the lake shore, a proper park would include both a bathhouse and a canoe house, as well as a comfort station and a large, grassy area enclosed by tall shrubbery. Several oiled-gravel roads and paths and a designated parking area would give the public easy access to the site. As a good Pipestone resident, Boomer included in his report a history of the area and a summary of the quarries' legends, as relayed to him by Charles Bennett. The *Star* contended that Boomer's park plan would not interfere with the Indian school or activities at the quarries.[12]

As a gesture of goodwill and in hopes of generating support for the idea, town leaders forwarded the report to Sen. Knute Nelson and to the Indian Office, expecting that the federal government would be responsive to their plans. However, although both recipients appreciated the interest in a park, they recognized that no such plans could develop on disputed tribal land. In response, the Pipestone Businessmen's Association discussed the issue at their annual meeting and circulated a petition with a limited request for a free public bathing area that could be supervised by the boarding school's superintendent. When this plan also met with resistance, the merchants tried a new tactic: they approached the state with a recommendation for a "tourist rest camp" by the falls.[13]

The idea of state involvement at the site found a warmer reception in St. Paul, Minnesota's capital. By the 1920s many in state offices acknowledged the growing importance of tourism. The Minnesota Historical Society recognized the quarries' imagery as part of state tradition and encouraged the use of the place as a romantic backdrop for novels set in Minnesota. To represent the state, Masons sent a Bible carved of catlinite to Alexandria, Virginia, for incorporation into the cornerstone of a memorial to George Washington. Minnesotans became increasingly aware of Pipestone's growing national reputation and readily accepted the town's interpretation of the quarries' Indian past as something that gave their state a place that contributed to America's sense of itself.[14]

In 1924 officials in St. Paul sought to help the state capitalize on any possible development on the reservation. At the urging of the ad hoc Pipestone County Park Committee, a group composed of local businessmen and elected officials, the Minnesota Highway Department circulated a petition to the legislature in favor of a state park at the quarries. The petition argued for Minnesota's government to preserve this "spot of special historic interest" and also to create from it "a lasting monument to the pioneers who opened up the southwest territory." In support of the historical significance of the site, W. E. Stoopes, the assistant state park engineer, submitted a report to the state auditor. Stoopes claimed that "historians say that there is no spot on the North American Continent better known" among tribes, whose dwindling numbers could no longer preserve their own traditions at the quarries. The report included plans similar to Boomer's for a beach, a bathhouse, roads, a picnic area, and an outdoor theater. A supplementary document highlighted familiar local "Indian Legends," referring often to Catlin's and Nicollet's visits, Abbie Gardner-Sharp's captivity, and Longfellow's poetry, using European American historical experiences at the place to bolster claims of the quarries' national significance, just as Pipestone residents had done for fifty years.[15]

Interested persons at the state level hoped that the federal government might grant Minnesota the portions of the reservation either not used by the school or bordering directly on the quarries. Although the U.S. government was both unwilling and legally unable to relinquish land, the idea of creating some form of a park had drawn extensive public attention. By the mid-1920s people in Pipestone increased their organized efforts to preserve the quarries. In an era of intensified assimilation policies, which included the Indian Citizenship Act in 1924, the federal government began to renew efforts to resolve the issue of reservation title. A successful elimination of the tribal claim to the land could further integrate the Yankton into the larger society, relegate the quarries thoroughly to the past, and serve as a first step in making the area more accessible to other Americans interested in visiting places of general national heritage.[16]

RESOLVING THE YANKTON CLAIM

From the time of the 1858 treaty onward, the Yankton had been in almost constant legal negotiations with the United States and in disputes about local use of the reserved land. When they were finally ready to resolve the issue in 1899 through the agreement mediated by James McLaughlin, Congress failed to ratify the settlement. At the time, many of the older members of the tribe still made the journey to Minnesota to quarry and carve pipestone. By the 1920s, however, no Yankton had visited the site in almost a decade. Assimilation policies, geographic distance from the quarries, and the death of elders who had direct ties to the area diminished the tribe's interest in retaining title to the section and increased the desire for a claim settlement. Other Dakota bands continued to object to the Yankton hegemony over the quarries, particularly as Flandreau Sisseton and Wahpeton men quarried periodically, in the absence of the legal tribal representatives.[17] A new generation of Yankton prepared for the final resolution of the seventy-year-old issue.

In the early 1920s the tribe pressed to have its case for settlement heard by the Indian Claims Commission. The commission decided in 1925 that the 1858 treaty granted the Yankton quarrying rights only. Upholding the interpretation that the federal government had always maintained, the decision reiterated that the treaty reserved Yankton cultural and economic rights to the land but did not provide for residence or occupancy, as with most reservations. With characteristic persistence, the tribe urged its attorneys to appeal the matter to the Supreme Court. A year later the Court reversed the judgment of the Indian Claims Commission, stating that the Yankton had indeed held title to the land, and it ordered the commission to assess proper compensation. Because the tribe considered the Indian school an encroachment for which it never received reparations, 1891 served as the basis for evaluations of the reservation's worth, to which the Court added the government's accrued interest for the use of borrowed land. A year after the 1928 ruling by the court of claims, Congress appropriated funds for the accumulated award of over $300,000 to the Yankton. This action finally settled the issue of title to the reserved section, while also acknowledging the continuing cultural and spiritual significance of the quarries. The land passed into the jurisdiction of the BIA, rather than into the public domain, and the boarding school continued in its role as custodian.[18]

While the Yankton and the United States resolved the question of title to the quarries, changes occurred in Pipestone. In 1926 Charles Bennett, the town's founder and most influential resident, died. Over half a century earlier he had crossed the prairies from Iowa to visit the quarries about which he had read in Catlin and Longfellow. Over the next fifty-three years Bennett had devoted himself to popularizing Pipestone and the tribal legends interpreted by earlier explorers and writers. He profited directly from the promotion of the quarries and the sale of pipestone carvings, but he was not motivated solely by economic incentives. He also led preservation efforts and believed that his private artifact collection was a storehouse of local tribal heritage.[19] He was, in a real sense, the father of the town.

During the 1920s fraternal groups in town, such as the Businessmen's Association, the American Legion, and the Masons, remained supportive of the idea of a park. Leadership in the matter of preserving the quarries, however, came from others in town. Across the country in the early decades of the twentieth century, women, working in groups and on their own, acted to identify and to preserve sites with natural and historical importance. In preservation work, they found a public outlet for political expression and an evolution of their earlier traditional roles as educators and moral bastions in the community.[20] Like their peers, women in Pipestone increasingly appointed themselves guardians of the local past within its national context and served as stewards of public heritage, seeking to uphold tradition for future generations.

As a town with strong Yankee roots, Pipestone was home to the Catlinite Chapter of the Daughters of the American Revolution (DAR). In addition to general civic service, the DAR in the East labored to protect eighteenth-century battlefields and buildings important to the beginnings of the United States. Elsewhere in the country DAR women concerned themselves primarily with places related to European American history, supporting a national sentiment of Americanization by stressing the importance of the country's shared heritage. For the Pipestone Catlinite Chapter, enmeshed in local lore, the quarries held obvious significance within that larger context.

When the exploration and cartography party led by Joseph Nicollet and John Frémont visited the Côteau in the late 1830s, they left an early tourist mark. On the top of a prominent outcrop along the quartzite ledge above the quarries, Nicollet had carved his name, and the others in the party had chiseled their initials. The deep incisions weathered a century of erosion by wind and harsh winters but faced an increasing threat as later travelers followed the map to the site and sought to leave evidence of their own visits.

Someone in town might have moved more quickly to preserve the site had the beloved Catlin made a physical impression at the quarries rather than just leaving behind essays and paintings housed in distant libraries and museums. Representing the United States in what was then remote territory, the Nicollet-Frémont expedition held almost as much romantic appeal. Throughout the country the DAR as an entity sought to preserve sites of national rather than Native historical importance. In deeming such places worthy of preservation, the organization demonstrated a typically ethnocentric European American assumption that "real" history, written by their ancestors, differed significantly from the Indian "lore" that was part of an indistinct past outside recorded time. Within this context, protecting the stone carved by representatives of the United States seemed an obvious patriotic duty to the Catlinite Chapter and one that complemented local interest in the preservation of the quarries themselves. Had it been possible to remove the stone and place it in a museum, an individual such as Bennett—who safeguarded the area's petroglyphs in his store—would have done so earlier. But protecting the top of a quartzite pillar required more organization and financial resources than removing rock carvings. The DAR could provide both and could also use a sentimental appeal to tangible national heritage preservation in order to garner support.

Because of the delay in clearing the title to the reservation, the local DAR turned first to the superintendent at the Indian boarding school, in his capacity as official guardian of tribal land. After their initial appeal to Superintendent Ora Padgett in 1923 provoked no interest, the women of the group, led by Allie Davies—the widow of real estate agent and Pipestone promoter E. W. Davies—renewed their efforts two years later with Padgett's successor, James Balmer. Inclined to cultivate good relations with townspeople, Balmer responded positively within three days. He approved of the chapter's plans to retrace the carvings with a chisel in order to make them more legible for tourists (an act that would make professional preservationists cringe), to erect a barrier in front of the stone, and to place on the cliff a bronze marker describing the rock's importance in American heritage. After sending his immediate reply to Davies in April 1925, Balmer forwarded her group's request to the commissioner of Indian Affairs with his recommendation for approval of the project. By the autumn of that year the DAR's plaque was in place and the Nicollet-Frémont stone was safeguarded for the benefit of posterity.[21]

The DAR expanded its interests in the quarries beyond protecting the carved stone. Locally, the Catlinite Chapter sought to preserve native plants and wildflowers on portions of the reserved section, one of the few remaining areas of tall-grass prairie in the region not plowed under by farmers. Because earlier residents had planted trees along the quartzite bluff, thereby altering the "historic" landscape, maintaining part of the legendary place as it might have looked when Catlin and Nicollet visited would enhance its authenticity for tourists. At the state level, the DAR members advocated the establishment of a national park at the quarries. Although they did not overlook the tribal legends associated with the quarries, they endorsed the land's preservation because of its role in attracting national explorers and pioneers and in hastening the development of that corner of Minnesota.[22] Like similar women's groups in other parts of the country, Pipestone's DAR selected as significant the natural scenery and national associations of the quarries, marginalizing the majority of human history that occurred there before the arrival of European Americans.

WINIFRED BARTLETT AND THE PIPESTONE INDIAN SHRINE ASSOCIATION AS GUARDIANS OF TRADITION

While the DAR pursued its complementary goals, others in Pipestone revitalized earlier efforts to preserve the area because of the cultural and economic value of the quarries' tribal heritage. In the early 1930s a loosely structured group of members belonging to various civic organizations formed the Pipestone National Park Federation. They retained their objectives for federal recognition and protection of the site but soon changed their name to the Pipestone Indian Shrine Association. This name described less a concrete preservation goal than a local proprietary sentiment of responsibility for the quarries and an emphasis on the cultural significance of the mythic place.[23] After fifty years people in Pipestone had developed a strong tradition of interpreting the area and acting as caretakers of the popularized tribal past. Over the decades they had built up layers of beliefs about the significance of the quarries, based on repeated versions of legends transmitted by Catlin, Nicollet, Schoolcraft, and Longfellow. For members of the Shrine Association the quarries drew historical importance from both their perceived value to tribes and the attention from nineteenth-century men of letters. By the 1930s they could not have thought of the quarries without reference to earlier Americans who documented the place's spiritual allure. The Shrine Association considered the quarries nationally important because of their human history in a culturally inclusive sense.

Unlike the DAR, the Shrine Association was a group of both women and men, and unlike previous attempts to establish a national park, it focused specifically on historical and cultural preservation. Its organizer was the woman who stepped in to fill Bennett's role as a town leader, G. Winifred Bartlett. Born near Pipestone in the 1880s and educated in town, Bartlett visited the reservation often as a child, playing by the falls and watching activities at the quarries. She trained as a teacher but found her adult career in law firms and courts; in 1927 she became the first woman county clerk of court in Minnesota. Through her position, Bartlett made professional acquaintances in places such as St. Paul and New York, many of whom shared her interest in Indian history and looked to her for ethnological information. Although she later described preservation as a hobby she picked up because she had to have something to do, both her childhood explorations and her adult occupation influenced her choice of civic activism. In the mid-1920s she worked as a court reporter for the Yankton settlement case and learned details of the tribe's history at and beliefs about the quarries. Her leading role in preservation efforts developed slowly, but her knowledge and enthusiasm made her a local expert and a charismatic spokesperson for the Shrine Association.[24]

From its beginning the Shrine Association assumed the stance of a guardian in relation to the quarries. Reflecting the widespread mentality that had created the Antiquities Act and similar legislation, Bartlett and her colleagues were convinced that tribes in the region had either no desire or no ability to preserve the site, despite their continued quarrying and presence in the area. The association perceived its mission as a necessity. Assuming they knew what was best for the regional tribes, despite independent tribal decisions and actions, the group's members saw themselves as acting on behalf of tribal interests, protecting the sacred place for those who could not do so for themselves.[25] In this they manifested locally the renewed national trend of salvage ethnography, which regained momentum in the early twentieth century. A similarly paternalistic perspective had previously coincided with the outlook of the BIA, which considered its boarding school education of tribal children essential and beneficent. Persuading the federal government that it shared Pipestone's preservation priorities required more effort.

Toward this end the Shrine Association chose an immediate plan of action. Preservation served as a local rallying cause as the Depression intensified nationally. Expecting prosperity to return and the federal government to resume its responsiveness, the association sought to garner interest in preserving the site. In 1932 it published two thousand copies of a forty-two-page booklet that described the quarries (or "shrine"), the creation legends, mentions of the site in national literature, the reservation's history, and the association's goals. Much of the booklet typified Pipestone promotional literature and built on the foundation of earlier pieces. It contained long excerpts from Catlin and Longfellow, retold the legends with an emphasis on the pantribal importance of the quarries, and summarized the area's history since European exploration west of the Mississippi. Resembling the earlier biblical allusions in descriptions of the place as an "Indian Eden," the booklet encapsulated the universal message of the site as "Peace on Earth, Good Will toward Men."

In other ways, however, the text clearly revealed the group's mission to preserve the quarries as a sacred Indian site within the context of American cultural history, familiar to a literate public. Written mostly by Bartlett, the essays told of "individual and sporadic" past efforts to protect the tribal cultural landscape, including earlier petitions and Bennett's "salvage ethnographer" activities. Following a section on "Indian Pipestone Lore" that heavily quoted Catlin, Nicollet, Hayden, and Powell and preceding excerpts from Longfellow, an essay on the reservation explained its legal history and relationship to the town and the federal government. Bartlett's prose exuded unself-conscious paternalism, typical of the Indian reform movement revitalized in the Depression era. The brochure noted that the tribes were helpless to care for the place and that their "white friends were divided in what was best for the Indians" in their early preservation activities but stressed that "both races" wished to protect the quarries. The initiative to acquire federal protection of the quarries came from the residents of Pipestone, who sought to "honor the race that established its Shrine at this place" and to "spread real understanding of the Indian beliefs" associated with the place since "ancient times." Although the Shrine Association obtained pipestone samples to accompany the booklets from tribal members such as the Mdewakanton men who quarried and carved catlinite trinkets for local merchants to sell, the group did not include a Yankton or other tribal member on whose behalf they considered themselves to be working.[26]

Despite a lengthy precedent of petitions and meetings, the association's objectives and actions differed from those of earlier efforts. The group wanted the public to visit the park, and it never denied the economic advantages of tourism for Pipestone, but with reformist zeal, Shrine Association members preferred education to simple recreation and stressed the cultural values of the quarries. Bartlett believed that as "knowledge of the Quarry's historical significance became general," the resulting widespread interest would ensure protection. In accordance with their progressive beliefs, the Shrine Association's goals included preventing vandalism, preserving the natural prairie, spreading an understanding of Indian legends associated with the quarries, and honoring tribes, through assuring their continued right to quarry, if desired.[27] They expected such broad ideals to generate a large base of support.

Rather than mailing their booklets to legislators and waiting for Congress to acknowledge the worthiness of the park proposal, members of the Shrine Association took direct, personal action. They consulted with James Balmer, superintendent of the boarding school, to determine how receptive the Indian Office might be. Although Balmer recommended the NPS as a more fitting Department of the Interior bureau, he and another Indian Affairs official submitted a joint report to their superiors, advocating establishment of a "National Indian Shrine." The cultural and historical aspects of the quarries emphasized by the association fit the mission of the Park Service, which in 1933 assumed management of the national monuments created through the 1906 Antiquities Act.[28]

Meanwhile, in late 1933, Winifred Bartlett took the message in person to those in prominent political positions. Using professional contacts, she arranged meetings with Park Service and Indian Affairs officials and members of Congress. In the hectic days of New Deal program development and plans for social change and economic revitalization, Bartlett and other Americans had high hopes that the government would be responsive to local needs and community-designed improvement plans. The public expected the government to provide funding and program assistance for deserving citizens and, increasingly, to support contributions to and the growth of national artistic and cultural life. In the mid-1930s the Pipestone preservation proposal corresponded well with the Park Service's goals. It also fit in with the New Deal's emphasis on local development and new federal programs such as the Civil Works Administration and the Indian Emergency Conservation Work. Within Franklin Roosevelt's administration, the new commissioner of Indian Affairs, John Collier, knew little of northern Plains cultures, but he believed strongly in revitalizing tribal arts and crafts traditions as an essential element of American heritage. His view of preserving native cultures and land resonated with the spirit of Catlin's early call for a national Indian park and the Shrine Association's contemporary mission. Bartlett included Collier in her list of officials before whom to plead the Pipestone case, and she found little persuasion was necessary to gain his approval.[29]

By 1935 administrators at the NPS's regional office in Omaha had become sufficiently interested in the quarries to take action. They sent their assistant historian, Edward A. Hummel, to survey the reservation and to assess its historical and cultural significance. In his thorough report of the land's attributes, its national importance, and its potential as a park, he borrowed from earlier writings of John Wesley Powell and described it as "incomparable" from the perspective of tribal lore. Although Hummel was a historian, his interpretation of the quarries' past differed little from the popularly accepted lore, an early indication that the Park Service would not always provide a more objective perspective than Pipestone's portrayal of the place's heritage. For context he explained the past preservation efforts of the DAR, the local residents, and the Indian school, and he described the limits of these groups' ability to maintain the area. Hummel agreed with the Shrine Association that the quarries required a structured, funded program, including a permanent custodian to prevent vandalism, to interpret the site for visitors, and to oversee tribal digging—in essence, the kind of sustained supervision that local residents and the school superintendent could not provide.[30] Within the Park Service the only issue under serious discussion was not whether the pipestone quarries merited some form of preservation but how to proceed with the task.

An easily designed, satisfactory plan for preserving the quarries also eluded members of Congress. Beginning in 1934, one member of Bartlett's audience, Minnesota's Sen. Henrik Shipstead, eagerly sponsored a series of three bills aimed at establishing the Pipestone Indian Shrine within the Park Service. Ordinarily, the president designated as a national monument a portion of the public domain with natural or cultural significance, while Congress legislated the creation of a national park. Because the area surrounding the quarries met the qualifications for a monument but lay outside the public domain, the usual methods did not apply in this case, even though the BIA agreed to cede the land. In addition, members of Congress remained unclear about the terms of the sponsored legislation. Shipstead initially considered the quarries and surrounding land as a potential "national Indian park" but could convince few of his colleagues that a deposit of unusual stone on the vast prairie compared favorably to the majestic Yosemite or Yellowstone. To have Congress create a national monument would be a somewhat unorthodox approach, but Shipstead found more support, including cosponsorship in the House by Minnesota's Rep. Paul Kvale, when he modified his approach and proposed the quarries as a monument.[31]

Throughout the process of securing federal preservation, the language involved reflected its users' views. After decades of local reference to the quarries as a sacred site for all tribes, Bartlett's group built on the tradition of seeing the place as spiritually significant. The site also served as the goal of tribal pilgrimage from afar. Pilgrimage became a popular term in the writings of nineteenth-century explorers, who made their own kind of long journey to the quarries, a sacred space on the periphery of industrializing society. By the 1930s constant use of the same images had made them normative for anyone who thought about the quarries, even members of the federal government who had never visited them. Because the association wished to emphasize the cultural values of the quarries, they stressed preservation of the "Pipestone Indian Shrine." Traditional, local use of *shrine* designated the quarries as a romantic place apart—a site outside recorded history and off the rational grid of surrounding farmland. Others in government offices, such as Hummel and the Indian school's Superintendent Balmer, also used the term as an image that alluded to tribal legends and their timeless past at the quarries. In the 1930s, however, legislating the establishment of an Indian shrine exceeded the bounds of congressional imagination. Instead, Shipstead and other elected officials continued to use the term *shrine* interchangeably with *park* and *monument*. In the end, the *park* designation proved too grand for such a small place as the quarries. *Monument* better approximated the shrine idea and situated the site on a par with birthplaces and battlefields and other loci of national importance.[32]

Reference to an Indian shrine and carved sacred pipes coincided well with Indian Commissioner Collier's romantic beliefs in earthy tribal religious practices, but tribe members themselves did not necessarily agree with him. When word of the proposed monument legislation reached southeastern South

Dakota, the Yankton followed their own legal tradition and lodged a protest. But other tribes throughout the region supported the congressional proposal and, after decades of Yankton hegemony, eagerly awaited the legal opening of the quarries to all tribes. From a Yankton perspective, the 1928 settlement reserved quarrying rights for them, in accordance with precedent and to the exclusion of other tribes. Influenced by the national growth of pantribalism and by traditional descriptions of the quarries as important to all tribes, Collier and others in Indian Affairs interpreted the ruling to mean that any tribal member held quarrying rights. They refused to entertain a Yankton appeal for additional compensation, and the bureau continued its endorsement of the park plan.[33]

While bills proposing federal preservation of the quarries bounced back and forth among committees and congressional houses in Washington, Pipestone's business and civic leaders continued their traditional use of the place for promotion and recreation. They did this in much the same ways they always had but adapted their efforts to their current audience and to opportunities that arose. In summer 1932 the town began hosting a Plains tribal powwow, or cultural gathering, at the quarries, which attracted tourists who wanted to see the friendly, competitive dancing. In a promotional tradition begun with the Close brothers in the 1880s, the Civic and Commerce Association mailed samples of pipestone to Philadelphia to represent Minnesota in the creation of a national rock garden. When the principals from BIA schools around the country convened at the boarding school, the town provided amenities and tours of the area around the quarries. For a meeting of the National Women's Auxiliary in northern Minnesota, Pipestone supplied a carved pipe. Civic leaders commissioned a carved catlinite shield to be sent to Oklahoma for the president of Phillips Petroleum; the elected officials of Pipestone probably saw nothing odd in this gift to an industry engaged in scandals over oil leasing from tribes such as the Osage. The *National Geographic* planned an article on Minnesota that would include coverage on Pipestone, but at the end of the year the writer canceled his visit. Instead, an article in the Standard Oil Company's *Stanolind Record*—which spread over four pages and compared Pipestone to "ancient Nineveh"—and an illustrated recommendation for tourists to visit "Pipestone national park" in the *Minneapolis Tribune* sufficed for press coverage. In 1936 the American Legion held its district convention in Pipestone, and members celebrated the event by dressing in feather headdresses, two years after an enthusiastic group of Boy Scouts acted similarly on their visit. Analyzing such behavior as part of a national pattern,

Philip Deloria argues that dressing as Indians allowed white Americans to escape into what they perceived as an authentic, natural past.[34] In these ways, tourism and methods of promotion through generic Indian imagery continued to be "business as usual" in Pipestone.

Tourism remained the leading contributor to damage inflicted on the quarries and the incentive for making physical changes to the landscape. By 1934 a New Deal Indian Emergency Conservation Work team descended on the reservation land to begin restoration of "one of the oldest Indian shrines in America," according to the Indian New Deal publication *Indians at Work*. At the urging of the Shrine Association and Superintendent Balmer, the BIA assigned a work team to help beautify the area in preparation for federal protection. Tribal workers voiced their ideas for changes, which included removing shrubs, planting trees, and creating graded footpaths to guide tourists along the quartzite ledge and falls, and then they performed the required labor. In an attempt to deter further vandalism, the group also erected fences and grates to prevent direct access to sensitive areas.[35] The work team's activities provided an early example of what New Deal programs and funding could offer Pipestone and the quarries.

A NEW FEDERAL PRESENCE

In 1937 the decades of effort by Pipestone's citizens came to fruition. When the third draft of a bill to create a national monument at the quarries moved from the Senate Public Lands Committee onto the floor in August, a majority of senators approved it. Within the month the House of Representatives and President Roosevelt concurred, creating the first NPS unit in Minnesota— the 115-acre Pipestone National Monument (PNM). As with other national monuments established in the 1930s, individuals with authority in the federal government chose to preserve a site with historical and cultural value, rather than solely with scenic splendor. After the House passed the bill, Rep. Paul Kvale, who had supported the measure throughout the attempts at passage, celebrated publicly by smoking a "peacepipe" with the House Speaker in front of an assembly of curious photographers.[36] Although the legislation reserved quarrying rights for tribal members only, Kvale's response and the actions of the Shrine Association and their predecessors demonstrated that the creation of PNM resulted from the quarries' significance on a national level, not its significance to regional tribes.

Little changed in Pipestone immediately following passage of the bill. Although the official name of the national monument omitted any spiritual reference, locals and occasionally people in federal positions persisted in referring to the "Pipestone Indian Shrine" and the less formal "sacred area." Having achieved its primary goal, the Shrine Association slowly disbanded, leaving Bartlett as the spokesperson for preservation issues and the local liaison with the Park Service. Town promoters added the lure of Minnesota's only federally designated cultural site to their advertisements, claiming further legitimacy for the same Indian imagery employed since the earliest days.[37]

Despite its official establishment, PNM existed only on paper and in the minds of concerned citizens for several seasons. Within the Department of the Interior, national parks held priority status, and their higher profile ensured appropriations, while national monuments received only minimal amenities. By 1937 much of the flurry of funding in the early years of the New Deal had subsided, leaving less support for recently established programs and projects. As had long been the arrangement, the Indian school's superintendent continued as the informal custodian of the quarries after the property's shift from Indian Affairs to the Park Service.[38] Without an operating budget, the new Park Service unit remained undeveloped and only nominally supervised.

Like other national monuments, Pipestone could have remained in stasis indefinitely, but its unusual attributes spurred federal action. The section of the 1937 bill that guaranteed tribal quarrying rights placed the Park Service in a legal relationship to tribes. Human use of the quarries necessitated appropriate policies and a degree of maintenance, independent of recreational interest in and tourist traffic to the place. Park Service officials did not have the option of devoting only minimal attention to tourism, as happened at other remote monuments. The proximity of the town and its promotional efforts ensured that tourists continued to learn of the quarries; they wanted to experience the "Indian Eden," as well as to buy catlinite souvenirs. Pipestone provided a multifaceted human factor that other rural national monuments lacked, which hastened development planning.[39]

During his brief three years as de facto interim custodian, the school superintendent, James Balmer, acted much as he had since his arrival in the mid-1920s. He maintained his reputation for fairness but experienced some tensions with the town. Following the law, Balmer allowed growing numbers of Wahpeton and Sisseton tribe members to camp on the Park Service land and work in the quarries for extended periods. Some, such as Moses and Estella Crow (Santee), worked at the school and began quarrying after moving to Pipestone. Later, Estella and her second husband, Robert Wilson, taught their children to extract and carve the stone, and they slowly established a permanent tribal presence in town. Others, among them Joseph Taylor (Mdewakanton) and his relatives, lived in Flandreau and spent their summers at the quarries. Seasonal rains often flooded the stone pits, increasing the labor necessary to excavate stone and lengthening the visitors' stay. Although many local merchants profited from the carvings sold to tourists after such encampments, which took place in government-sanctioned tipis intended to lend an "authentic" atmosphere, some voiced their concerns, continuing the old distinction between "good Indians," who behaved according to expectations, and "bad Indians," who did not embody the prescribed image. Too many tribal members who congregated by their own initiative rather than at the town's invitation constituted a less welcome presence. In response, civic leaders registered their complaints with Balmer. His ability to maintain good relations with the local people waned somewhat as he defended federal policies, but his general popularity persisted beyond his temporary dual position. After his three years of custodian duty, Balmer received thanks and praise from Park Service and Indian Affairs officials, but he gladly relinquished the responsibility when the new development plans included a part-time resident custodian.[40]

Beginning in January 1940 PNM entered its formal custodial phase with the arrival of Albert F. Drysdale, a new federal employee from Winona in southeastern Minnesota. With the guarantee of its first appropriation for the unit, the Park Service funded Drysdale's seasonal employment at the quarries. For seven years, Drysdale lived in Pipestone, during which time he made physical improvements at the site and provided an official presence for visitors in the warm months. Although Balmer no longer served in an official relationship to the national monument land, he continued to assist the Park Service, offering advice, tools, and even horses to Drysdale, as well as storage facilities and nominal supervision in the winter; he also provided an element of continuity, particularly when Drysdale took leave for military service during World War II.[41]

Many of Drysdale's concerns resembled those expressed by Balmer and previous Indian school superintendents. Lobbying and promotional efforts by local people had been largely responsible for the establishment of the national monument, and its creation intensified the proprietary sense that Pipestone's residents had long felt for the quarries. Whereas the BIA had spent over forty years negotiating its school's position in regard to the town, the Park Service had no local precedent on which to rely; instead, the influence of its own institutional culture complicated its officials' relationship with the people in Pipestone. Although staff at the regional office in Omaha wished to be responsive to local concerns and interests wherever feasible, the Park Service stressed that the national monument existed as a separate federal entity, governed by its own policies and priorities and not by popular or local demand. The organization also emphasized the primary nature of the quarries as a cultural and historical area, rather than as a recreational park. This difference in perception about the national monument's role generated a degree of tension between some local residents and employees of the Park Service.

Most of the issues that Drysdale faced in his years as custodian concerned use of the national monument land. In Balmer's earlier situation with tribal encampments, some Pipestone residents thought that too large a number of Indian families deterred local and tourist recreation near the quarries. Drysdale's problems did not involve the tribes but did put him in a similar position of enforcing Park Service policy contrary to local wishes. Since the Indian school superintendency of DeWitt Harris in the 1890s, public access to the quarries and falls had been a contentious subject. Indian Affairs had attempted to limit points of entry to the reservation, and the Park Service sought to do the same with the national monument. Automobiles had worn three roads into the section, allowing tourists and locals to wander unmonitored and limiting the custodian's ability to gauge accurately the number of visitors to the unit. Officials in Omaha sought to restrict access to a single entry point, despite the popular preference, and in doing so, they used earlier local complaints about insufficient protection of the quarries as justification.

Shortly after the establishment of the national monument, a contingent of Pipestone's citizens expressed their concern to the Park Service that the unit had no facilities and no one to interpret the site for tourists. A year later Drysdale and the NPS historian, Edward Hummel, noted that a single road would route all visitors past the custodian's contact station at the south gate, allowing them to receive directions and interpretation. The Park Service took a less conciliatory stance in requiring that the custodian remove a baseball diamond and discourage general public recreation. As the *Star* noted, people in town persisted in seeing "the state's only national park" as "a place of beauty and convenience" for themselves and tourists. In response, the acting regional director, Howard W. Baker, asserted that the Park Service would not "convert the national area into a local picnic ground."[42] With only a seasonal custodian, compliance with federal policy remained inconsistent, and Drysdale returned each spring to new problems, including continued vandalism, graffiti, and wheel ruts.

Funding remained limited during the 1940s due to national economic difficulties and World War II. Plans for development remained on hold, but the Works Projects Administration (WPA) and the Park Service took the initial steps toward providing interpretation for tourists, though not in response to the urging of Pipestone residents. While formality and a more scientific approach characterized the government's research of the quarries' physical and human history, its resultant presentation of the site's significance closely resembled the town's traditional interpretation. For decades Pipestone had used images of the quarries created by outsiders to support claims of the place's national importance. After creation of the national monument, federal agencies continued employing the same representations and legends to explain the quarries' Indian heritage to Americans and other visitors.

In 1938 the Federal Writers' Project published its state guide to Minnesota and thereby provided the kind of national publicity Pipestone promoters had sought continuously. An aspect of the New Deal climate of support for public culture that had been partly responsible for establishment of the national monument, the WPA guide included a variety of information about Pipestone within many of its sections. References to the "famous quarries" appeared under the headings of "Geology," "First Americans," and "Mining"; in this last section, the writers noted catlinite's "great interest to the student of American history." Pipestone also qualified as a topic under "Education and Religion," due to the boarding school, and under "The Arts," because of catlinite carving. The guide's authors lamented the decline of tribal craftsmanship and recommended museums for the best specimens of pipes, echoing earlier writings by the Shrine Association.[43]

One of the local tours recommended in the WPA guide began at the Pipestone Indian Training School, then led travelers to the quarries, "famous in Indian legends and historic documents." The writers summarized the tribal past of the "sacred and neutral ground" as lore, including the hardening of flesh into red stone when a great flood covered the site of creation. After white bison's hooves later unearthed the stone, tribes used it "for many centuries." Moving rapidly from the vague realm of romanticized prehistory, the guide then provided details of "the travelers and explorers who followed George Catlin," with dates of their visits and their birth and death years. The tour information concluded with a lengthy segment that highlighted the town (population 3,489), "set on the western slope of the Côteau des Prairies." Pipestone's buildings, constructed of "the beautiful red granite quarried here," received special attention. Finally, the writers mentioned again the carved catlinite articles on display and for purchase.[44] The WPA guide borrowed heavily from the traditional Pipestone interpretation of the quarries.

The NPS similarly institutionalized the existing popular perception of the quarries as having no real human history prior to Catlin's arrival. Three years after the Federal Writers' Project publication, the NPS published its first brochure, entitled simply "Pipestone National Monument." Although it contained a fairly specific section on the geology and geography of the quarries, the brochure resembled earlier writings by Pipestone promoters and preservationists, perhaps in part because the NPS had cooperated with Winifred Bartlett in obtaining information and photographs. It began with an excerpt from Longfellow, who "immortalized part of the lore associated" with the quarries. After a brief mention of tribal reverence for the pipe and the stone, the brochure explained that PNM was established "to memorialize their significance in the religious and social life of the American Indian and to commemorate the legends associated with the red pipestone quarries." The publication gave special attention to explorers and ethnographers, particularly Catlin, Schoolcraft, and Prescott, and then provided overviews of legends about the blood of warring tribes and the role of the Three Maidens. Throughout the brochure, the Yankton were mentioned only in regard to their claims and court case, actions that intersected with documented American history at a national level. Otherwise, compared to the explorers, tribe members appeared in the brochure only as if they existed in the customary timeless prehistory; they remained absent as individuals in the present with quarrying rights, living cultures, and evolving traditions.[45]

During Drysdale's seasonal custodianship in the early 1940s, the townspeople continued to press their proprietary stance toward the national monument. Members of the Old Settlers Society repeatedly requested that a Park Service official, preferably from the regional headquarters in Omaha, attend their meetings to discuss their interest in better interpretation at the quarries, but the office declined. After Charles Bennett's death in the 1920s, the Old Settlers had acquired some of his collection of petroglyphs and carvings. In 1940 they approached Drysdale with a proposal to build a museum for the Indian artifacts on Park Service land, staffed by locals. Hoping to increase the chances that their plan would succeed, they also contacted James Balmer at the Indian school and their representative in Congress, H. Carl Anderson. The acting regional director expressed an interest in meeting with the group at some point but also discouraged ideas of a museum. Any such facility on national monument land would belong to the federal government and not be a city-sponsored museum. While the issue dissolved, the Old Settlers stored the collection in the courthouse. After a few years, town physician Walter Benjamin tried again, writing directly to Newton Drury, NPS director. Benjamin stressed the importance of "the only National Park in Minnesota" and its "unusual interest from many standpoints because of its interest historically in the life of the Indian." He argued that "increasing interest in the shrine has been shown by local people and tourists," necessitating some sort of museum. A bland official response about appropriations and delayed plans effectively ended the idea of a joint interpretive project by local citizens and the federal government, but it did little to diminish the townspeople's convictions that the national monument needed better management.[46] *WWII/peace shrine"*

After a slump during the World War II years, PNM increased in popularity and began attracting more visitors. The quarries' reputation as the "Indian Peace Shrine" may have held special appeal to Americans weary of conflict and postwar tension and nostalgic for a romantic past. Pipestone's Civic and Commerce Association capitalized on the image, referring to the quarries as the "First American Site dedicated to Eternal Peace." In 1949 the federal government began to emphasize the place as a "peace site," and the Park Service published a new self-guiding tour leaflet for the national monument, labeling it "America's original peace shrine." State officials also took an interest in the quarries' symbolism. That same year, Louis H. Powell, director of the Science Institute in St. Paul, wrote to Sen. Hubert H. Humphrey about the need for a museum at the national monument. Powell argued that "in a period when such vast Federal expenditures for the prevention of war are being made . . . it would be a worthy objective to adequately publicize and interpret for the public this important national monument which has been traditionally dedicated to the quarrying and manufacturing of peace pipes." Local residents had previously marked the site of the Inkpaduta encampment after the so-called Spirit Lake Massacre of 1857 with a sign commemorating the conflict and the ensuing captivity of Abbie Gardner-Sharp. In response, NPS Region II's administrative assistant recommended that a small, temporary sign with only two words—"Inkpaduta Campsite"—sufficed.[47] References to any specific

[handwritten margin note: ensure o violent past]

tribal activity, particularly one tinged with violence, interfered with the peaceful, nontemporal atmosphere of the national monument.

INVENTIVE INTERPRETATIONS AT THE OLD INDIAN SHRINE

The postwar growth of interest in the quarries and improved economic conditions brought an end to the seasonal custodial period at the national monument and the beginning of full-time funding. The NPS transferred Drysdale to Mount Rushmore and replaced him in 1948 with a year-round superintendent, Lyle K. Linch. Prior to his Pipestone assignment, Linch had served at national parks and monuments throughout the country, including the Natchez Trace, Rocky Mountain National Park, and the Badlands of South Dakota. Although he was a Park Service veteran who enforced the agency's policies with vigor, Linch often exhibited a strong individualism and an enthusiasm for local interests in and interpretations of the quarries. Perhaps because of the full-time nature of his position, he became more involved in the community than Drysdale had been, joining fraternal organizations and composing a column for the local newspaper. Linch occasionally seemed more of a zealous promoter of Pipestone's image than the town's residents, often to the dismay of his supervisors, who received a steady stream of correspondence filled with exaggerated descriptions of life and events the "old Indian shrine"— a contrast to Drydale's sober reports.

[handwritten margin note: Superintendent w/ full-time funding 1948]

From his first days at the quarries, Linch associated himself with the Pipestone perspective and worked diligently to improve the situation at the Park Service unit. He looked to Winifred Bartlett as "the unquestioned God Mother of the National Monument" and considered her "words, thoughts, and visions" with characteristic hyperbole as "tremendously important to our Côteau Country, to the whole state, and to our nation." Linch consistently referred to the quarries as the "Pipestone Indian Shrine." Like his nineteenth-century predecessors, he imbued the landscape with cultural virtues. Given the vast prairie surrounding him, he considered the national monument's location one that provided "a physical, a mental, and . . . a moral break in this terrible monotony." Arriving at a time when local people such as Bartlett had begun to lose hope in physically developing the national monument, Linch placated townspeople by immediately clearing overgrown paths, making signs to mark points of interest, and consulting with Bartlett and others about tourists' needs. Until the Park Service constructed a superintendent's residence, he lived at the Calumet Hotel on Main Street and took advantage of the opportunity to get to know local residents.[48] Through personal involvement Linch began to change the somewhat distant relationship between the Park Service and the people of Pipestone.

Considering the American people "shareholders in a unique shrine," Linch put his considerable energy into making the national monument as appealing as possible to the largest conceivable audience. Toward this end, his presentation of the quarries often diverged from the official perspective and exaggerated local interpretations. Linch created signs about the site for window displays along Main Street to inform visitors and townspeople about improvements and any special events at the quarries. With Bartlett's assistance he developed a new nature trail at the national monument that identified native plants along the route and included a cardboard "poison ivy jail" to confine the nefarious plant and keep it away from tourists. Linch also set up an archery range, which he thought natural for a place associated with Indian lore. With haste, his supervisors in Omaha instructed him to remove both the jail and the archery range; the former they considered "not appropriate" and the latter "not in keeping with our policy and . . . hazardous." At the same time, Linch received orders that he should "curb the enthusiasm . . . developed for picnic use of the area." After a 1950 visit the NPS acting regional director, Howard Baker, observed that at Pipestone "the National Park policies are not always given due weight in arriving at solutions to or methods of handling some matters."[49] Linch's zeal for appealing to the public often eclipsed agency protocol, but it entertained and attracted visitors, making him a vibrant presence at the national monument.

Linch concentrated many of his efforts on new ways to present traditional information about the quarries. He made arrangements with the *Pipestone County Star* to publish a regular column that he would write, called "Tepee Smoke," which other regional newspapers reprinted. In the summer, Linch initiated a series of campfire talks, and he gave regular interpretive talks to tourists, groups of schoolchildren, and anyone else who would listen. In true American style he donned a feathered headdress for a visiting Boy Scout troop and dramatized the quarries' standardized tribal lore. The NPS regional historian, Olaf T. Hagen, wrote an interpretive statement for Linch's review that mentioned Longfellow's verse, as well as Catlin's "classic ground" and his influential statement, "This place is great, not in history, for there is none of it, but in traditions and stories." But Hagen's draft was too limited and dry for

Linch's style. Linch preferred to call the national monument "The Red Man's Garden of Eden" and to provide an amalgamation of legends about great floods and tribal creation, mixed with demons and French explorers, all in a landscape of "mysterious relief" and an "awe inspiring sense of strangeness."[50] His attempts to make the national monument as appealing to the public as possible were in keeping with the local view of its heritage and were built on Pipestone's traditions of representing the quarries as unique and timeless.

One of Linch's efforts at embellishing the quarries' imagery proved too creative for the Park Service, though it was not exceptional by local standards. In his eagerness to emphasize the antiquity of the quarries, he attributed new meaning to a symbol carved on some of the rocks near Winnewissa Falls and the Nicollet Marker. During Linch's first year at Pipestone, Maurice Pratt Dunlap, a regional resident, a former American consul to Sweden, and an avid Egyptologist, visited the national monument and met the superintendent. Impressed by Dunlap's claim to be the sole survivor of the King Tut expedition, Linch became adamant about Dunlap's theory that the rounded symbol on the rocks was really an ankh and thus evidence that an ancient Egyptian tribe or its descendants had migrated to North America and become the ancestors of all Indian tribes. Through Dunlap's suggestion, Linch conflated disparate cultural icons. Egyptian sun worshipers, referred to by some scholars as Titans, bore a close enough linguistic resemblance to the Grand Tetons in Wyoming and the Teton Lakota of the Plains for Linch to believe in a connection to Plains tribal sun dances and the related ceremonial use of pipes carved from catlinite at the quarries. Before the next summer Linch formed the Ankh Society and began including the story of the symbol and his version of its significance in his interpretive talks and on a map of national monument land.[51]

Such an oddity might have remained anecdotal for Linch's supervisors had it not been for media interest in the idea. Since the establishment of PNM, state tourism and government offices, including the Science Institute and the Minnesota Historical Society, had devoted more attention to the quarries and helped to promote the federal unit to Minnesotans. In 1950 the *Minneapolis Sunday Tribune* published two illustrated articles on the subject, including one entitled "Pipestone Indian Cult from Egypt?" which newspapers throughout the region reprinted. The state was fertile territory for such notions. In 1898 a farmer in the north-central section of Minnesota claimed that he discovered a rune stone in his field, purportedly left in the fourteenth century by visiting Vikings. Although controversial, the stone story acquired loyal believ-ers in all parts of the state, even on the tourist board. Alleged evidence of an earlier visit by Norsemen bolstered Minnesotans' sense of their touted Scan-dinavian heritage and of their collective identity and importance in much the same way that Pipestone's residents had long associated themselves with and promoted the quarries' legendary past.[52] Even in 1950, few in the state would turn a wholly skeptical eye toward Pipestone and the possibility of a visit by ancient Egyptians. (NHS)

Press coverage of the ankh theory prompted a stern response from Omaha. When Linch proudly referred his supervisors to the newspaper articles, not-ing that the story had been picked up by a paper as far away as Topeka, Kansas, the regional director reacted in writing: "That! The heck of it—this article should not have been written." Both the acting associate regional director, Jerome C. Miller, and the regional historian, Merrill J. Mattes, responded to Linch's actions with blunt memos. Miller stressed the reliance of the official NPS interpretation on credible sources and called the idea of Native Ameri-can descent from Middle Eastern peoples "preposterous." While Miller did not disdain attempts to make interpretive talks interesting, he discouraged Linch from including the ankh as a subject because "the net result is to cast doubt on the professional integrity of our programs everywhere." Mattes more directly discredited Dunlap and Linch's ideas about a connection between Ti-tans and Tetons. He considered it "a fallacy common among popular writers of assuming that where there is a similarity of spelling, there must be a histori-cal relationship." Not only did the Teton Lakota not live near western Wyoming but the French etymology of *Teton* shared no origins with *Titan*. Mattes con-cluded his memo with advice that Linch "adhere to commonly accepted sci-entific concepts rather than harken to . . . theories" and desist from mention of ankhs.[53] Traditional Indian mythology about the quarries was acceptable Park Service policy, but creatively constructed new narratives were not.

So long as Linch remained within the standard interpretation and ade-quately maintained the national monument grounds, his superiors overlooked his somewhat unorthodox and gimmicky approach to popularizing the unit. To the delight of Pipestone promoters, Linch continued to develop new ways to use old images and draw public attention to the quarries. Every summer he celebrated the "Monument Birthday" with special guest Winifred Bartlett, the "Monument Mother." Linch also declared August 21 as "Indian Day" and obtained the voluntary assistance of an Ojibwe man from Flandreau and a former student at Haskell Indian School, George Bryan, also called Standing Eagle. Bryan was married to Clara Crow, who was the daughter of Moses and Estella Crow, from whom she learned quarrying, and an employee at the Indian school. As part of Linch's regular interpretive program, Bryan acted as a guide on the trail through national monument land and participated in fully promoting the quarries' Indian imagery. He also served as a "living history" demonstrator, carving pipes and other items from pipestone that he quarried in the presence of visitors, similar to Native cultural demonstrations at other NPS units, such as Hopi craftspeople at the Grand Canyon. To promote Indian Day in 1949 Bryan wrote the "Tepee Smoke" column for Linch. Addressing his "paleface friends," he employed the full range of popular Indian imagery in stereotypical language, including phrases such as "heap big smoke sign float out over distant prairie" and "get papoose ready," as well as the repeated use of "ugh." More than eight hundred visitors attended Indian Day, many of whom took tours with Standing Eagle. As a result of the day's success, Linch became a more recognized personage in the state and appeared as a character in the *Minneapolis Morning Tribune*'s iconic Indian cartoon, *Smorgy.* The illustration featured a stereotypical, scantily dressed "brave," as well as peace pipes, tomahawks, and the threat of scalping, all at the quarries under the watchful eye of Linch, whose theatrics upheld such popular images.[54] As a sidekick to the real national monument superintendent, Bryan/Standing Eagle provided an entertaining spectacle and an impression of authenticity that supported both Linch's and Pipestone's efforts to attract tourists.

Other tribal activities at the quarries, though they differed from those of the cartoon characters and from Bryan's performances, continued to shape perception of the quarries. Members of tribes throughout the region continued to visit and to extract stone for ceremonial purposes and for carving and selling. By provision of the 1937 act to establish PNM, only registered tribal people possessed the right to dig by permit. The development of a policy for granting quarrying permits fell to the Department of the Interior, which delegated responsibility for creating guidelines to the Park Service. New to the task of managing the quarries, the Park Service requested advice from James Balmer at the Indian boarding school, after which it still took years to establish quarrying regulations.

While the Park Service deliberated possible policies, life in and around Pipestone did not remain static. Tribal people continued to visit the quarries and to camp there for as long as necessary or desired, which attracted tourists (though some locals worried it might deter them for fear of "unregulated Indians"). The establishment of PNM increased interest in and requests for carved catlinite items, and merchants in town grew impatient for access to prepared trinkets and to unworked stone. Finally, in 1946, almost a decade after passage of the PNM bill, the Park Service guidelines—"designed to preserve the historic and prehistoric values of the red pipestone quarries"—became effective. Only registered tribal members could apply for a quarrying permit, which the NPS superintendent issued and which remained valid for a year. Policy required all carving to be done on site, by hand methods characteristic of the "Early American Indian" and in forms "associated with Indian folklore and legend." In an effort to terminate decades of nontribal profit from pipestone, the policy prohibited the sale of unworked stone and granted the superintendent strict oversight of quarrying camps and use of national monument land.[55]

Although its policies appeared rather stringent, the Park Service strongly encouraged continued quarrying and pipe carving. It also closely monitored all activity at the quarries, particularly the amount of stone removed. No one ever accurately estimated the amount of pipestone in the quarries or its sustainability, but Drysdale speculated that several tons had already been removed at a rate of three or four tons per year, mostly after Pipestone's settlement, to be marketed across the country. He and other Park Service officials opposed the sale of unworked stone to town merchants and therefore supported a policy that limited the sale of any pipestone item on national monument land. As the Park Service curtailed local profits from pipestone and increasingly controlled the market for carved items, it also incorporated contemporary quarrying into its official interpretation. George Bryan served as the first paid tribal interpreter, but others soon joined him and became seasonal spectacles for tourists. With the help of one of the men, Ephraim Taylor (also known as Looking Eagle), Linch reopened a neglected quarry and cleared it out so that visitors could clearly see the strata of rock and better understand the geological qualities of the site.[56] As its policy developed more coherently and fully, the Park Service sought to preserve both the physical integrity of the quarries and the distribution of the handicraft associated with them.

By 1950 Pipestone's residents, especially those interested in promoting the town, found themselves in an unanticipated situation. After decades of both casual and well-organized efforts to bring to the area a federal presence that would protect the quarries from vandalism and neglect, they experienced the disadvantages of success. In the postwar years, steady annual funding and full-time staffing allowed improvements at the national monument that made it more attractive and interesting for tourists. Federal development of the unit created a viable entity separate from its community context, and the Park Service interpretation stressed the quarries' tribal and national past, with little or no mention of Pipestone. Winifred Bartlett continued to serve as the liaison to the Park Service, providing her considerable knowledge as an interpretive resource for the superintendent and the regional historian. The town itself moved increasingly to the margins of popular perception of the quarries. Merchants and civic leaders found that the community's material interests in the quarries as a recreational area and a cultural commodity had fewer benefits than anticipated, even though they were legitimized by federal recognition and preservation. Having succeeded in preserving the quarries, these groups renewed their efforts to promote the town and to attract tourists to its amenities and commercial offerings. Although the typical Pipestone interpretation of the quarries never differed greatly from the official Park Service presentation, townspeople resisted any substantive change at the quarries, a place that they considered timeless and unchanging. In response, they sought to regain some of their authority as locals and their birthright as descendants of the old settlers. Another generation worked to build on the foundation of earlier claims of the place's importance and to preserve the imagery of the quarries further as a usable resource for their communal development and identity.

1. Banusia Wakefield, G. W. Wakefield, G. E. Culver, C. L. Bristol, and G. S. Agersborg seated at the base of Catlin Ledge at the pipestone quarries, 1889. Minnesota Historical Society.

2. Children on the steps of the Pipestone Indian Training School, 1893. Minnesota Historical Society.

3. Charles H. Bennett with pictographs on rocks removed from the Three Maidens in the 1880s, 1902. Minnesota Historical Society.

4. Men and tourist markings on the rocks at Winnewissa Falls, ca. 1908. Photo by Clifford Peel, Minnesota Historical Society.

5. Ferris Grand Opera, Moore Building, and Calumet Hotel on Olive Street, looking east, Pipestone, ca. 1914. Minnesota Historical Society.

6. Children at the Three Maidens, ca. 1935. Minnesota Historical Society.8. Roe's 8.

7. DAR's Nicollet expedition marker at Pipestone National Monument, ca. 1940. Minnesota Historical Society.

8. Roe's Trading Post and Indian Museum, postcard, ca. 1960. Minnesota Historical Society.

9. Roe's Indian Trading Post promotional brochure, ca. 1937. Minnesota Historical Society.

PIPESTONE

MINNESOTA 1937

Legendary Home of Peace
to All Tribes

Home of the World-Famous Red
Pipe Stone, Longfellow's Falls of
Winnewissa and the Sacred
Indian Quarries

Compliments of

Roe's Trading Post
Free Indian Museum
Pipestone, Minn.

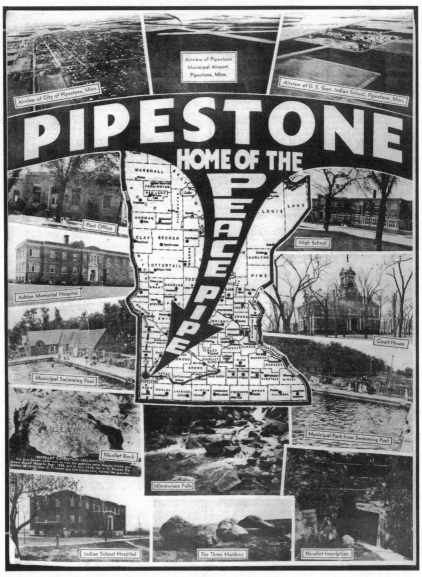

10. Civic and Commerce Association stationery and promotional pamphlet, ca. 1941. Minnesota Historical Society.

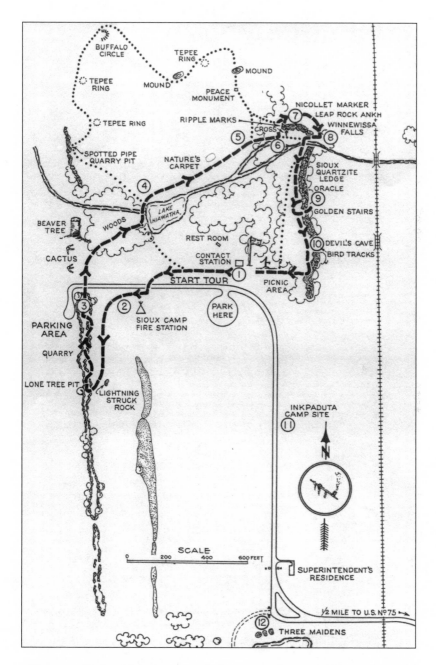

11. Pipestone National Monument map for visitors designed during Lyle Linch's tenure as custodian, National Park Service, late 1940s. Collection of the author.

The Red Stone Indian Peace Pipe

A symbol of all the mysticism embodied in the world's most stoic race—the North American Indian.

It echoes the merciless, stalking fierceness of the Red Man's warfare. Around a thousand camp fires, it carried through hundreds of years, a tribute to peaceful relations between tribes and later to the invading white race.

The pipe stone quarries and Winnewissa Falls, at Pipestone, in Minnesota, are accepted by all the Red Race as sacred ground—their Garden of Eden.

Henry Wadsworth Longfellow, the beloved poet, in his "Song of Hiawatha," wrote:

On the Mountains of the Prairie,
On the great Red Pipestone Quarry,
Gitche Manito, the mighty,
He the Master of Life, descending,.
On the red crags of the quarry,
Stood erect and called the nations,
Called the tribes of men together.

Down the rivers, o'er the prairies,
Came the warriors of the nations,
All the warriors drawn together
By the signal of the Peace Pipe,
To the Mountains of the Prairie,
To the great Red Pipestone Quarry.

In writing of "The Coming of the First White Men in 1837," George Catlin, the historian relates the following Indian legend concerning the birth of the Peace Pipe:

"The Great Spirit at an ancient period here called the Indian nations together, and, standing on the precipice of the red pipestone rock, broke from its wall a piece, and made a huge pipe by turning it in his hand, which he smoked over them, and, to the north, the south, the east, the west, told them this stone was red—that it was their flesh—that it belonged to them all, and that the war-club and the scalping knife must not be raised on its ground. At the last whiff of his pipe his head went into a great cloud, and the whole surface of the rock for several miles was melted and glazed; two great ovens were opened beneath, and two women (guardian spirits of the place) entered them in a blaze of fire; and they are heard there yet (Tso-mec-cos-tee and Tso-me-cos-te-won-dee) answering to the invocations of the high priests or medicine men, who consult them when they are visitors to this sacred place."

We invite you to visit Pipestone and inspect our wonderful display of pipestone peace pipes, arrow heads, Indian hand made jewelry, Navajo rugs, Indian bead work, hand made baskets, pottery of all kinds, hand carved figures, maple sugar, wild rice, etc.

Roe's Indian Trading Post

| Mail Orders Filled and Satisfaction Guaranteed | **Pipestone, Minnesota** | Free Indian Museum Open Evenings and Sundays |

12. Roe's Indian Trading Post promotional brochure, early 1950s. Collection of the author.

FIVE

Re-creating the Image

After the successful 1952 production of Pipestone's *Song of Hiawatha* pageant, Pipestone National Monument (PNM) superintendent Lyle Linch described the evening's experience with his customary hyperbole, claiming that "the all-permeating mystic hovering Indian Spirit of the majestic Three Maidens and America's Original Peace Shrine weaves an awe inspiring spell over every intelligent patron capable of absorbing the finer inspirational things of life." Linch continued, "Codgers and kids alike thrilled as the opening Indian battle between the valley and hill tribesmen was stilled by the superbly costumed Great Indian God, Gitche Manitou in person."[1] The pageant, which became an annual event in Pipestone in the late 1940s and into the 1950s, represented a new phase in uses of the quarries. The town play re-created the image of the sacred site for the community's cultural and economic needs after the earlier success of its preservation efforts. In an era of victorious postwar prosperity that nurtured popular belief in American exceptionalism, Pipestone's social club participants, church congregants, and civic leaders found another way to promote the natural and historical attributes of their locality as nationally significant. The quarries attracted growing numbers of middle-class tourists with incomes for leisure activities and an interest in seeing places that they believed made their country special. This national atmosphere encouraged the use of the kind of images and promotion that had always characterized Pipestone. Pageant visitors from the Midwest and other regions of the United States supported the local economy, while the show's annual production sustained a sense of community based on the quarries' legendary past and continued repetition of related Indian imagery.

With the establishment of the national monument, the town of Pipestone became increasingly peripheral to the National Park Service's (NPS) presence at and association with the quarries. The community's economy and sustainability depended on federal protection of the heavily promoted place. Successful local preservation efforts during the 1920s and 1930s resulted, however, in the Park Service's drawing visitors to the national monument in the 1940s and separating the quarries from the community. As the federal presence loomed larger than anticipated, Pipestone's merchants and active residents such as Winifred Bartlett found the town and its identity becoming overshadowed by the government's representation of the quarries. By the end of the 1940s Bartlett and her neighbors sought to reassert Pipestone's identity. They selectively overlooked the U.S. government's role in presettlement territory acquisition and exploration and emphasized Pipestone's precedence over Park Service and other federal activity in the area. After securing the preservation of the quarries, renewed communal efforts returned to the town's original focus on promotion and tourism and to benefiting as a community from proximity to the enshrined "sacred site." Previously useful methods of promoting Pipestone continued to be employed in various forms, while the town's citizens adapted old ideas to a contemporary national audience and developed new ways of expressing their place-based identity. In his six years as superintendent at the national monument, Linch proved that theatrical behavior and imaginary Indian gimmicks captured tourists' attention. His example helped Bartlett and other Pipestone leaders develop their own dramatic representation of the past. They built on Pipestone's established tradition, once more re-creating and marketing imagery of the quarries and their Indian heritage to serve new local needs for economic growth and community cohesion.

MARKETING PIPESTONE'S IMAGE

The tradition of image promotion and repetition began in Pipestone's first days, when Charles Bennett single-handedly established a marketing standard for the town, to be upheld by others long after his death. Town founder, druggist, general merchant, and amateur ethnologist, Bennett combined his vocation and avocations in a museum store. More than any other early resident,

he worked to create a popular, national association of his town with generalized Indian lore about the quarries. Bennett shared many attributes with the
growing number of collectors of Indian artifacts in the late nineteenth and
early twentieth centuries, including acquisitiveness, a desire to educate the
public, and strong business acumen. In his drugstore he not only housed his
substantial permanent collection of artifacts from the quarries, meant to en-
chant and impress tourists, but also offered for sale a large inventory of carved
pipestone trinkets and other items related to the romantically interpreted
local past. Bennett advertised widely, traveled with the more spectacular pieces
of his collection to expositions and other gatherings throughout the country,
and made as many connections among the political and cultural elite as he
could, all with the intent of promoting Pipestone through its image of the
quarries as a place sacred to all Indians.[2]

Following Bennett's established pattern, members of the Old Settlers Society hoped to preserve some of the material culture of the area and to use artifacts to attract tourists. In the 1940s it appeared logical to many in town, as
well as to state figures such as Sen. Hubert Humphrey, that Pipestone needed
an Indian museum at the quarries and that Bennett's collection, housed by the
Old Settlers since his death in 1926, should constitute much of the inventory.
Local overtures to cooperate with the Park Service in establishing such a museum met with the federal assertion of complete control over the quarries and
the demise of proposals for joint efforts. The refusal by the Park Service to
allow a local presence at the national monument revived the town's proprietary
feelings about the quarries. More than half a century of control over the interpretation of the tribal site had created in Pipestone's residents a strong sense
of ownership over local heritage. As a response to federal policy, they founded
an informal historical museum for Bennett's collection in town, first in the
courthouse basement and later more permanently housed in the city hall.[3] A
public museum asserted a communal claim to the interpretation of the place's
past.

The collection, didactic display, and sale of Indian artifacts to the interested public became a widespread trend in interwar America, a period with
undercurrents of antimodernism and nostalgia for what was believed to have
been a simpler past. While profit motivated many museum store owners, curiosity about the continent's Indian heritage and a desire to accumulate certain kinds of cultural items spurred a majority of collectors. Like their predecessors, the nineteenth-century salvage ethnographers, the new generation of

collectors believed they were preserving vanishing Indian traditions and making them available to the public. Through their interpretation of diverse artifacts, collectors participated in shaping national culture and the popular perception of America's Indian heritage.[4]

After Bennett's death early in the twentieth century, other local merchants carried on his tradition of the museum store. During the 1920s and 1930s Eli H. Swenning and his wife also collected, displayed, donated, and sold relics and carved catlinite objects at their Pipestone Novelty Company, though on a smaller scale, and they displayed some of Bennett's objects. The Swennings' eagerness to travel and take their collection to anyone willing to hear about Pipestone spread word of the town in an age of rapidly growing tourism in North America. One of their gift pipes worked its way to England, intended for the Prince of Wales, while other parts of the collection awed schoolchildren in surrounding states. After the Swennings moved to Michigan in the late 1930s, they continued to speak as self-professed Indian experts, telling schoolchildren and tourists legends of the quarries associated with their carved pipestone pieces.[5]

The Swennings maintained local continuity in marketing pipestone crafts and filled a temporal gap between Bennett's original museum store and its bigger, bolder successor. Opened in 1937, Roe's Indian Trading Post contained an extensive collection of artifacts and crafts acquired from tribes throughout North America during the course of four decades. Far from unusual, Roe's Trading Post resembled other museum stores in the Northeast, Southwest, and Northwest, where tourists provided a steady market for commodified tribal crafts. The Roe collection contained baskets, pottery, rugs, beadwork, arrowheads, dolls, clothing, and carved figures. With its recognizable name and reputation and the recent addition of the national monument, Pipestone seemed like an ideal location for the business. The Roe family—John S. and Ethelyn and their son, John Hollister—hailed from Iowa, as had Charles Bennett, and operated the trading post as a definitive museum store, combining their complementary educational and profit motives. They offered guided tours of their vast collection to tourists and visiting groups, as well as souvenirs for sale both on site and through mail order. After their arrival in Pipestone, the Roes continued to expand their collection, providing more local character by adding an array of carved catlinite items based on popular Indian imagery, from the expected peace pipe to war clubs and tomahawks, as well as bookends, paperweights, candlesticks, and ashtrays. Although Pipestone's museum store phenomenon never matched the national attraction of other commodified tribal landscapes, such as the southwestern pueblos' popularity in the early twentieth century, marketing artifacts remained a central element of the town's identity. It also met tourists' expectations in an era when automobiles made seeing America more possible and desirable; within their first season of operation in Pipestone the Roes claimed to have had over ten thousand visitors from all over North America.[6]

Although they acquired artifacts initially because of their interest in tribal crafts, the Roes were also good business owners. They recognized that their economic success depended in part on the familiarity of Pipestone and the attraction of the town's image to people throughout North America, the same appeal that had drawn them to the long-celebrated place. They advertised boldly and widely, much as Close Brothers had done fifty years earlier. In their brochures the Roes promoted their trading post and Pipestone inseparably. Some of their literature borrowed verbatim from the nineteenth-century pamphlet "Legends of the Pipestone Quarry," published by Close Brothers and Company and the *Pipestone County Star*. The literature referred to Pipestone as the "legendary home of peace to all tribes" and "home of the world famous red pipe stone, Longfellow's falls of Winnewissa and the sacred Indian quarries." Continuing the local tradition of promoting popularized, generic Indian imagery, one flyer featured a page about the peace pipe, calling it "a symbol of all the mysticism embodied in the world's most stoic race" and offering the same excerpts from Longfellow and Catlin quoted by the town's earliest residents. On the brochure's reverse side, the Roes advertised Pipestone as "rich in Indian lore." Short paragraphs summarized legends of creation and attractions at the quarries and offered an overview of the site's significance, largely borrowed from previous promotional literature prepared by the town newspaper and railroads. All of the ads concluded with an invitation to visit the free Indian museum, with its store of items for sale. Annoyed by the store's aggressive marketing, Albert Drysdale informed his Park Service superiors that the Roes' efforts to commercialize Pipestone led Ethelyn Roe to advise tourists to avoid the Park Service unit because they could get all they wanted at the trading post. As tourism to the national monument increased, Roe's advertisements became more elaborate, enticing travelers into town to view the cornucopia of the collection within the context of the quarries' Indian heritage and then, the Roes hoped, to purchase souvenirs.[7]

Pipestone's Civic and Commerce Association followed not only the Roes' pattern but that of previous generations of townspeople. Throughout the late

1940s and early 1950s, a period of rapid urbanization and the decline of small towns, the organization and its members increased efforts to publicize their community by combining local business advertising with widespread Pipestone promotion to tourists and potential investors. The association published a brochure almost identical in text and design to some of the Roes' pamphlets. Still using reference to the "Indian shrine," an early brochure described the place as "a square-cut jewel displayed upon folds of shimmering green velvet," an image worthy of Victorian-era railroad publications. Slowly the association's literature grew in size and scope, incorporating several contemporary and historical photos of the town and features of the quarries. Like most other publications about the place, the brochures of the businesspeople of Pipestone relegated tribal history to the customary timeless past and considered as the site's "early history" the visits of Catlin and Nicollet. A reciprocal gesture and good business practice, the advertisements always added a short paragraph about Roe's Indian Trading Post, blending it smoothly into other local attractions associated with Indian imagery.[8]

Through their publications, both Roe's Trading Post and the Civic and Commerce Association strove to increase recognition of Pipestone and to augment business revenue. They may not have realized fully that in the process of pursuing these goals they were marketing the past as they and others in town had come to perceive it, influenced by previous promoters of the area, while also contributing to standard Indian images in America. Even if aware of the effects of their language or of the layers of meaning in some of their literature, they created brochures that invited tourists to visit Pipestone "with its mystic, fascinating store of legend and tradition." Other businesses that did not benefit directly from the local custom of commodifying the perceived tribal past of the quarries indirectly staked much of their success on the town's associations with the expected images.

Like the county business directories of the 1880s through the 1930s, the postwar Pipestone telephone directory combined its primary informational function with the promotional identification of the town with the quarries. On its introductory page describing Pipestone, only two short paragraphs made specific reference to the town's attributes, such as the library, hospital, and public school. The remainder of the essay featured excerpts from the promotional publications of Roe's Trading Post and the Civic and Commerce Association. A sentence near the beginning explained that "the history of Pipestone is completely centered around the Indian stories of the red pipe stone," a statement emphasizing the centrality of the quarries to the identity of the town. With lines borrowed from other brochures, the telephone directory also asserted that "the history of Pipestone differs entirely from that of all other points in America." Such proclamations of uniqueness within a national context complemented the growing postwar, popular sense of American exceptionalism. Many in Pipestone viewed the place's mythic past as distinctive to and inseparable from the town. In the essay's only mention of the national monument, referred to as the "Pipestone National Shrine," its authors credited the Pipestone Indian Shrine Association with securing passage of the bill that established the Park Service unit. Like the brochures by the Civic and Commerce Association, it identified Pipestone's concerned citizens with the preservation of the quarries so that all tribes could worship there, making townspeople's actions part of the blurry, celebratory past of the place.[9]

Regardless of its authoring organization, the promotional literature generated in the 1940s and early 1950s built on the traditions of previous Pipestone booster material, particularly from the nineteenth century. Brochures consistently referred to the town rather than the quarries as the home of the "world famous" stone and stressed pipestone's importance to "all Indian tribes." Actual tribal members were never mentioned as historical actors, nor did the publications distinguish among tribes, whose members were always generically referred to as "the early Red Man," with the exception of "a band of Sioux Indians" who warned Catlin away from the "forbidden ground." As actors in the unfolding American drama, Catlin and Nicollet appeared as the chief figures whose presettlement visits placed Pipestone within the context of documented national development and lent authority to images of the quarries. No brochure ever quoted a tribal member about the quarries' legends or importance, but almost every page featured excerpts from Catlin and Longfellow, the acknowledged experts on Indian lore. The same legends—of the flood and creation and of the Three Maidens—reappeared year after year, as they had in publications since the town's early days. When not quoting either of the two widely read authorities, the publications borrowed phrases directly from nineteenth-century pamphlets, scientific essays, and previous writings by the Shrine Association. Familiar phrases such as "from time immemorial," "to this spot . . . every Indian made regular pilgrimage," and "the awesome effect upon the savage mind of a visible shrine" appeared repeatedly, with no reference to their sources, reinforcing images used in local promotional literature for over seventy years and accepted and expected by a receptive public.

In their descriptions of the place's past, Pipestone's residents were part of the larger pattern of popular-heritage creation in the United States; they accepted earlier European Americans' understandings of Native history and culture without consulting living tribal members for interpretation.[10]

SPREADING MATERIAL REPRESENTATIONS

In addition to publishing literature that associated Pipestone with images of the quarries, civic organizations continued another promotional tradition. They presented notable public figures with special pipestone carvings, typically supplied by Roe's, as symbolic gifts from the town. Most often, the carved gift was the characteristic peace pipe. Within the state, people such as the Rebekah Assembly's president, Dorothea Schmidt of Minneapolis, received a pipe from George Bryan, dressed for the photo opportunity in full Plains Indian garb and headdress, despite his Ojibwe heritage. At their annual football banquet in 1950 the Pipestone Jaycees made a gift of a carved pipe to Bernie Bierman, the former football coach of the University of Minnesota. Pipes from America's "peace shrine" seemed appropriate gifts to give military dignitaries in the Cold War era. A former Pipestone resident stationed at Walker Air Force Base in Roswell, New Mexico, and editor of the *Atomic Blast* newspaper presented Col. William Blanchard with a peace pipe from Roe's. Even the commander in chief, President Dwight Eisenhower, like Calvin Coolidge and Herbert Hoover before him, received a pipe with a carved buffalo on it while at a national 4-H conference. Outside the United States catlinite curiosities continued to promote the association of pipestone with America, as the Close brothers had done in the 1880s when they sent tons of samples to Europe. Sen. Hans Pedersen selected a pipe from Roe's to present to King Frederick of Denmark for a wedding gift. In the late 1950s the governor of Minnesota, Orville Freeman, took pipes with him on an Asian tour and bestowed them as a gesture of peace on heads of state along the Pacific Rim, further spreading the reputation of the distinctive stone as part of America's identity.[11]

Other carved gifts came in unusual forms. During the 1948 presidential campaign the Pipestone Republicans commissioned a catlinite elephant from George Bryan and presented it to the Republican candidate, Thomas Dewey, who had long claimed an interest in Indian lore. Locally, a stockholder of the Farmers' Creamery received a carved pipestone clock. Roe's provided a number of odd trinkets as honorary gifts for such occasions, particularly paperweights and ashtrays. Only the Science Museum of Minnesota criticized "the production of a great number of bizarre objects," including bookends and doorstops. With ethnological acuity, it observed: "Frequently made by Indians, these objects lacked any connection with aboriginal culture patterns except through the material itself."[12] Never having attempted to learn much valid information about tribal cultures, few in Pipestone noticed anything bizarre about the gifts but considered their gift giving both appropriate and, when their recipients made the desired association between the stone and its eponymous town, successful.

THE QUARRIES AS NATIONAL STAGE

Promotional brochures and presents offered a degree of name recognition, but Pipestone merchants wanted something that would draw greater national attention and many more tourists. Since the town's beginnings, its residents had associated the place with Longfellow's *Song of Hiawatha* and referred to the poem as an authoritative interpretation of the romantic Indian past of the region, even though the majority of the poem concerns Hiawatha's life far to the north along the Great Lakes, where the tale originated. Memorized by generations of children in schools or in scout troops, Longfellow's verses continued to possess wide recognition in popular American culture. The opening stanzas about the creation of tribal people "on the great Red Pipe-stone Quarry" and the general appeal of the Hiawatha story provided usable promotional material.[13] By the late 1940s Pipestone's residents had acted to capitalize on the recognizable poem and its associated imagery that stressed the quarries' significance.

During the early twentieth century pageants gained popularity in America, often produced in small towns as a way to express local interpretations of and participation in the drama of national history. Groups throughout the country performed versions of *The Song of Hiawatha* as a pageant. Periodically, tribal groups took advantage of what they perceived as the poem's positive portrayal of Native people, with its wise, loyal, and appealing hero, and performed Hiawatha plays for largely white audiences. In 1913 a troupe of Iroquois actors staged a version of the tale in upstate New York. During the next summer an Ojibwe group toured as part of a chautauqua and performed the Hiawatha saga in Pipestone for a large, pleased audience. In a period of renewed policy reform, the U.S. government deemed the poem important for

Indian schoolchildren, who also enacted the familiar poetic saga across the country. In 1928 the tribal pupils at the Haskell boarding school in Kansas performed the play in what one reviewer considered "an atmosphere of reality," though far removed from the poem's Great Lakes setting. The Pipestone Indian School soon followed the example. Since the school's establishment in the 1890s its pupils had presented an annual play, open to the general public. For spring commencement in 1932 the school produced its first *Song of Hiawatha* play along the creek below Winnewissa Falls, using red lighting for the Dakota characters and white lighting for the Ojibwe ones, disregarding the actual tribal affiliation of the children. As always the school invited local residents, and people from the larger vicinity attended the open-air production, which the school thereafter produced repeatedly in the 1930s as the weather permitted. The local newspaper observed that "the entire surroundings were sufficiently rustic in their natural beauty, to aid materially in the successful presentation."[14] The pageant demonstrated the potential of the quarries as a dramatic setting, although no one in Pipestone explored that potential at the time, and it reaffirmed the consistent public interest in productions of that type.

As early as 1924 Pipestone residents, including Charles Bennett, had considered participating in the national trend by producing some sort of historical pageant. A few people in town formed an ad hoc committee to "proceed with the work of securing definite historical data that could be used in a pageant," but nothing came of their initiative.[15] Like other inventive ideas of ways to promote the town and to continue to affirm its identity, the pageant proposal lay dormant for years before being reconsidered and reinvigorated. Then, in the late 1940s, members of fraternal organizations and business leaders in town observed the federal government's increasingly active role in interpreting the quarries and sought ways to reassert Pipestone's identity. The town had long controlled most of the interpretation and presentation of the place's Indian heritage, a popular tradition that did not always coincide congenially with the Park Service's view. With some of that control usurped by the federal operation of PNM, museum stores and promotional literature proved important but were an insufficient counterweight. The local view of the quarries' significance had always relied heavily on Catlin and Longfellow and the popular writers' belief in the drama of the site's tribal past. Suddenly, the idea of a pageant offered the possibility of garnering publicity and enhancing identification with the perceived and popularized history of the place.

The year 1949 marked the centennial of Minnesota's organization as a territory, and people in Pipestone viewed it as an auspicious time for the production of a historical pageant that would attract visitors from throughout the state. Founded in 1917 as a service organization with a focus on celebrating American heritage, the National Exchange Club's newly organized Pipestone chapter seemed to be the appropriate group to oversee the creation of a pageant. The club officially sponsored the production, but members of other civic organizations and prominent merchants also participated in the pageant's development. Despite advice from his supervisors in Omaha not to be too involved in local activities, Lyle Linch, the gregarious superintendent of PNM and honorary member of the Exchange Club, eagerly volunteered to help with the production, from recruiting actors to promoting the event. Linch used his "Tepee Smoke" column in the *Pipestone County Star* and his contact with local residents and tourists to generate interest and enthusiasm in the pageant. Having a representative from the national monument, even one who had been privately discouraged by the Park Service, added credibility to the developing project. While the officials in Omaha did not approve, Linch's excitement about the pageant aided Exchange Club members in launching Pipestone's first substantial promotional effort in the twentieth century not related to the national government.[16]

Northwest of town, beyond the Milwaukee Road railroad tracks but south of the national monument boundary, lay an old quartzite quarry. Formerly owned by Leon Moore, the nineteenth-century stone merchant and sculptor, it had since fallen into disuse and seasonally filled with enough water to make it a favorite swimming hole for children from town and from the Indian school. Of less interest to recreating youths but of significance to parties concerned with attracting tourists, the granite boulder formation called the Three Maidens rested on the land adjacent to the quartzite quarry. Although a quarter mile removed from the pipestone quarries, the Three Maidens featured prominently in many of the popularized legends of the site and were the primary source of the petroglyphs collected in the 1880s by Charles Bennett. The boulders sat outside the reservation boundary of the 1858 treaty and across the road from the designated Park Service area; though mainly on privately owned land, the formation was always associated with the larger quarries' area. In the late 1940s Robert Owens, the county register of deeds and president of the Exchange Club, purchased the Moore property containing the old quartzite quarry and the Three Maidens.[17] For the locals eager to produce a pageant, the site, with its small "lake" and ethnologically significant backdrop, seemed a natural stage.

With some effort the core group of pageant organizers transformed the area around the Three Maidens into an amphitheater. The Exchange Club, Boy Scouts, and city and county personnel spent spring 1949 enlarging the pond and reinforcing its edges, mowing grass for the semicircular seating area on one side of the water, and leveling a space for the stage on the other side. The main local newspaper, the *Star,* advertised the pageant heavily and encouraged readers to invite friends and family from other parts of the country. Lyle Linch eagerly encouraged visitors to the national monument to return to the area for the pageant. When off duty, he assisted in recruiting volunteers and designing the production. Linch's assistant, George Bryan, known as Standing Eagle, who carved pipes and led interpretive tours of the quarries, offered to play the roles of both Gitche Manito, the Creator who gave the first pipe to the tribes, and the Arrowmaker, father of Hiawatha's Dakota bride Minnehaha; his image, in full regalia with feathered headdress, appeared on the cover of pageant programs for several years. Town churches organized groups of children for scenes requiring crowds, and adults from the vicinity filled the remaining roles, often sewing their own costumes.[18] The first production included approximately sixty actors and was truly a communal effort.

Because of the length of the poem, the pageant version of *The Song of Hiawatha* contained only a selection of scenes from the work. It concentrated heavily on the opening stanzas that took place at the pipestone quarries, then featured some of the more dramatic episodes of the saga. The Exchange Club set up tipis near the Three Maidens. For scenes that took place by Lake Superior, actors floated across the pond in canoes. Instead of having actors memorize and speak parts, they pantomimed, accompanied by a taped narration and an "authentic" musical score created by a nontribal composer.[19]

The pageant ran for six evenings in June and, despite rain, drew a paying audience estimated at five thousand people. The Exchange Club immediately declared it a success and commenced planning for a bigger, better pageant for the following summer. Always prepared to promote Pipestone and the "peace shrine" with creative symbolism and syncretism, the *Star* ran an enthusiastic review that declared the production "as inspirational as a lovely rainbow, a great dramatic play, and a church service combined." With the background of the Three Maidens, "the music enters one's soul and lifts him on enchanted wings like a magic carpet to the yesteryears of the red men." In his characteristically dramatic language, Linch reported to his supervisors that the pageant "introduced a virgin Siamese Twin attraction for the monument with unlimited possibilities for future development and refinement." Linch had no need to exaggerate the effects of his activities or the success of the pageant. In 1949 PNM led other Park Service units in the annual number of visitors gained— over sixteen thousand—and proved the ability of the projected quarries' imagery to continue to attract tourists.[20]

With each summer, the *Hiawatha* pageant grew, both in the scale of production and promotion and in the size of the audiences. Regional newspapers reproduced photographs from the first summer that enticed new visitors. For the next year's show, local musicians organized the Southwest Minnesota Shrine Club Band to give prepageant concerts, while the Civic and Commerce Association provided free buffalo burgers to the waiting crowds. The 1950 production included seven evenings, featured "mounted Indian warriors" and tribal dances, and drew over eighty-five hundred people. The following year's pageant benefited from the services of the high school drama teacher, Robert Colburn, who volunteered as the director of a cast that had grown to two hundred. Phillip J. Smith from the University of Minnesota succeeded Colburn. The pageant also added more tribal participants, including Bea Burns, a Peoria tribal member originally from Oklahoma, who began what became her annual appearance as Hiawatha's grandmother, Nokomis. Over ten thousand visitors from twenty-seven states attended the pageant. With greater resources for leisure travel in the booming 1950s' economy, including cash and cars, Americans eager to escape the monotony of work and to experience the "real" Indian heritage of what they considered their exceptional country traveled to Pipestone in droves. A front-page item in the *Star*'s August 9, 1948, issue told the story of a woman from Twentynine Palms, California, who was driving across the country. While in Ohio, she read about the quarries in a newspaper and turned back, driving several hundred miles out of her way to visit the place. Although the story is plausible, the column did not list the woman's name or any details about her to bolster its veracity, but it illustrated local beliefs about the national importance and appeal of the quarries during a time of increased tourist visits. People in Pipestone seized the opportunities offered by Americans' interest in national places. Linch continued his promotional efforts and increased the frequency of his newspaper column, in which he referred effusively to the pageant as "the finest outdoor grass-roots home-talent production ever presented in our great grain basket prairie cornucopia."

He also persuaded local merchants to display related, familiar Indian images, such as pipes and headdresses, in their windows. The Civic and Commerce Association thanked the producers for their efforts to "advertise Pipestone and its people."[21] The dramatized *Song of Hiawatha* was rapidly becoming integral to Pipestone's tradition of expressing its American identity through localized versions of nationally recognizable tribal imagery.

CLAIMING AUTHENTICITY FOR THE PRODUCTION

Although many American writers had chosen tribal subjects for their works, Longfellow's saga attained greater popularity and became more familiar than other pieces. Based on the accepted, authoritative writings of Schoolcraft, the poem acquired a public reputation as the "most realistic account of the Indian." Longfellow's work received praise as the American equivalent to the national heroic epics of the *Iliad,* Beowulf, or, more appealing to those of Minnesota's largely Scandinavian heritage, the Finnish *Kalevala.* Despite scholarly criticism, this popular perception of the work persisted well into the twentieth century, reaffirming the nineteenth-century view of "real" Indians as existing nobly in a static, timeless past, untainted by evolving history. Pipestone's residents considered Longfellow's poem and their derivative pageant in the same way that they had always perceived the quarries—as part of the realm of mythical Indian prehistory—and they employed the same images in describing the play as they did in representing the legends of the quarries. Pageant promotional material proclaimed the familiar phrases used in other promotional literature, "from time immemorial to the present," "tradition has it that . . . ," and "the awesome effect on the savage mind of a visible shrine endowed with mysterious features can hardly be imagined."[22] The pageant provided Pipestone with yet another means of expressing its association with the quarries and their images.

Because Pipestone's identity was so inextricably enmeshed with representations of the quarries' past, townspeople concerned themselves with perceptions of the pageant as the "most realistic account of the Indian." Civic leader and preservationist Winifred Bartlett worked with the Exchange Club to make annual improvements to the pageant until she found it "quite authentic." In all of their printed promotions, the Exchange Club and its successor, the Hiawatha Club, emphasized the "many authentic properties" of the production, from its quarry setting to the costuming and music. They based their concept of authenticity on Longfellow's reputation and connections to School-craft and other nontribal experts, rather than on any research or discussions with tribal historians. The presence of tribal actors George Bryan and Bea Burns in the pageant lent further credibility to the production; although neither acted as cultural consultants but filled their prescribed roles just as their nontribal colleagues did, their participation confirmed assertions of the pageant's authenticity. Because the pageant conformed to popular perceptions of an "Indian epic"—images established in decades of American literature and art and reinforced by western dramas in cinemas and on television—no one criticized the production or acknowledged the obviously contrived atmosphere. In the American Midwest of the 1950s, a group of nontribal people dressed as generic Indians and performing a pageant based on a poem by a Victorian Yankee could call their activities authentic and draw large crowds willing to accept the artificial activity as realistic.[23] The production met the audience's expectations and offered unusual summer entertainment. Thousands flocked to Pipestone annually, primarily from area farms and towns and larger midwestern cities but increasingly from other regions of the country, as automotive vacations became a summer standard for middle-class families.

The Hiawatha Club used the pageant's popularity as a promotional tool. By 1957, the production's ninth year, the program's introductory essay claimed that the local attraction garnered "nation-wide attention." Of importance to the purpose of the pageant, the club also noted that "vacationists plan to visit the Southwestern Minnesota city during one of the three weekends when they will have the opportunity of seeing 'The Song of Hiawatha.'"[24] Although the annual production mattered as a financial success, it held a deeper, less tangible importance. From its conception, the pageant existed as a means for the town to benefit more directly from the quarries than it had been able to do since the establishment of the national monument. Townspeople never ceased to advertise the Park Service unit as significant, but they sought to return attention to Pipestone and its original association with the quarries, making the town a primary destination for tourists rather than a filling station peripheral to federal land and enhancing their authority as the primary interpreters of the place's Indian heritage. Pipestone's civic and commercial leaders wanted the town's name to be synonymous with the quarries and their legendary past and for visitors to look to Pipestone first for interpretation of the place's significance. While financially beneficial, the *Hiawatha* pageant supported continuity in communal identity and in the town's sense of ownership of the local historical landscape. The annual event developed during an era of dissolving small-town communalism, as nuclear families isolated themselves in front of televisions each evening and federal programs invested more in suburban development than in declining agricultural areas. The production brought people from all parts of town out of their homes to work together on a community project that helped Pipestone maintain a strong sense of itself.

An active participant in the community until his transfer to Louisiana in 1954, Lyle Linch promoted the pageant unofficially. As noted earlier, his Park Service superiors occasionally advised him to limit his local involvement, and their response to the pageant remained neutral, despite Linch's assertions that the production's success resulted in increased visitation at the national monument. Although the Park Service had no stated position on the pageant, its location caused a degree of contestation between federal representatives and the townspeople. From the earliest days of research into the site's potential as a Park Service unit, regional officials in Omaha viewed the Three Maidens as culturally significant and expressed interest in acquiring them. Outside reservation boundaries, they rested on private land that could not be transferred to the Park Service as part of the public domain under Department of the Interior jurisdiction as the former reservation land had been. With a low budget and no means to develop facilities at the quarries or to acquire additional land, the Park Service delayed consideration of annexing the Three Maidens until it seemed a viable option.[25]

By 1950 PNM had proven itself popular enough for Park Service officials in Omaha to pursue formal inclusion of the boulders in the Pipestone unit. Ten years earlier, in hopes of increasing visitation to the newly preserved site, the city council had offered to find the means to donate the land to the Park Service, but the idea never reached fruition. When approached with a renewed offer, the council conferred with Owens. After deliberation, both Owens and the city strategized and expressed a willingness to donate the land surrounding the Three Maidens to the Park Service under one condition. Unwilling to lose the town's access to the financially and communally important location, Owens would transfer fee-simple title only if the federal agency agreed to allow the Exchange Club to perform the *Hiawatha* pageant annually on the grounds. In just over a decade the people of Pipestone had shifted from petitioning the national government to assist them in preserving the quarries to a position of bargaining over the use of culturally significant land, calling on the tradition of the federal government as the servant of the people. Their sense of ownership over the area and their communal identification with the place remained strong and grew with the positive public reception of the pageant. After negotiations, Owens agreed to donate the land, and the Park Service granted a special-use permit for the pageant, renewable annually for twenty years. The transfer became official in 1951, but the grounds continued to be perceived as pageant territory rather than part of the Park Service domain.[26] Pipestone had succeeded in extending the association of the town with a major landmark of tribal heritage, an act that reinforced local proprietary feelings toward the quarries.

DRAMATIZING THE LEGENDARY INDIAN PAST

The pageant continued as a work in progress, changing and expanding each year. New sound systems and improved lighting provided technical advancements for the growing crowds. For the fifth anniversary in 1953 the producers attracted the attention of a Sioux Falls radio station, KSOO, which broadcast the show across the region, reaching a larger audience. Those attending the live production received programs that offered a synopsis of Longfellow's tale, summaries of the legends of the quarries, and several photographs of the site to entice them to stay longer, explore more of the area, and enjoy other local attractions. In addition to serving buffalo burgers, pageant participants organized a parade that featured floats and displays by dozens of merchants, fraternal and church groups, and anyone else who wanted to join in. Getting in the spirit, townspeople erected "wigwams" and hosted another summer event, the Winnewissa Frolic, similar to a street fair.[27] All of the activities revolved around the quarries' mythic past, as they complemented the primary event—the pageant—and reinforced Pipestone's sense of itself.

Pipestone came late to the American historical pageant movement, but the production suited its purposes well and attracted consistent crowds each summer. Like pageants of the early twentieth century, *The Song of Hiawatha* served as a defining public image that reflected a shared view of the local past. Through pageantry, middle-class European Americans defined their national identity and their place within the larger societal drama. Having a theme or a cast perceived as authentic—in this case, a poem accepted as realistic and several tribal participants—gave the experience a sense of validity. Actors and dancers provided a commonly accepted spectacle in performing Indian roles conceived by nontribal people, a popular public activity throughout the country.

Pipestone's pageant combined a celebration of the quarries' special role in America's heritage with national themes from collective culture.[28]

In the postwar period the Hiawatha saga also appealed to its annual audience on two emotional levels. As the Cold War intensified, the pageant's location at "America's First Monument to Peace" and the pipe's symbolic role in resolving hostilities provided some sense of solace and an evening's respite from the worries of the world. During the same period, national policymakers involved with Indian matters initiated another in a series of assimilation policies. The termination of government responsibility toward tribes, such as the Menominee in neighboring Wisconsin, and the relocation of individuals from reservations into urban areas, including the Twin Cities, aimed at dissolving Native cultures and absorbing tribe members into the larger society. Pageants emphasized the unique qualities of communities while simultaneously participating in the unfolding drama of American history and culture; the *Hiawatha* pageant reinforced the ideas of contemporary Indian policy. A century after he wrote it, Longfellow's work continued to reflect a persistent national perception that precontact tribal cultures embodied much that was noble and heroic but that they were destined to vanish with the perceived advance of American society. The pageant upheld the accepted belief in the inevitability and necessity of assimilation while alleviating guilt through its emphasis on a golden past. Audience members could celebrate what they believed was the essence of a generic Indian heritage without feeling guilty about the phases of termination within their own nation's development.[29]

Unlike most communities, particularly in the Midwest, Pipestone's use of pageantry to work out its local place within national culture occurred in close proximity to two federal presences. In their original petitions for an Indian school and a park, townspeople, perhaps naively, had considered their nation's government a public servant that existed to respond to their needs. They had not anticipated an independent entity that would follow its own agenda and begin to overshadow the community that initially invited it into its midst. The tensions between Pipestone and the Park Service never escalated to rivalry, but area residents maintained that they had brought the government in to help them, and they never yielded their sense of ownership over local lore. They expected federal employees to preserve and to enhance the quarries, but Pipestone continued to assert its tradition and authority in interpreting local legends and the Indian past.

Although townspeople bristled at what they considered Park Service encroachment in the area of quarries' interpretation, Pipestone had always incorporated externally created narratives of the place into its site-specific identity, and it continued that communal custom throughout the twentieth century. The *Hiawatha* pageant declared the town's association with local Indian legends, but it derived from a poem written in New England by a nationally acclaimed poet who had never been to Minnesota. For the state centennial in 1958 Pipestone published a town history. Similar to the nineteenth-century imagery of the quarries, the publication devoted one section to theories from outside "scholars" about the site's significance in antiquity. In addition to the popular ankh idea were suggestions that the petroglyphs resembled Tibetan symbols and Norse runes, the latter a cultural reference that was more familiar to Minnesotans. Another "scholar and poet" speculated that the quarries had been the Garden of Eden, expanding its sacred designation while keeping it firmly situated in mythic prehistory.[30] Pipestone's interpretation of the quarries remained ready to incorporate any new images that might complement traditional ones and attract more public interest in and attention to the site.

The centennial publication also included a time line with synopses of local events deemed significant by the commemoration organizers. Like the promotional literature of previous decades and despite its title, the historical overview—"From Indian Country to Indian Reservation to Indian Shrine Monument"—concentrated heavily on the actions of European Americans and virtually excluded any tribal events. Similar to other American heritage literature, the time line began with 1650, when "white men heard about the red pipestone off to the west." Thus the publication regulated centuries of tribal activity at the quarries to a compressed and timeless period before popularly recognized history, which began with non-Indian awareness of the place. Most of the history's dates highlighted the area's exploration, government activities regarding the quarries, and local cultural developments, such as preservation efforts and the production of the pageant. The chosen dates involved almost no tribal action but much external validation of local events. Through its selection and omission of certain kinds of human activities at the quarries, the time line revealed the connection of Pipestone's identity to a particular historical narrative—one that relied on written records as repositories of truth about the past. Within the preferred narrative white men with national reputations and power, whether explorers or legislators, affirmed the quarries' importance through their words and deeds, while local people acted to keep the place's significance known throughout the country and to preserve their version of its past for other Americans. The lack of active Native individual or collective actions or influences reinforced the perceptual difference between tribal history, classified as enchanting but unrealistic myth or legend, and European American history, accepted as quantifiable reality or documented truth.[31]

The centennial history of Pipestone, like other promotional efforts by local residents, provided another example of imagery that met the expectations of outsiders. Townspeople had always considered the place unique, through its geography and cultural references, despite the existence of catlinite deposits elsewhere and of hundreds of other tribal creation narratives associated with other sites. Pipestone drew tourists who sought unusual experiences and who chose to believe the quarries were as exceptional as its promoters claimed. The various attractions—the pageant, Roe's Indian Trading Post, PNM—all expressed the essence of the place's past and commodified it for consumption by visitors. People from other parts of the country accepted the locals as experts and their interpretations as valid, an authority that Pipestone's residents had claimed since Bennett first arrived at the quarries. In addition to a mythic pan-Indian past, the place offered entertaining performances such as the pageant with its drama and dancing and the spectacle of quarrying and pipe carving, both of which functioned as local rituals expected by tourists and open to their observation.[32] Pipestone continued to project its traditional interpretation and to attract visitors whose interest affirmed the place's identity and the popularity of generic Indian images.

While Pipestone celebrated its past within the context of Minnesota's centennial, the state continued its inclusion of the quarries and legends as part of its promotion. Tourist guides regularly featured Pipestone as one of the state's key attractions. Newspapers from the Twin Cities printed special articles highlighting the area's uniqueness, while public schools recommended the quarries for families' summer educational outings. The Minnesota Historical Society included the quarries and the town on its historical tours, and the state's archaeological society published articles and offered lectures on the site. As a cooperative venture, the Science Museum in St. Paul designed a temporary exhibit for the national monument to use until the Park Service created its own.[33] This combination of local, state, and federal promotion provided a fairly consistent representation of the quarries and drew tourists by the thousands each year, making the place far more popular than any other in the state and comparing roughly with visitation to the Black Hills.

By the mid-1950s Pipestone had become an established attraction on the Minnesota prairie. The national monument maintained its budget and operations, while the pageant expanded every summer and became an expected part of the Pipestone experience. The Indian boarding school took a different course. After more than sixty years in operation it had long outlived similar institutions and could not avoid the federal trend of terminating services for tribes. The Department of the Interior had deliberated closing it for almost a decade. Despite pressure from Pipestone to retain the school, it finally closed in 1953. Although the Park Service expected to benefit from the closure, the city of Pipestone, which had been instrumental in establishing the school, negotiated to purchase much of the land and the buildings. Business and civic leaders hoped to create a state industrial school at the facility, but no concrete plans developed immediately.[34] With the loss of a central, long-standing attraction, Pipestone's residents shifted their energies to other promotional pursuits, such as the pageant and a renewed involvement at the national monument.

TRIBAL PARTICIPATION IN PIPESTONE PROMOTION

The success of the pageant and the draw of the quarries attracted thousands of tourists to Pipestone, eager to see Indians digging and to acquire souvenirs of their visit. George Bryan and other tribal members continued to quarry and to carve pipes and other items for sale, but they did so with little scheduling or consistency in pricing. In 1954 Winifred Bartlett and her associates decided to revive the Pipestone Indian Shrine Association as a vehicle for organizing and marketing catlinite products at the quarries. As at other Park Service units the national monument could not buy or sell artifacts, regardless of tourist demand, so Bartlett's group operated in cooperative association with the Park Service as the only concession at the quarries. Unlike concessions at other units, which sought only to profit from sales of park-related merchandise, the Shrine Association retained the goal set at its 1930s' inception. As it had twenty years earlier, the group considered itself a guardian of tribal culture and the main local supporter of tribal crafts. Although it operated cooperatively with the Park Service, the Shrine Association maintained its affiliation with the town of Pipestone, and wherever possible, it sought to influence the interpretation of the quarries by the national monument staff. The group quickly published its own trail guide and began to draft brochures and other interpretive pamphlets for sale at the unit.[35] The reorganization of the Shrine Association provided local residents the element of authority at the quarries that they had enjoyed before the national monument was established and that they had sought to recover for almost twenty years.

Although they frequently lacked any overall organization, tribal people in Pipestone also continued to participate in the interpretation of the area's past. Anyone with skill at digging and carving could not only earn a small income from the practice but also work as a virtual living history exhibit at the national monument, providing the human spectacle that tourists expected while answering visitors' questions and retelling legends that sometimes varied from the standard local version. When not carving or interpreting as Chief Standing Eagle, George Bryan acted in the *Hiawatha* pageant with other tribal participants such as Bea Burns, who played the part of Nokomis for decades. Some Native Americans saw such pageants as a depiction of positive Indian values and chose to lend their presence to make the production appear more authentic to the audience—a fairly common choice by tribal people who wished to help shape white perceptions. Philip Deloria aptly describes such actions by Native people as "imitating non-Indian imitations of Indians."[36]

Bryan, Burns, and other tribal members who took active roles in the pageant or at the national monument differed from the previous generations of tribes who had associated themselves with the quarries. Few Yankton made the drive from southeastern South Dakota, leaving mainly nearby Flandreau Santee and the small Sisseton and Wahpeton community at Pipestone, mainly the Crow and Derby families, to work the quarries and continue carving traditions while also taking a more active role in marketing their crafts. Much oral history became interwoven with local nontribal interpretations, giving the area a different significance than it had when previous generations of Yankton had struggled over cultural and legal title to the land. The larger American culture continued to extract from tribal cultures whatever it found useful or valuable and to sanction that appropriation with the rationale of cultural preservation.[37] With Yankton representatives no longer regularly present to influence the activity and still years before the emergence of tribal activist groups, nontribal Americans continued their commodification of the timeless tribal past of the quarries.

By the mid-1950s Pipestone's residents had devoted almost a century to various efforts to enhance the town's identity and to promote it nationally. Finally they settled into a comfortable pattern. American postwar prosperity provided a steady influx of tourists each year, eager to experience a connection with the Indian past at the quarries. Roe's and other merchants continued successfully marketing the imagery of the quarries, while the pageant served as the annual centerpiece attraction. Cooperation between the Shrine Association and the Park Service allowed townspeople to exercise interpretive influence at the national monument with direct economic benefits. Pipestone had secured the desired ownership of local heritage and established the association of the town with the Indian place on the national cultural map.

Conclusion

Sense of place is not something that people know and feel, it is something people do.

—Albert Camus

Changes in recent decades in Pipestone have followed familiar patterns and revealed how historical narratives shape the political present. Founded amid the civil rights movement of the late 1960s and based in Minneapolis, the American Indian Movement (AIM) focused not only on urban problems but also on historical developments at the pipestone quarries. The activist group used continued national interest in *The Song of Hiawatha* to draw public awareness to tribal issues. During summer 1970 AIM staged a televised protest at the pageant in Pipestone. Thirty AIM members took control of the production area to express their opposition to Longfellow's and local representations of tribal traditions. While in town, the group also evaluated the exhibits at Pipestone National Monument (PNM) and criticized the National Park Service (NPS) for its emphasis on European American exploration to the place and its limited inclusion of tribal perspectives in its interpretive displays.[1] This act marked a new phase of more active tribal political and cultural participation at the quarries and a renewed presence based in diverse views of the site's traditions.

The marketing of pipestone crafts, long a point of contention, has become increasingly controversial. In 1986 the National Congress of American Indians passed a resolution calling for a ban on sales of pipes to nontribal people. A year later the Yankton tribal council petitioned the Senate Select Committee on Indian Affairs to evict the Pipestone Indian Shrine Association and its operation of the Midwest Indian Cultural Center from the national monument and to return the quarries to tribal control. Drawing on their own traditional identity and referring to themselves as "Keepers of the Red Sacred Pipestone," the Yankton considered the establishment of the Park Service unit an unlawful act and the sale of pipes "illegal commercial exploitation" of the quarries. To demonstrate support for the petition, regional tribes organized a symbolic "run" from Greenwood, South Dakota, on the Yankton reservation to the quarries the following summer. From 1987 to 1994 the run was an annual event, drawing media attention to the controversy. Although none of the tribal councils in the area seriously expected the federal government to cede the quarries, they hoped to exert sufficient pressure to sever the Park Service's working relationship with the Shrine Association and to cease all sales of pipestone. A representative of the St. Paul American Indian Center described the historical and contemporary vendor situation as "a Plantation economy with White people setting the prices and in fact doing the marketing."[2]

Within town some tribal groups have begun to provide alternative opportunities for interested tourists. Since 1988 members of the Pipestone Dakota (Tiospaye) Community, many of whom are descendants of Moses and Estella Crow, have operated their own cultural center, currently known as the Little Feather Interpretive Center. At the community's Spirit of Peace Indian Museum, located at the edge of downtown and organized by Chuck Derby, the Crows' grandson, local Dakota people explain to visitors their tribe's history at the quarries and beliefs about the pipe. Each year they hold their *wacipi* ceremony and powwow on land near the quarries. In 1996 several individuals from outside the community who were interested in promoting pipe making and selling pipestone crafts independent of official representation at the national monument formed their own religious organization as the Keepers of the Sacred Tradition of Pipemakers and opened membership to Native Americans and nontribal people from the United States and other countries. The following year the group purchased the old Rock Island Railroad depot as the center from which to hold pipe-related programs, including their annual "Share Our Heritage Gathering." The differences among these perspectives and actions and the willing participation of various Sisseton, Wahpeton, and Ojibwe people in both the pageant and the demonstration carving at the national monument have revealed to the Park Service and the public that tribal perspectives on the quarries vary greatly and cannot be generalized.[3]

Conflicting cultural opinions also made it more difficult for the Park Service to respond to requests for policy changes. Despite the historical precedent of the 1858 treaty and subsequent negotiations, it could not concede to continued Yankton assertions of the right of determination at the quarries. The federal government representatives at the unit had a long-standing working relationship with the local community and with tribe members from throughout the country. Furthermore, Native people employed at the national monument not only did not object to their conditions but also opposed any outside group that tried to advocate on their behalf for changes they did not want. Given these circumstances, the Park Service was not compelled to sever its ties with the Shrine Association at the time. In other ways, however, it did seek to honor the requests made by AIM and regional tribal councils, particularly with respect to the 1978 American Indian Religious Freedom Act. National monument personnel accommodated the annual demonstrations associated with the summer runs from South Dakota. In 1991 AIM began an annual sun dance ceremony on high ground near the quarries. The Park Service cooperated by keeping tourists from interfering in the event and offered an open invitation for tribal people who wished to use national monument land for spiritual practices. With limited funding for changes, the Park Service also initiated plans to change the interpretive displays in its museum.[4]

As had always been the case at the quarries, tribal people found the federal government more receptive to their views than the residents of Pipestone were. After the first AIM protest in 1970, townspeople did nothing to alter their "beautiful pageant" but continued the annual summer production with technological improvements and no discernible interpretive changes. Promotional literature continued to refer to the town as the "home of the renown [sic] peacepipe." In the language of previous booster brochures, it touted the importance of "traditional" ceremonial carving that visitors could experience firsthand at the quarries, a significance that "goes back beyond recorded history, before the first European set foot on this continent. To the Indian, it goes back to the beginning of time." The tribal members' participation in the pageant and in carving for the Shrine Association validated local beliefs about the authenticity of their interpretation of the quarries' Indian heritage.[5]

During the period of growing tribal protests, Pipestone added more tourist attractions and built further on its traditional representation of the quarries' past. In the mid-1970s, at the intersection of Hiawatha Avenue and Reservation Avenue—the two roads leading to both the pageant grounds and the national monument—entrepreneurs from town used old telephone poles to construct "Historic Fort Pipestone." Although no fort had existed within a hundred miles, few visitors to town questioned its authenticity; rather, they stopped at the fort to buy souvenirs, such as buffalo jerky and rough-cut catlinite. After the Roe family heirs sold much of the store's collection in the early 1960s, an Indian trading post continued to operate in some fashion until 1981, finally ending the museum store era. Since then local residents have considered reestablishing some form of Native American living history center or a theme store to take greater economic advantage of continued tourist interest in Pipestone's well-crafted image. While some people in town were creating new versions of popular heritage, a historic preservation movement began in Pipestone, one focused on restoration and promotion of the quartzite buildings at the town's heart. Approximately thirty of the red stone structures qualified as "architecturally important" in historical resources studies. As a result, the National Register of Historic Places nominated most of the buildings for preservation as the Pipestone Historic District. This action added further national legitimacy to the claims of Pipestone's historical significance and its connections to the landscape. Later, the town began to host summer Civil War reenactments, furthering the Grand Army of the Republic legacy of its founders and their interplay of the local and the national. In 1979 the Pipestone County Historical Museum moved into its current location in the old city hall, one of the buildings on the National Register. The move created permanent exhibits of Bennett's pipestone collection and other displays related to prairie settlement history, including a replica of the shanty in which Daniel Sweet lived in the early 1870s as the first Pipestone County resident. The museum further assumed the mantle of local tradition, marketing the town as "Pipestone: Where History Is in Store," while the chamber of commerce summarized the past as "Peacepipes, Pioneers, and Progress." Business in Pipestone has been good, based on decades of what one Yankton referred to as the "old legends that they sell there."[6]

Meanwhile, the national fascination with the quarries and associated imagery continues to thrive and to find new expressions. In summer 1991 a New Jersey–based group of largely middle-class, white Americans held their own "spiritual gathering" at PNM, modeled on generalized tribal traditions. A film company based in New York is producing a documentary about the annual

Song of Hiawatha pageant and its history. PNM records up to one hundred thousand visitors each year, many of whom spend at least some of their time in the town learning about the local interpretation of the place's past.

From Pipestone's beginning various people of the town took images about the area created prior to the community's founding and used them to develop and define local identity within a larger national context. Because the representations of the quarries captured the awareness of a broad audience before the town's founding, Pipestone began as an idea about a place and its past. People such as Charles and Adelaide Bennett believed the legends and interpretations were authentic and presumed the place held national importance before any urban settlement occurred there. The images that drew them to the quarries might have made the site only a passing curiosity to others, one of countless other mildly interesting tribal places across the country. After the Bennetts and their neighbors had invested themselves, not just financially but also socially and psychologically, in the idea of Pipestone's Indian past, they devoted their energies to ensuring the perpetuation of something they were certain others would recognize and appreciate as significant.

The Bennetts' faith in Pipestone and their subsequent booster activities set a precedent for a succession of townspeople. Decade after decade, local residents—from newspaper editors and merchants to voluntary preservationists and church groups—reinforced and built on the inherited images of the quarries that had proven successful and reassuring. They used the local tradition of a timeless past as a stable reference point and a source of cohesion amid a changing society. In newspapers, promotional literature, and correspondences various people in Pipestone repeated versions of the legends and generated new ones, stressing the universal significance of the "sacred site of peace" and the uniqueness of the quarries in myth and geology. Even as the twentieth century progressed, civic and commercial leaders perpetuated the language used by nineteenth-century explorers, scientists, artists, and poets, drawing on a view of history that embodied respected cultural authority and knowledge. This practice solidified accepted images of the quarries, reaffirmed local traditions (including the tradition of seeing the place as significant in the context of national heritage), and limited receptivity to any alternative interpretations. Rather than attempting to understand Native historical practices at the quarries, Pipestone's residents translated unfamiliar tribal customs about sacred land into recognizable concepts such as an "Indian Eden," a universal strategy for responding to the unfamiliar and to cultural differences. In nineteenth- and twentieth-century America, however, the racially based im-balance of power gave this common interpretive behavior lasting consequences for relationships surrounding the quarries and their use.

Each new group of local people built on accepted traditional perceptions of the quarries' importance, acting on their own beliefs about what was needed to establish Pipestone's future and continued national awareness of the place. Town founders and merchants enticed railroad and land companies to invest in and promote Pipestone. Later they joined with local teachers, clergy, and church congregations to petition for an Indian boarding school. Women preservationists led efforts to establish a national park or monument to pre-serve the quarries physically, after which a wide array of townspeople joined them to maintain local interpretations of the past through the production of *The Song of Hiawatha* pageant. Regardless of the group composition, Pipe-stone's residents always sought to attract attention and tourists, providing them with samples of the carved stone—whether obtained through illegal quarrying and sale or through museum stores or the Pipestone Indian Shrine Association's concessionaire arrangement. People and their ways of expressing their beliefs about the place overlapped as they continued to build on the foundation of local identity within a national context. In less conscious ways their actions also shared characteristics with tribal responses to the quarries. The secular religious impulse that inspired townspeople to perform rituals ex-pressing nationalism mirrored tribal traditions in its repetition of time-honored beliefs about the place, its reliance on authoritative legends passed down from earlier generations, and its use of iconographic images.

Despite tribal activities and repeated attempts to popularize indigenous perspectives on the area's history, aspects of local tradition, based in the nine-teenth century, persist in Pipestone. Members of the Yankton and other tribes still have more substantial relations with Park Service personnel than with townspeople and often express their beliefs about the quarries with coopera-tion from the federal government. Meanwhile, members of the Hiawatha Club and other Pipestone residents similarly continue to promote their in-terpretation of the place's past and enjoy a symbiotic relationship with the national monument. The varied views of tribal groups abide in juxtaposi-tion with Pipestone's tradition—coexisting cultures that comprise separate but overlapping worlds that affect each other constantly, though not always consciously or intentionally. To some degree each group has embraced a be-lief in a "timeless tradition" at the quarries and works within historically based identities that can obscure the need for living cultures to adapt to changing circumstances.

After more than a century, Pipestone's quarry-based identity is authentic for the people of the town. Reference to and repetition of a selectively perceived, stable past for self-representation characterizes identity formation for localities, ethnic groups, and regions. Americans participate in their pluralistic society in part by resisting total immersion through the use of a particular view of history to reinforce distinctiveness within a larger cultural context. Pipestone's residents continue to perceive the past and the landscape around them from within local tradition, expressing their experience in the place melded with expectations shaped by a sense of the past. Recently, many in town have begun to accept that perpetuation of their place-based identity also carries the responsibility to acknowledge and respect other narratives and other realities at the quarries. This development marks the beginning of a meaningful cultural dialogue and furthers Pipestone's tradition of adapting national cultural trends for local use.

Two centuries after Lewis and Clark's expedition the Côteau landscape remains amenable to American ideals projected onto it, just as it has long been to tribal values. People of all cultures act continually to create place and identity, building on beliefs of and about the past. At the quarries common interest in a special landscape reinforces divergent cultural values. The land abides as a useful resource, both in its physical stone and in the images created from it.

NOTES

1. The Pipestone Indian Shrine Association (hereafter PISA), *The Pipestone Indian Shrine, Pipestone, Minnesota: Indian Legends and Historical Facts Regarding the Red Pipestone Quarry, Winnewissa Falls, and the "Twin Maidens,"* 1; Edmund C. Bray and Martha Coleman Bray, eds. and trans., *Joseph N. Nicollet on the Plains and Prairies: The Expeditions of 1838–39, with Journals, Letters, and Notes on the Dakota Indians,* 54.

2. Bray and Bray, *Joseph N. Nicollet,* 83. Although extensive and illustrated, Nicollet's journal remained unpublished until the 1970s. A condensed version of his observations appeared in his 1841 report to Congress.

3. Hal K. Rothman, *Managing the Sacred and the Secular: An Administrative History of Pipestone National Monument,* 10–14; Andrew Gulliford, *Sacred Objects and Sacred Places: Preserving Tribal Traditions,* 167–70. For an overview of the variations in historical and current beliefs among Plains tribes, see David T. Hughes, *Perceptions of the Sacred: A Review of Selected Native American Groups and Their Relationships with the Catlinite Quarries,* 10–20, 101–5. The term *Dakota* is used here to refer to the Dakota/Lakota/Nakota linguistic and cultural groups of the region, the eastern Dakota (Santee) bands being most prevalent in western Minnesota.

4. Marcia Crosby provides a First Nations' perspective on the current academic trend of inclusivity in "Construction of the Imaginary Indian," in *Vancouver Anthology: The Institutional Politics of Art,* ed. Stan Douglas (Vancouver, BC: Talonbooks, 1991), 267–91. For a discussion of tribal views of scholarship in the United States, refer to Devon A. Mihesuah, ed., *Natives and Academics: Researching and Writing about American Indians.* See also Barry Lopez, *About This Life: Journeys on the Threshold of Memory,* 3–15. On uses of the term *Indian,* see Daniel Francis, *The Imaginary Indian: The Image of the Indian in Canadian Culture,* and Robert F. Berkhofer Jr., *The White Man's Indian: Images of the American Indian from Columbus to the Present.* My perspective on the issue of tribal inviolability evolved from time spent among Rosebud Lakota and Diné people. Within both of these cultures, it can be considered offensive to speak on behalf of another individual or to try to represent someone else. Prior to beginning my research on this subject,

I wrote to the Yankton Tribal Council, describing my project and explaining that I did not intend to speak on behalf of the tribe.

5. Robert A. Murray, "Administrative History of Pipestone National Monument, Minnesota" (typed manuscript, 1960), 66–67, in General Collections, Minnesota Historical Society, St. Paul (hereafter MHS).

6. Philip J. Deloria, *Playing Indian*; David Lowenthal, *Possessed by the Past: The Heritage Crusade and the Spoils of History*, and "Identity, Heritage, and History," in *Commemorations: The Politics of National Identity*, ed. John R. Gilles (Princeton, NJ: Princeton University Press, 1994). Similar to Lowenthal's distinction between history and heritage, David Glassberg describes his personal experiences of the differences between academic training as a historian and popular depictions of tribal prehistory presented to the American public at a National Park Service unit. He explores these themes and the relationship between place and past in his *Sense of History: The Place of the Past in American Life*, 3–6, 122–27. In "Fantasy Echo: History and the Construction of Identity," Joan W. Scott urges other historians to examine the complex ways in which people create and sustain historical identities. She argues that the extraction of and identification with selected representations of the past constitute an imaginative act, or fantasy, that compresses time, overlooks differences, and implies continuity. When repeated or echoed over generations, the "retrospective identifications" become increasingly distorted but retain their cohesive effects. Scott offers a useful framework for analyzing the process of identity formation and adaptation in Pipestone.

CHAPTER ONE

1. A version of this chapter was presented at the American Heritage Center's Sixth Annual Symposium on American Culture, "American Places," held in September 1997 in Laramie, Wyoming. George Catlin, *Letters and Notes on the Manners, Customs, and Conditions of North American Indians*, 2:164 (emphasis in original). Catlin first published his work, with illustrations, in London.

2. Archaeologists have done and continue to do a variety of research both at the quarries and through oral histories. The most thorough ethnographic approach is Hughes, *Perceptions of the Sacred*. See also Alan R. Woolworth, comp., "The Red Pipestone Quarry of Minnesota: Archaeological and Historical Reports," in *Minnesota Archaeologist* 42 (1983), and Craig M. Johnson, "An Analysis of Prehistoric Ceramics from the Pipestone National Monument, Pipestone County, Minnesota," brochure published by the Midwest Archaeological Center, Lincoln, Nebraska, 1998.

3. For an examination of the similar process through which visitors to and writers about the Grand Canyon transformed it into images and imbued it with

meaning relevant to American culture, see Stephen J. Pyne, *How the Canyon Became Grand: A Short History.*

4. Anne Farrar Hyde, *An American Vision: Far Western Landscape and National Culture, 1820–1920,* 13, 19, 110; Hal K. Rothman, *Devil's Bargains: Tourism in the Twentieth-Century American West,* 15, 23; David Lowenthal, "The Place of the Past in American History," in *Geographies of the Mind: Essays in Historical Geosophy,* ed. David Lowenthal and Martyn J. Bowden (New York: Oxford University Press, 1976), 101–2, and "Past Time, Present Place: Landscape and Memory," 13, 31; John F. Sears, *Sacred Places: American Tourist Attractions in the Nineteenth Century,* 4–7, 23, 123; David B. Danbom, *Born in the Country: A History of Rural America,* 66–85; William H. Goetzmann, *Exploration and Empire: The Explorer and the Scientist in the Winning of the American West,* 181.

5. Berkhofer, *White Man's Indian,* 73–80, and "White Conceptions of Indians"; Frances K. Pohl, "Old World, New World: The Encounter of Cultures on the American Frontier"; Julie Schimmel, "Inventing 'the Indian,'" in *The West as America: Reinterpreting Images of the American Frontier, 1820–1920,* ed. William Truettner (Washington, DC: Smithsonian Institution Press, 1991), 149–90; and Deloria, *Playing Indian,* 63.

6. Father Louis Hennepin, *Description of Louisiana by Canoe to the Upper Mississippi in 1680,* trans. Marion E. Cross (Minneapolis: University of Minnesota Press, 1938), 43, 94–96; Herbert T. Hoover, *The Yankton Sioux,* 25; John Parker, ed., *The Journals of Jonathan Carver and Related Documents, 1766–1770,* 138, 126. Carver spent most of his life in Massachusetts and fought in the Seven Years' War before traveling west. Parker contends that Carver's mention of the quarries "brought them to the world's attention" (148). Mary Louise Pratt expands on ideas of the cultural effects of such journals in *Imperial Eyes: Travel Writing and Transculturation.*

7. Gary E. Moulton, ed., *The Journals of the Lewis and Clark Expedition: August 25, 1804–April 6, 1805,* vol. 3, 355; Samuel Lewis after William Clark, "A Map of Lewis and Clark's Track" in Nicholas Biddle and Paul Allen, *History of the Expedition under the Command of Captains Lewis and Clark to the Sources of the Missouri . . . ;* Elliott Coues, ed., *The History of the Lewis and Clark Expedition* (1893; reprint, New York: Dover Publications, 1965), 1:80; Yi-Fu Tuan, *Space and Place: The Perspective of Experience,* 91–107, 161–65. For an examination of the relationship between perception and description of place, see William L. Lang, "Lewis and Clark on the Columbia River: The Power of Landscape in the Exploration Experience," *Pacific Northwest Quarterly* 87 (Summer 1996): 141–48.

8. Lucille M. Kane, June D. Holmquist, and Carolyn Gilman, eds., *The Northern Expeditions of Stephen H. Long: The Journals of 1817 and 1823 and Related Documents* (St. Paul: Minnesota Historical Society Press, 1978), 274, 293; Giacomo

Beltrami, *A Pilgrimage in America: Leading to the Discovery of the Sources of the Mississippi and Bloody River* (1828; reprint, Chicago: Americana Classics, Quadrangle Books, 1962), 218–19, 314 ; Maximilian, Prince of Wied, "Travels in the Interior of North America," trans. Hannibal Evans Lloyd, in Reuben Gold Thwaites, ed., *Early Western Travels: 1748–1846* (Cleveland, OH: Arthur H. Clark, 1905), 12:321–22. Thwaites identifies Catlin as the first white person to visit the quarries and also notes that the stone can be found in other areas of the upper Midwest.

9. Henry Rowe Schoolcraft, *Narrative Journal of Travels from Detroit Northwest through the Great Chain of American Lakes to the Sources of the Mississippi River in the year 1820* (Albany, NY: E. and E. Hosford, 1821), 299. In *Space and Place* Tuan asserts that officials in the nineteenth century held the authority and power to create a place, as Schoolcraft did at the Mississippi headwaters at Lake Itasca in northern Minnesota (165).

10. John Brinckerhoff Jackson, *The Necessity for Ruins and Other Topics,* 89–102; David Lowenthal, *The Past Is a Foreign Country,* 43, and "Past Time, Present Place," 11–13; Hyde, *An American Vision,* 214, 231–39.

11. Rayna Green, "The Indian in Popular American Culture," in *History of Indian-White Relations,* ed. Wilcomb E. Washburn (Washington, DC: Smithsonian Institution Press, 1988), 587–606; Berkhofer, *White Man's Indian,* 44–52, and "White Conceptions," 528–32; Lowenthal, "The Past in the American Landscape," 96–99, 104–5; Deloria, *Playing Indian,* 71–90; Schimmel, "Inventing the Indian," 153–54. Robert Berkhofer summarizes this notion in "White Conceptions": "The history of White imagery reveals at its core that the quintessential Indian was and is thought outside the dictates of time and history in Western thought" (528).

12. Donald Dean Parker, ed., *The Recollections of Philander Prescott: Frontiersman of the Old Northwest, 1819–1862,* 136–39, 149; Bray and Bray, *Joseph N. Nicollet,* 19; Philander Prescott, in Henry Rowe Schoolcraft, *Information respecting the History, Condition, and Prospects of the Indian Tribes of the United States: Collected and prepared under the direction of the Bureau of Indian Affairs per act of Congress of March 3, 1847* (Philadelphia: Lippincott, Grambo, 1852), 2:176. Many scholars note Prescott's unverified claims, but few take him at his word; among those who do are John Wayne Davis, "A History of the Pipestone Reservation and Quarry," 26–29, and Paul A. Kelley, "The Pipestone Quarries: An Historical Geography," 28–35, whose thesis uses Prescott's account as a historical reference. For an account of the rivalry and ill will between Schoolcraft and Catlin, see Brian W. Dippie, *Catlin and His Contemporaries: The Politics of Patronage,* 54–57; Dippie characterizes Schoolcraft as an intellectual who denigrated Catlin's romantic tendencies.

13. Joseph N. Nicollet, "Report Intended to Illustrate a Map of the Hydrological Basin of the Upper Mississippi River," 11, 15–16; Bray and Bray, *Joseph N. Nicollet,* 42–108.

14. Bray and Bray, *Joseph N. Nicollet*, 40–41, 75–76.

15. Dippie, *Catlin and His Contemporaries*, xvi. Sherry L. Smith traces persistent romanticized images of Indians in popular writings later in the nineteenth century and into the twentieth in her *Reimagining Indians: Native Americans through Anglo Eyes, 1880–1940*.

16. In her work on cultural cannibalism, *Cannibal Culture: Art, Appropriation, and the Commodification of Difference*, Deborah Root defines appropriation as "not only the taking up of something and making it one's own but also the ability to do so. People have always shared ideas and borrowed from one another, but appropriation is entirely different from borrowing or sharing because it involves the taking up and commodification of aesthetic, cultural, and . . . spiritual forms of a society. Culture is neatly packaged for the consumer's convenience" (70). See note 1 in this chapter; In "Imperialist Nostalgia" (*Representations* 26 [Spring 1989]: 107–22), Renato Rosaldo refers to "salvage ethnography" as the doctrinal effort to "record the precious culture before it disappears forever" (115); Deloria, *Playing Indian*, 63–64, 101–6; Lowenthal, *Possessed by the Past*, 63, 85–87; Martha A. Sandweiss, "The Public Life of Western Art," in *Discovered Lands–Invented Pasts: Transforming Visions of the American West*, ed. Jules David Prown (New Haven: Yale University Press, 1992), 117–33; Nancy K. Anderson, "Curious Historical Artistic Data," in *Discovered Lands—Invented Pasts*, esp. 5–8; Gregory H. Nobles, *American Frontiers: Cultural Encounters and Continental Conquest*, 146–48; William H. Goetzmann and William N. Goetzmann, *The West of the Imagination*, 15–35; Dippie, *Catlin and His Contemporaries*, xvi, 16, 39–42, 189; William H. Truettner, *The Natural Man Observed: A Study of Catlin's Indian Gallery*, 69–80. For discussion of the appropriation of tribal culture as part of salvaging, see Crosby, "Construction of the Imaginary Indian." Catlin's "Notes of Eight Years Travel amongst the North American Indians" appeared in newspapers occasionally between 1832 and 1837.

17. Catlin, *Letters and Notes*, 2:163–68 (emphasis in original).

18. Ibid., 2:165, 168, 201; Marjorie Catlin Roehm, *The Letters of George Catlin and His Family: A Chronicle of the American West* (Berkeley: University of California Press, 1966), 91–101; Pohl, "Old World, New World," 154–56; Kathryn S. Hight, "'Doomed to Perish': George Catlin's Descriptions of the Mandan," *Art Journal* 49 (Summer 1990): 119–24; Hyde, *An American Vision*, 28–29; and Truettner, *The Natural Man Observed*, 35. In *Sacred Places* Sears contends that writers and artists helped to make certain sites in the American landscape famous and sacred by use of the language of pilgrimage (5). Catlin's descriptions of his travels to visit the quarries qualify as this sort of writing and effect. Glassberg describes the effects of writers and artists in creating known places in his *Sense of History*, 116–17.

19. Catlin, *Letters and Notes,* 2:170, 202–3; Dippie, *Catlin and His Contemporaries,* 40–43; George Gurney and Therese Thau Heyman, eds., *George Catlin and His Indian Gallery,* 204. The Smithsonian Institution's National Museum of American Art has created a series of lesson plans based on Catlin's Indian Gallery, "Campfires with George Catlin: An Encounter of Two Cultures," http://www.nmaa.si.edu, accessed on December 29, 2003.

20. Dippie, *Catlin and His Contemporaries,* 40–43; Charles T. Jackson, "Catlinite or Indian Pipe Stone." Jackson's article describes catlinite as "not steatite, but a new compound very similar to agalmatolite," consisting mainly of silica and alumina and overlaid by quartz rock. For more on Catlin's patronage woes and controversy surrounding the naming of the stone, see Dippie, *Catlin and His Contemporaries,* 63–67. Deposits of catlinite occur not only at Pipestone but also in Minnehaha County, South Dakota, and in quartzite beds near Jasper, Minnesota. Various tribes carved pipes out of similar, noncatlinite stone found in Ohio, Kansas, Wisconsin, and Arizona; see John S. Sigstad, "A Field Test for Catlinite."

21. Dippie, *Catlin and His Contemporaries,* 49–56, 79–80; Alan Trachtenberg, "Singing Hiawatha: Longfellow's Hybrid Myth of America," 15–17; Berkhofer, *White Man's Indian,* 87–89; Richard Bauman, "The Nationalization and Internationalization of Folklore: The Case of Schoolcraft's 'Gitschee Gauzinee'" *Western Folklore* 52, "Theorizing Folklore: Toward New Perspectives on the Politics of Culture" (April–October 1994): 247–70; Alvin M. Josephy Jr., "The Real Hiawatha," in *The Patriot Chiefs: A Chronicle of American Indian Resistance* (New York: Viking Publishers, 1961), 1–30; Christopher Vecsey, *Imagine Ourselves Richly: Mythic Narratives of North American Indians,* 100–106; Richard G. Bremer, *Indian Agent and Wilderness Scholar: The Life of Henry Rowe Schoolcraft;* Basil Johnston, *The Manitous: The Spiritual World of the Ojibway,* 51–95. Wub-e-ke-niew, in *We Have the Right to Exist: A Translation of Aboriginal Indigenous Thought,* argues that Schoolcraft used his tribal connections to give his "agenda an aura of legitimacy" but that his interpretations of Ojibwe culture reflected his own interests and not tribal traditions (75–85).

22. Henry Wadsworth Longfellow, *The Song of Hiawatha,* 23–28; Eric L. Haralson, "Mars in Petticoats: Longfellow and Sentimental Masculinity," 346–49.

23. Trachtenberg, "Singing Hiawatha," 1, 16–18.

24. Cecil B. Williams, *Henry Wadsworth Longfellow,* 157–59; Chase S. Osborn and Stellanova Osborn, *Schoolcraft-Longfellow-Hiawatha,* 108–9. The Osborns write admiringly of Schoolcraft. Longfellow used Schoolcraft's 1839 *Algic Researches: Indian Tales and Legends* and Catlin's *Letters and Notes* as his primary material (Osborn and Osborn, 13). See also Joseph S. Pronechen, "The Making of Hiawatha," *New York Folklore Quarterly* 28 (June 1972): 151–59; Rev. Benjamin

Franklin DeCosta, *Hiawatha, or the Story of the Iroquois Sage in Prose and Verse* (New York: Anson D. F. Randolph, 1873), 1–13.

25. Berkhofer, "White Conceptions," 532–33. In *Days of Obligation: An Argument with My Mexican Father,* Richard Rodriguez sees this as a global phenomenon, in that "the industrial countries of the world romanticize the Indian who no longer exists, ignoring the Indian who does" (5–6). Also see Michael Kammen, *Mystic Chords of Memory: The Transformation of Tradition in American Culture,* 83–87. Kammen charges Longfellow with "cultural co-optation," in his translation of Native American legends to form an origin myth for the American continent and to assuage the guilt lingering in Anglo-American middle-class popular culture (83). In *Reimagining Indians,* Sherry Smith notes that writers in the nineteenth century assumed the power and the cultural authority to define Indians and "to relegate them to a supposedly traditional past" (9–10).

26. Jacob Ferris, *The States and Territories of the Great West,* 261; Moses K. Armstrong, *History and Resources of Dakota, Montana, and Idaho,* 2–7, and *The Early Empire Builders of the Great West* (St. Paul, MN: E. W. Porter, 1901), 160. Leah Dilworth analyzes the appeal of images of a premodern, edenic Indian past to American anxieties in her essay "Tourists and Indians in Fred Harvey's Southwest," in *Seeing and Being Seen: Tourism in the American West,* ed. David M. Wrobel and Patrick T. Long (Lawrence: University Press of Kansas, 2001), 144–54.

27. See notes 18 and 20 in this chapter; Keith R. Burich, "'Stable Equilibrium Is Death': Henry Adams, Sir Charles Lyell, and the Paradox of Progress," *The New England Quarterly* 65 (December 1992): 631–47. For a thorough overview of the changes in scientific culture in the nineteenth century, see Stephen Jay Gould, *Time's Arrow, Time's Cycle* (Cambridge, MA: Harvard University Press, 1987).

28. Ferdinand V. Hayden, "Sketch of the Geology of Northeastern Dakota, with a notice of a short visit to the celebrated Pipestone Quarry." See chapters 2 and 3 for further discussion of the influence and repeated uses of Hayden's observation.

29. Charles A. White, M.D., "A Trip to the Great Red Pipestone Quarry."

30. Charles Rau, "Red Pipestone," 368–72.

31. John Wesley Powell, Letter to Commissioner of Indian Affairs W. A. Jones, quoted in "Title of Yankton Indians to the Pipestone Reservation in Minnesota," Senate Document 55, 57th Cong., 1st sess., 1901, 1–8.

32. Newton H. Winchell, "The Geological and Natural History of Minnesota," 97–109. Extensive petroglyphs mark the quartzite outcrops near Jeffers, Minnesota, seventy miles east of Pipestone. Throughout the southwest corner of the state, numerous quartzite deposits at and above the ground's surface have markings.

33. Henry H. Sibley, letter to the Legislative Council of Minnesota Territory, September 11, 1849, 30–31. In "The Minnesota Marker in the Washington Monument"

(*Minnesota History* 8 [June 1927]: 176–77), Bertha L. Heilbron explained to a curious reader how pipestone came to represent Minnesota in the monument and commented that "no material could be more appropriate for a Minnesota marker" (176). See Dippie, *Catlin and His Contemporaries*, 184–91, for an expanded explanation of Catlin's ability to offend most men of status in Minnesota Territory.

34. Catlin, *Letters and Notes*, 2:166–67; Henry H. Sibley, "Reminiscences: Historical and Personal," in *Collections of the Historical Society of Minnesota* 1 (1902): 393. Sibley complained that Catlin's letters "abounded with mis-statements. . . . The people in this quarter were absolutely astounded at his misrepresentations of men and things."

35. Hoover, *The Yankton Sioux*, 48–51; Hughes, "Perceptions of the Sacred," 9–23. Hughes examines the oral traditions of several bands of Dakota/Lakota and other tribes on the northern Plains and provides summaries of their beliefs about the pipe and the quarries.

36. Research data obtained through the archives of the South Dakota Oral History Center, Institute of American Indian Studies, University of South Dakota, Vermillion, South Dakota, American Indian Research Project (hereafter AIRP) Tape no. 67, Paul Picotte, Yankton, interviewed by Joseph Cash, 1968; Hoover, *The Yankton Sioux*, 16, 28, 30, 40–41, and "Yankton Sioux Tribal Claims against the United States, 1917–1975," 127–28.

37. "Treaty with the Yankton Sioux, 1858," in Charles J. Kappler, comp. and ed., *Indian Treaties, 1778–1883* (Washington, DC: U.S. Government Printing Office, 1903), 586–90; Hughes, *Perceptions of the Sacred*, 25–34; Davis, "History of the Pipestone Reservation," 43–52; Rothman, *Managing the Sacred*, 26–30. For a Yankton oral history account of the treaty process, see Renée Sansom-Flood, *Lessons from Choteau Creek: Yankton Memories of Dakota Territorial Intrigue* (Hills, MN: Crescent Publishing, 1986), 27–38, 87–89.

38. Gary Clayton Anderson, *Kinsmen of Another Kind: Dakota-White Relations in the Upper Mississippi Valley, 1650–1862*, 217–18; AIRP Tape no. 1026, Winifred Bartlett, interviewed by William Corbett, April 17, 1976; Abbie Gardner-Sharp, *History of the Spirit Lake Massacre and Captivity of Miss Abbie Gardner* (Des Moines: Iowa Printing, 1885), 168–72. Greg Olson examined Gardner-Sharp's efforts to gain local fame through exaggerating her ordeal in his paper "Exhibiting History: A Case Study of the Preservation Efforts of Abigail Gardner-Sharp and Charlotte Kirchner Butler," presented at the Women in Historic Preservation Conference, Mesa, Arizona, March 1997.

39. Gary Clayton Anderson and Alan R. Woolworth, eds., *Through Dakota Eyes: Narrative Accounts of the Minnesota Indian War of 1862* (St. Paul: Minnesota Historical Society, 1988); William E. Lass, *Minnesota: A Centennial History*, 117–35; Francis Paul Prucha, *The Great Father: The United States Government and the*

NOTES TO PAGES 32–35

American Indians, 143–46; Angie Debo, *A History of the Indians of the United States,* 184–90, 233–66; Nobles, *American Frontiers,* 215–20.

CHAPTER TWO

1. Winifred Bartlett, "Pipestone County," 784; Arthur P. Rose, *An Illustrated History of the Counties of Rock and Pipestone, Minnesota,* 320–21, 263–65; Pipestone County Historical Society, Pipestone, Minnesota (hereafter PCHS), *A History of Pipestone County,* 9, 74; Kelley, "The Pipestone Quarries," 100–101; Lass, *Minnesota,* 136–52.

2. Liza Nicholas, "Wyoming as America: Celebrations, a Museum, and Yale"; Anne F. Hyde, "Cultural Filters: The Significance of Perception in the History of the American West"; Martha A. Sandweiss, "Looking at the West from Here and There," in *A New Significance: Re-envisioning the History of the American West,* ed. Clyde A. Milner II (New York: Oxford University Press, 1996); Kevin Lynch, *The Image of the City* (Cambridge, MA: MIT Press, 1960), 126–27.

3. For a discussion of the development of national culture after the Civil War and local communities' participation in developing common national experiences and symbols, see Kammen, *Mystic Chords,* 17, 96, 141–45; Lowenthal, *Possessed by the Past,* 61–63, 121–26; Alan Trachtenberg, *The Incorporation of America: Culture and Society in the Gilded Age,* 16–26; Peirce F. Lewis, "Small Town in Pennsylvania"; Martin E. Marty, convocation lecture, Macalester College, St. Paul, Minnesota, November 1997. For a more generalized analysis, see Benedict Anderson, *Imagined Communities: Reflections on the Origin and Spread of Nationalism.*

4. Gratia Frances Ferris, unpublished letter to her sister, November 30, 1907, General Collections, MHS; Ernest V. Sutton, *A Life Worth Living* (Pasadena, CA: Trail's End Publishing, 1948), 34–36; Rose, *Illustrated History,* 261, 333; James P. Reed, "The Role of an English Land Company in the Settlement of Northwestern Iowa and Southwestern Minnesota: A Study in Historical Geography," 40; Paula M. Nelson, *After the West Was Won: Homesteaders and Town-Builders in Western South Dakota, 1900–1917,* 82–99; Robert V. Hine, *Community on the American Frontier: Separate but Not Alone,* 123–24, 128–49. In 1873, Sutton's father took him to the quarries, which he remembered as surrounded by endless prairie "just as God made it." For examples of a sense of regional distinction, see Frederick Manfred's "Siouxland" novels about settlers in the area and its unique geography. My thanks to Garneth Peterson, a fellow native of the region and Minnesota landscape historian, for many discussions about the area and its sense of place.

5. Charles B. Howard Papers, "Recollections of Pipestone, 1911–1928," Manuscripts Collection, MHS; G. Ferris, letter; Bartlett, "Pipestone County," 785; Rose, *Illustrated History,* 266–71; PCHS, *History,* 9, 74; Richard White, *"It's Your*

Misfortune and None of My Own": A New History of the American West (Norman: University of Oklahoma Press, 1991), 181–99. Howard spent much of his youth in Pipestone and recalled what he learned of the town's history while growing up there, as well as his own childhood memories.

6. Rose, *Illustrated History,* 266–71; PCHS, *History,* 9, 74. Other towns in southwestern Minnesota and on the Great Plains followed similar growth patterns; see John Radzilowski, *Prairie Town: A History of Marshall, Minnesota, 1872–1997,* and Nelson, *After the West Was Won.*

7. *Pipestone County Star,* June 19, 1879, 2. The following statement appeared on the same page: "The Pipe-Stone quarry near here is bound to bring a fortune to this place in the near future. We shall have more to say of this in some future issue." This statement was also far-sighted; the *Star* faced competition from two or three other newspapers at various points during its publication, but it continues to the present time to be the main publication in town, and it has always featured commentary on and promotion of the quarries. A self-professed booster paper, like others in small towns, it served as a consistent source of information from the perspective of the Republican business class and as a fairly accurate gauge of general public sentiment throughout Pipestone's history.

8. John G. Rice, "Old Stock Americans," in *They Chose Minnesota: A Survey of the State's Ethnic Groups,* ed. June Drenning Holmquist (St. Paul: Minnesota Historical Society Press, 1981), 55–72; John C. Hudson, "Yankeeland in the Middle West," *Journal of Geography* 85 (September–October 1986): 195–200; Jon Gjerde, *The Minds of the West: Ethnocultural Evolution in the Rural Midwest, 1830–1917;* Kammen, *Mystic Chords,* 228. Marshall closely paralleled this kind of population and town structure; see Radzilowski, *Prairie Town,* 85–121.

9. *Illustrated Album of Biography of Southwestern Minnesota* (Chicago: Occidental Publishing, 1889), 200, 304–5, 366, 468, 646, 651–54, 746–47, 774–75, 779–80; Minnesota State Census, 1880, Pipestone County; Pipestone County Genealogical Society, *Biographies of the Civil War Veterans who Came to Pipestone County, Minnesota,* 13, 15, 31; "David and Janet Fyffe reminiscences" (typed manuscript, 1880s or '90s), Manuscripts Collection, MHS, 152–62; Nelson, *After the West Was Won,* 82–85.

10. Rose, *Illustrated History,* 299–300, 294–95, 381, 656. For a fictionalized account of the British colonies in southern Minnesota, see Maud and Delos Lovelace, *Gentlemen from England* (New York: Macmillan, 1937).

11. AIRP Tape no. 1026; Wanita Beal, *I Have a Story to Tell about Pipestone,* 2; *Star,* August 14, 1879, 2; Rose, *Illustrated History,* 321; PCHS, *History,* 74, 160. Beal's work is an oral history, compiled from her interviews with older town residents, particularly Winifred Bartlett, about memories of the town's past and its founders. Its tone is not unlike early booster material in its glowing descriptions and uncritical acceptance of perceptions of the area.

12. *Star,* August 14, 1879, 2; Rose, *Illustrated History,* 321; PCHS, *History,* 74, 160.

13. *Star,* August 14, 1879, 2; Cordenio A. Severance, *Indian Legends of Minnesota* (New York: D. D. Merrill, 1893).

14. PCHS, *History,* 9; *Star,* March 11, 1880, 3; Rothman, *Managing the Sacred,* 30–32; Kelley, "The Pipestone Quarries," 102–5; William P. Corbett, "The Red Pipestone Quarry: The Yanktons Defend a Sacred Tradition, 1858–1929"; Robert A. Murray, *A History of Pipestone National Monument, Minnesota,* 23–25. Claussen's name also appeared as Cluensen. Rothman notes that the refusal of the federal government to allow unrestricted settlement clashed with American expectations of the West as wide open and free, a tension that marked later relations between the Yankton and the residents of Pipestone. Corbett gives a thorough explanation of the course of the legal actions of the Yankton, with extensive footnotes for his research in the National Archives in Washington, D.C.

15. *Star,* July 17, 1879, 3. The paper also observed that "the rising generation among them are making rapid strides toward civilization," as were the Flandreau Santee, who quarried at the same time.

16. *Star,* July 24, 1879, 3, and October 14, 1880, 3; Leah Dilworth, "Tourists and Indians," 146–52; Derek Bousé, "Culture as Nature: How Native American Cultural Antiquities Became Part of the Natural World"; Root, *Cannibal Culture,* 82–87.

17. *Star,* July 17, 1879, 3.

18. An extensive literature examining white perceptions and representations of tribes explores the differences between imagery and living people, including the following: Smith, *Reimagining Indians;* Curtis M. Hinsley Jr., "Zunis and Brahmins: Cultural Ambivalence in the Gilded Age"; Leah Dilworth, *Imagining Indians in the Southwest: Persistent Visions of a Primitive Past;* and Berkhofer, "White Conceptions," 528–38. See also Scott, "Fantasy Echo," 284–304.

19. *Star,* October 9, 1879, 3, October 16, 1879, 3, and November 27, 1879, 3; Rose, *Illustrated History,* 279–81.

20. Howard, "Recollections of Pipestone"; Bartlett, "Pipestone County," 785; Rose, *Illustrated History,* 279–81; PCHS, *History,* 11; *Star,* October 9, 1879, 3, October 16, 1879, 3, and November 27, 1879, 3; Nelson, *After the West Was Won,* 85–86; Lewis, "Small Town," 325–27, 333; Minnesota State Census, 1880, Pipestone County, Sweet and Gray Townships; National Register Minnesota, *Rails across the Prairie* (St. Paul: State Historic Preservation Office, Minnesota Historical Society, n.d.); Danbom, *Born in the Country,* 132–60. The Chicago, St. Paul, Minneapolis and Omaha Railway bought the St. Paul and Sioux City company shortly before the completion of its line to Pipestone.

21. *Star,* March 18, 1880, 3, and March 17, 1881, 1; PCHS, *History,* 26.

22. For a discussion of Richardson's style and popularity in the Midwest, see James F. O'Gorman, *Living Architecture: A Biography of H. H. Richardson* (New

York: Simon and Schuster, 1998), and Paul Clifford Larson with Susan M. Brown, eds., *The Spirit of H. H. Richardson on the Midland Prairies: Regional Transformations of an Architectural Style.* For analyses of Sioux quartzite, see George S. Austin, "The Sioux Quartzite, Southwestern Minnesota," in *Geology of Minnesota: A Centennial Volume,* ed. Paul K. Sims and Glenn B. Morey (St. Paul: Minnesota Geological Survey, 1972), 450–55. Quartzite is a metamorphic derivative of quartz sandstone, as its name implies; the variety known as Sioux quartzite occurs in extensive deposits in southwestern Minnesota. Formed through intense pressure over time, it is an extremely hard but less common rock, composed of densely compacted and tightly fused, or recrystallized, sandlike grains. My thanks to David L. Southwick, former director of the Minnesota Geological Survey, for discussions about the geology of southwestern Minnesota and his encouragement of my interest in the relationship between architecture and geology. Some material for this chapter was adapted from my unpublished essay "'Proof of the Solidity of the Town': Quartzite Buildings and Local Identity in Jasper, Minnesota," written in 1998 with research assistance from the Society for the Study of Local and Regional History, and from a subsequent paper on quartzite buildings in Pipestone and Jasper, Minnesota, presented at the International Conference of Historical Geographers, in Québec, Canada, in August 2001.

23. *Star,* June 10, 1880, 3, June 24, 1880, 3, and September 16, 3; Rose, *Illustrated History,* 325; Beal, *I Have a Story,* 6–8.

24. *Star,* October 26, 1882, 1, February 8, 1883, 1, May 3, 1883, 1, and May 17, 1883, 3. The paper complained steadily that Sioux Falls was shipping stone of an inferior quality to Chicago and that Pipestone was lagging behind and losing business.

25. *Star,* September 7, 1882, 1, January 18, 1883, 1, and December 20, 1883, 3; G. Ferris, letter; Rose, *Illustrated History,* 325–27; Lawrence Durrell, *Spirit of Place: Letters and Essays on Travel* (New York: E. P. Dutton, 1969), 156–57; Tuan, *Space and Place,* 107–22, 159. Lowenthal, in "Past Time, Present Place," observes the effect of such buildings on the psyche of those new to a locale: "Simply to know that structures are durable may give residents a sense of being rooted in a place" (8). Some works on Richardson's place in American architecture include: Wayne Andrews, *Architecture, Ambition, and Americans: A Social History of American Architecture* (New York: Free Press, 1978), 144, 150, 161; Minneapolis Institute of Arts, *A Century of Architecture in Minnesota* (Minneapolis, MN: Minneapolis Institute of Arts, 1958), 12–15; Marcus Whiffen and Frederick Koeper, *American Architecture, 1607–1976* (Cambridge, MA: MIT Press, 1981), 224, 233; and Lewis Mumford, *Sticks and Stones: A Study of American Architecture and Civilization* (New York: Boni and Liveright, 1924), 99–105.

26. James F. O'Gorman, in *ABC of Architecture,* notes, "Architecture is a form

of language, of communication. It speaks. It can convey through its design its place in society, its content" (89).

27. *Star*, June 24, 1880, 3, and July 15, 1884, 3; Charles A. Chapman, *South Western Minnesota: The Best Farming Section in the World*, 26. Even Arthur Rose, in his 1911 *Illustrated History*, described the downtown district as constructed from "the red pipestone building stone" (300). Confusion about the two different stones continues. In an article about the quartzite petroglyphs at Jeffers, Minnesota, "Listen to Grandmother Earth" (*Minnesota History* 56 [Summer 1999]), Loris Connolly noted that Pipestone National Monument "is still used by American Indians for cultural and religious activities, including quarrying the Sioux quartzite to carve pipes and other objects" (326). The journal's editor readily acknowledged the mistake.

28. Howard, "Recollections of Pipestone"; Reed, "English Land Company," 144–58; Rose, *Illustrated History*, 284–86, 325; PCHS, *History*, 10–11. Reed examines the operations of Close Brothers in great detail and contradicts Rose's assertion that the company bought mainly excess Southern Minnesota Railroad lands.

29. Beal, *I Have a Story*, 5, 12–16; Howard, "Recollections of Pipestone"; Reed, "English Land Company," 178–81; Curtis Harnack, *Gentlemen on the Prairie*, 4–6, 188–89; J. M. Powell, *Mirrors of the New World: Images and Image-Makers in the Settlement Process*, 18, 56–59, 85–90; *Illustrated Album*, 381.

30. PCHS, *History*, 11; *Star*, April 12, 1883, 1, May 3, 1883, 1, July 5, 1883, 3, May 27, 1884, 3, May 30, 1884, 3, and June 6, 1884, 3; White, *It's Your Misfortune*, 194–97.

31. Close Brothers and Company, "Legends of the Pipestone Quarries" (Pipestone, MN: Close Brothers, 1880s). According to the Pipestone Indian Shrine Association, D. Ivan Downs was the pen name of D. N. Davidson, an attorney from Luverne, Minnesota; PISA, *The Pipestone Indian Shrine*, 36.

32. Howard, "Recollections of Pipestone"; Rose, *Illustrated History*, 288–94; National Register Minnesota, *Rails across the Prairie;* PCHS, *History*, 12. The James J. Hill Papers—in the James J. Hill Reference Library, St. Paul, Minnesota—contain expressions of his views on the extension into southern Minnesota and his interest in art depicting Minnesota Indian history. Selected letters on these themes include: James J. Hill to R. F. Pettigrew, August 22, 1889, Letterpress Books; James J. Hill to F. H. Welcome, April 14, 1887, Letterpress Books; Warren Upham to James J. Hill, March 30, 1906, General Correspondence; Frances B. Mayer to James J. Hill, October 30, 1891, General Correspondence; and John Wesley Bond to James J. Hill, April 13, 1878, General Correspondence. Hill and W. P. Clough also composed a short history of the Great Northern, dated March 1, 1906 (James J. Hill Papers, James J. Hill Reference Library, St. Paul, Minnesota).

33. General Collections, MHS; Chicago, Rock Island, and Pacific Railway Company, *The Land of Plenty* (Chicago: Clark and Longley Printers, 1885);

NOTES TO PAGES 50–53

Chicago and Northwestern Railway Company and Chicago, St. Paul, Minneapolis, and Omaha Railway Company, *A History of the Origin of the Place Names in Nine Northwestern States* (Chicago: C.S.P.M.&O. Railway, 1908); *Star,* February 5, 1884, 3, March 25, 1884, 3, and May 27, 1884, 3. Of Bennett's poem, the paper noted that she "does not seem to lack of subjects to write upon," March 25, 1884, 3. For a similar pattern of promotion by the Great Northern Railway Company, which used images of Blackfeet to advertise the railway and its tourist interests in Glacier Park, see Smith, *Reimagining Indians,* 46–62, and Ann Regan, "The Great Northern and the 'Glacier Park Indians,'" *Encounters* (Science Museum of Minnesota) (July–August 1985): 17–21, and "The Blackfeet, the Bureaucrats, and Glacier National Park, 1910–1940," paper presented at the Western Historical Association annual conference, Billings, Montana, October 1986.

34. *Star,* June 19, 1879, 2, November 6, 1879, 3, August 19, 1880, 3, January 6, 1881, 2–3, March 30, 1882, 1, September 7, 1882, 1, May 3, 1883, 1, and November 29, 1883, 2. In his 1867 report on his visit, "Sketch of the Geology," Hayden said that "nearly all of our writers on Indian history have invested this place with a number of legends or myths" (21). *Star,* Harvest Edition, August 12, 1880, 3, and September 7, 1882, 1; Kammen, *Mystic Chords,* 141–53, 165–66, 201–2; Sears, *Sacred Places,* 7–13, 23–24, 72–78, 140–55.

35. *Star,* June 19, 1879, 2, November 6, 1879, 3, August 19, 1880, 3, January 6, 1881, 2–3, March 30, 1882, 1, September 7, 1882, 1, July 12, 1883, 3, and November 29, 1883, 2; Rose, *Illustrated History,* 304; C. L. Wing, comp., *Pipestone County Directory,* 51.

36. *Star,* June 19, 1879, 2; Roy W. Meyer, *History of the Santee Sioux: United States Indian Policy on Trial,* rev. ed. (Lincoln: University of Nebraska Press), 257; Murray, "Administrative History," 12–13. Murray notes the massive removal of pipestone for sale by nontribal people began as early as 1864 and continued through the first decades of the town's existence.

37. *Star,* January 1, 1881, 3, March 2, 1881, 1, July 28, 1881, 1, February 23, 1882, 1, and August 3, 1882, 1.

38. Murray, *History,* 24–26; PCHS, *History,* 7; *Star,* September 6, 1883, 3, and September 13, 1883, 2–3.

39. Murray, *History,* 24–26; PCHS, *History,* 7; Corbett, "The Red Pipestone Quarry," 106–7; Rothman, *Managing the Sacred,* 33–41; Davis, "History of the Pipestone Reservation," 52–55; Martin Maginnis to James J. Hill, April 3, 1884, and J. D. C. Atkins to L. Q. C. Lamar, April 6, 1886, General Correspondence, James J. Hill Papers, James J. Hill Reference Library, St. Paul, Minnesota; Frederick E. Hoxie, *A Final Promise: The Campaign to Assimilate the Indians, 1880–1920,* 52–70; Hoover, *The Yankton Sioux,* 30–47.

40. Murray, *History,* 24–26; PCHS, *History,* 7; Beal, *I Have a Story,* 20–22; "Uncle Sam's Mandate," *Star,* October 14, 1887, 5; in *Managing the Sacred,* Roth-

man comments on the aberrance of the situation in terms of western history's general course of favoring settlement over tribal rights (37).

41. *Star,* September 13, 1883, 2, November 11, 1883, 3, and November 22, 1883, 3. Rothman, in *Managing the Sacred,* considers the townspeople as more typically "western" and supportive of the squatters but provides no substantiation for this view (35).

42. *Star,* May 3, 1883, 1; *Illustrated Album,* 779–80; Corbett, "The Red Pipestone Quarry" 106–7.

43. *Star,* June 29, 1882, 1; Berkhofer, *White Man's Indian,* 25–31, 96–111.

44. *Star,* September 7, 1882, 1, and November 15, 1883, 3.

45. PCHS, *History,* 26; *Star,* March 17, 1881, 1, June 16, 1881, 1, and June 14, 1883, 3; Kammen, *Mystic Chords,* 141–45.

46. *Star,* March 17, 1881, 1, June 16, 1881, 1, and June 14, 1883, 3; Lewis, "Small Town," 326–30; Deloria, *Playing Indian,* 4, 64, 103, 115.

47. Philetus W. Norris, *The Calumet of the Coteau, and other Poetic Legends of the Border,* 12, 17–39, 101–9, 171–74. For a discussion of the incorporation of writers and artists into the "storied landscape," see Sears, *Sacred Places,* 74–77, 149–55.

48. Ernest Ingersoll, "The Home of Hiawatha," *Harper's New Monthly Magazine* 67 (June 1883): 68–80; *Star,* February 17, 1881, 1; *Jasper Journal,* October 14, 1892, 1; Olson, "Exhibiting History."

49. Charles M. Skinner, *Myths and Legends of Our Own Land,* 2:151–64; Col. Henry Inman, *The Old Santa Fé Trail: The Story of a Great Highway* (New York: Macmillan, 1898), 244–50 (emphasis added).

50. E. W. Davies and Company, *Pipestone County and a Glimpse of Pipestone, Minnesota.* Davies also included "A Tribute to Minnesota" by Horace Greeley, who found Minnesotans "strong, elastic, active, vigorous, buoyant."

51. Ibid., 34; Rose, *Illustrated History,* 340–43; PCHS, *History,* 89–90; Radzilowski, *Prairie Town,* 105–12; Nelson, *After the West Was Won,* 110–12.

52. *Pipestone Farmers' Leader,* March 2, 1893, 3; Minnesota Board of World's Fair Managers, *Final Report of the Minnesota Board of World's Fair Managers,* 14, 56, 85; *Jasper Journal,* December 30, 1892, 1, and May 5, 1893, 1. The Pipestone and Jasper women's groups argued over the amount of each stone that the piece would contain, with Pipestone gradually crowding out the smaller Jasper contribution. Jasper residents felt vindicated when some of their quartzite formed the staircase in the Minnesota building, and the mantel found a limited audience in its display location in the women's restroom. See also William Cronon, *Nature's Metropolis: Chicago and the Great West,* 341–44, and Trachtenberg, *The Incorporation of America,* 217–19, 224–34.

53. Minnesota Board of World's Fair Managers, *Final Report,* 23, 56, 68, 133; Moses P. Handy, *The Official Directory of the World's Columbian Exposition* (Chicago: W. B. Conkey, 1893), 1098.

54. *Pipestone Farmers' Leader,* November 16, 1893, 3; Davis, "History of the Pipestone Reservation," 23–25. For examples of salvaging behavior throughout the country in this era, see Shepard Krech III and Barbara A. Hail, eds., *Collecting Native America, 1870–1960.*

CHAPTER THREE

1. Lass, *Minnesota,* 136–65.

2. David Wallace Adams, *Education for Extinction: American Indians and the Boarding School Experience, 1875–1928,* 8–9, 31–36, 51–59, 82–94; Hoxie, *A Final Promise,* 5, 43–50; Francis Paul Prucha, *Americanizing the American Indians: Writings by the "Friends of the Indian," 1880–1900,* 1–10, and *The Great Father,* 232–41; Robert H. Wiebe, *The Search for Order, 1877–1920,* 60–62, 166–77; Trachtenberg, *The Incorporation of America,* 140–47. Works on Indian schools either examine federal policy or analyze the adaptation and resistance of tribal pupils. They provide a good national context but rarely mention the perspective or interests of nontribal communities near the schools. Pipestone's early residents were aware of national developments, such as the establishment of Carlisle, and they discussed the possibility of a similar Indian boarding school in the first few years of the town's promotion; see Rose, *Illustrated History,* 333–34.

3. *Pipestone Farmers' Leader,* March 29, 1894, 1; *Star,* October 10, 1902, 5, and July 17, 1879, 3; Deloria, *Playing Indian,* 68–74, 103–6; Hoxie, *A Final Promise,* 13–33.

4. Rose, *An Illustrated History,* 333–34.

5. Lass, *Minnesota,* 200–209. At the MHS, the collected papers of members of Congress such as John Lind and James McCleary contain dozens of letters from residents of small towns throughout Minnesota, who wrote requesting attention and assistance from their representatives in local concerns.

6. *Star,* "Pipestone Review" edition, March 1887, 3–4, June 14, 1889, 4–6, January 21, 1890, 8, and February 21, 1890, 5.

7. *Star,* February 21, 1890, 5. The paper printed the petition in its entirety, accompanied by editorial urgings for support from all readers. In "Administrative History" Murray looked critically on the actions of the townspeople, considering them partly animated by reform zeal but mostly motivated by self-interest in the form of the profits to be gained by the presence of a federal institution (43–44).

8. *Star,* March 7, 1890, 4, March 14, 1890, 1, March 21, 1890, 4, and May 30, 1890, 5. Rose, *Illustrated History,* 334; Rothman, *Managing the Sacred,* 40–41. Notices of the petition appeared in immigrant presses, including the March 11, 1890, edition of the *Svenska Amerikanska Posten,* a Swedish paper published in Minneapolis that closely followed the professional activities of Rep. John Lind, a Swedish immigrant.

9. Murray, *History,* 33; Gaylord V. Reynolds, "The History of Pipestone Indian School" (MA theses, University of South Dakota, 1952), 14–15. Reynolds was employed as a teacher at the school at the time he wrote his thesis and took his master's degree at USD in Vermillion, near the Yankton reservation. His work offers no analysis and serves as a glowing report about the school, with considerable data on its history.

10. Report of the Commissioner of Indian Affairs, House Executive Document No. 1, 51st Cong., 1st sess., serial 2725; Thomas J. Morgan, "A Plea for the Papoose," in Prucha, *Americanizing the American Indians,* 239–51, and "Supplemental Report on Indian Education, December 1, 1889," in *Documents of United States Indian Policy,* ed. Francis Paul Prucha (Lincoln: University of Nebraska Press, 1975), 179–80; Prucha, *The Great Father,* 237–41; Wilbert H. Ahern, "Indian Education and Bureaucracy: The School at Morris, 1887–1909." At the meeting of the Friends of the Indian at the tenth annual Lake Mohonk conference in 1892, Morgan summarized the prevailing belief of Indian reformers. He maintained that "we must either fight the Indians, or feed them, or educate them. To fight them is cruel; to feed them is wasteful; to educate them is humane, economic, and Christian" (in Prucha, *Americanizing the American Indian,* 252).

11. *Star,* February 13, 1891, 5, March 27, 1891, 4, and August 14, 1891, 5.

12. Wilbur Mills Fiske, "Training the Red Children . . . on Historic Ground," *St. Paul Dispatch,* May 16, 1908. Several works analyze the boarding school system, including Margaret L. Archuleta, Brenda J. Child, and K. Tsianina Lomawaima, eds., *Away from Home: American Indian Boarding School Experiences, 1879–2000;* Scott Riney, *The Rapid City Indian School, 1898–1933;* Donal F. Lindsey, *Indians at Hampton Institute, 1877–1923;* Devon A. Mihesuah, *Cultivating the Rosebuds: The Education of Women at the Cherokee Female Seminary, 1851–1909;* Brenda Joyce Child, "A Bitter Lesson: Native Americans and the Government Boarding School Experience, 1890–1940" (PhD diss., University of Iowa, 1993); K. Tsianina Lomawaima, "Domesticity in the Federal Indian Schools: The Power of Authority over Mind and Body," *American Ethnologist* 20 (May 1993): 227–40, and *They Called It Prairie Light: The Story of Chilocco Indian School;* Michael C. Coleman, *American Indian Children at School, 1850–1930;* Sally J. McBeth, "The Primer and the Hoe," *Natural History* 93 (August 1984): 4–12; and Adams, *Education for Extinction,* 97–99, 142. Child's dissertation examines the schools at Pipestone and Flandreau, as well as Haskell, focusing primarily on the experience of the pupils and the schools' effects on their lives but also providing analysis of their curricula and policies. Federal statutes limited enrollment at the school at Pipestone, which increased from 100 in 1898 to 225 in 1910 and 250 in 1925. In "History of Pipestone Indian School" Reynolds provides lists of appropriations, enrollment figures, construction, and employees. A fire at the school in

1934 destroyed most of the school records, hindering Child's and Reynolds's research, as well as that of other scholars examining the institution and the agency. The Pipestone Indian School superintendent oversaw the reservation on which the school was located and the Santee or Lower Sioux Agency at Morton, with a day school at Birch Coulee on the Minnesota River.

13. *Star*, March 17, 1893, 2; Child, "A Bitter Lesson," 68, 74; Ahern, "Indian Education and Bureaucracy," 93–94; Riney, *Rapid City Indian School*, 18–29. School officials and tribal agents often used clothes, utensils, and children's photos as bribes. Parents sometimes took advantage of the competition between schools and used government bribes to alleviate the poverty that made boarding schools appear to be good options for large families.

14. *St. Paul Dispatch*, May 16, 1908; C. J. Crandall, "Report of School at Pipestone, Minnesota," July 25, 1893, *Reports of Superintendents of Schools to the Commissioner of Indian Affairs* (Washington, DC: U.S. Government Printing Office, 1894), 421–22; Reynolds, "History of Pipestone Indian School," 10, 17–21; *Star*, August 28, 1891, 5; Rose, *Illustrated History*, 329; PCHS, *History*, 80.

15. *Star*, February 13, 1891, 3–4; Davies, *Pipestone County*, 22, 28. Davies also happily mixed, in one sentence, Indian history with the organization of churches.

16. Kelley, "The Pipestone Quarries," 107–9; *Star*, August 14, 1891, 5, September 16, 1892, 5, March 31, 1893, 5, May 19, 1893, 1, and December 8, 1893, 5; *Pipestone Farmers' Leader*, November 30, 1893, 7.

17. Beal, *I Have a Story*, 6, 19, 44–46; PCHS, *History*, 76–79; Davies, *Pipestone County*, 33; John A. Jakle, *The American Small Town: Twentieth-Century Place Images*, 5–6, 18, 27–43; Sally J. Southwick, "'Proof of the Solidity of the Town': Quartzite Buildings and Local Identity in Pipestone and Jasper, Minnesota," unpublished paper presented at the International Conference of Historical Geographers, Québec City, Canada, August 2001. In 1903, Pipestone successfully applied to the Carnegie Foundation for library funds.

18. Reynolds, "History of Pipestone Indian School," 24, 30–32; *Star*, October 21, 1892, 10, and May 4, 1894, 1; PCHS, *History*, 80–81; F. T. Mann, Pipestone Indian Training School (hereafter PITS) Superintendent to Cato Sells, Commissioner of Indian Affairs, October 19, 1915, Letters Sent to the Commissioners of Indian Affairs, General Records, Bureau of Indian Affairs (hereafter BIA), Box 2, Record Group (hereafter RG) 75, National Archives–Central Plains Region, Kansas City, Missouri (hereafter NA). See also Riney, *Rapid City Indian School*, 167–92.

19. *Star*, December 8, 1893, 5, January 22, 1904, 1, and April 1, 1904, 8; *Pipestone Farmers' Leader*, May 12, 1904, 1, August 11, 1904, 1, and December 15, 1904, 5. The papers noted that the Minnesota exhibit also featured a sample of pipestone from the state capitol and that the Flandreau school displayed some carved

craft pieces, making "the products of the Pipestone quarries pretty well represented at the exposition in St. Louis" (*Star,* January 22, 1904, 1).

20. *Pipestone Farmers' Leader,* June 23, 1904, 1; *Star,* June 3, 1904, 1, and June 10, 1904, 6, 8.

21. Pipestone County Genealogical Society, *Biographies of the Civil War Veterans who Came to Pipestone County, Minnesota,* iii, 13, 25, 31; *Pipestone Republican,* September 29, 1885; *Star,* May 4, 1894, 1, June 3, 1904, 1, June 10, 1904, 6, and September 8, 1905, 5. On the relation of the GAR and a fraternal sense of national identity, see Mary Ann Clawson, *Constructing Brotherhood: Class, Gender, and Fraternalism,* 124–35.

22. *Star,* September 2, 1892, 5, September 30, 1892, 4, May 10, 1895, 1, June 12, 1896, 1, and January 8, 1897, 3.

23. *Star,* December 8, 1893, 5, April 21, 1899, 4, June 12, 1903, 5, January 7, 1908, 7, and September 15, 1908, 1.

24. Mary Catherine Judd, *Wigwam Stories told by North American Indians,* iii, 80, 91–102; Frederick Webb Hodge, *Handbook of the American Indians North of Mexico,* 217–19; Davis, "History of the Pipestone Reservation," 8–9. Holmes wrote the essay in 1905.

25. For discussion of Yankton assimilation efforts, see Hoover, *The Yankton Sioux.*

26. Corbett, "The Red Pipestone Quarry"; Davis, "History of the Pipestone Reservation," 55–57; Rothman, *Managing the Sacred,* 38–39; Murray, *History,* 27–28; Kelley, "The Pipestone Quarries," 104–5. Corbett and Kelley cover the legal aspects of the dispute and provide detailed narratives.

27. Murray, *History,* 29–33; Corbett, "The Red Pipestone Quarry," 110–11; Rothman, *Managing the Sacred,* 41–42; Kelley, "The Pipestone Quarries," 106–7.

28. AIRP Tape no. 67.

29. DeWitt S. Harris, PITS Superintendent, to Major James McLaughlin, United States Indian Inspector, March 8, 1899, Miscellaneous Letters Sent, BIA, Box 1, RG 75, NA; Murray, *History,* 32–35; Corbett, "The Red Pipestone Quarry," 112–13; Rothman, *Managing the Sacred,* 42–45; Kelley, "The Pipestone Quarries," 110–12.

30. Hubert Work, Secretary of the Department of the Interior, to Jennings C. Wise, Attorney for the Yankton Tribe, December 25, 1925, Miscellaneous Letters Sent, BIA, Box 1, RG 75, NA; Murray, *History,* 36; Corbett, "The Red Pipestone Quarry," 112–13.

31. *Star,* June 26, 1891, 5, April 14, 1905, 1, and November 10, 1905, 1; Mann to Henry Niemann, February 21, 1917, Miscellaneous Letters Sent, BIA, Box 2, RG 75, NA.

32. E. B. Meritt, Assistant Commissioner of Indian Affairs to Mann, August 7, 1914, Letters Received from the Commissioner of Indian Affairs, BIA, Box 1, RG 75, NA; Mann to Commissioner of Indian Affairs Cato Sells, November 2, 1915,

Letters Sent to the Commissioner of Indian Affairs, BIA, Box 2, RG 75, NA; Abstract of proposals for Pipestone School, n.d., Letters of the Commissioner of Indian Affairs, BIA, Box 1, RG 75, NA.

33. Abstract of proposals for Pipestone School, n.d., Letters of the Commissioner of Indian Affairs, BIA, Box 1, RG 75, NA; Meritt to Ora Padgett, PITS Superintendent, January 11, 1923, Letters Received from the Commissioner of Indian Affairs, BIA, Box 1, RG 75, NA; *Star,* January 16, 1912, 4. Many works examine the growth of pantribal consciousness in boarding schools, including Child, "A Bitter Lesson," 74, 158; Lomawaima, "Domesticity," 227–36; McBeth, "Primer and Hoe," 10; and Adams, *Education for Extinction,* 94–99. For an interesting memoir by a former pupil at the Pipestone Indian School, see Jim Northrup, *Rez Road Follies: Canoes, Casinos, Computers, and Birch Bark Baskets.*

34. *Star,* June 12, 1908, 1, January 22, 1909, 3, February 22, 1910, 1, and February 25, 1910. For further examples of ways in which Indian schools incorporated popular cultural images of Native Americans, see Rayna Green and John Troutman, "'By the Waters of the Minnehaha': Music and Dance, Pageants and Princesses," in Archuleta, Child, and Lomawaima, eds., *Away from Home,* 60–83.

35. *Star,* March 17, 1892, 2; Alice O'Hearn to James W. Balmer, May 11, 1938, Decimal Correspondence Files, BIA, Box 9, RG 75, NA.

36. Howard, "Recollections of Pipestone."

37. DeWitt S. Harris, PITS Superintendent, to William A. Jones, Commissioner of Indian Affairs, January 8, 1902, Letters Sent to the Commissioner of Indian Affairs, BIA, Box 1, RG 75, NA; *Pipestone Farmers' Leader,* July 12, 1894, 7; *Star,* June 15, 1894, 5, April 30, 1897, 1, July 29, 1898, 1, May 25, 1900, 9, September 21, 1900, 8, July 17, 1903, 2, January 29, 1904, 11, February 22, 1907, 4, and April 30, 1909, 1. One of Jim Northrup's memories of his time at the Pipestone school involves his attempt to return home to northern Minnesota by running away; see Northrup's *Rez Road Follies,* 4–9. Michael C. Coleman examines the choice to run away as a typical resistance action in *American Indian Children at School.*

38. *Star,* January 21, 1908, 1, and September 19, 1916, 8; Mann to Sells, November 2, 1915, Letters to the Commissioner of Indian Affairs, BIA, Box 2, RG 75, NA; Mann to Henry A. Larson, September 18, 1916, Miscellaneous Letters Sent, 1899–1926, BIA, Box 4, RG 75, NA.

39. *Chippeway Herald,* November 1902; Howard, "Recollections of Pipestone." Howard spent much of his youth in Pipestone and remembered the tribal children as good athletes who often played basketball against the Pipestone teams.

40. *Star,* December 8, 1893, 5, December 29, 1908, 1, and June 18, 1920, 1; *Pipestone Farmers' Leader,* March 26, 1936, 1.

41. Harris to McLaughlin, U.S. Indian Inspector, March 8, 1899, Miscellaneous Letters Sent, BIA, Box 1, RG 75, NA.

42. Mann to A. W. Leech, Yankton Agency Superintendent, July 1, 1915, Miscellaneous Letters Sent, BIA, Box 1, RG 75, NA; Mann to Henry Niemann, February 21, 1917, Miscellaneous Letters Sent, BIA, Box 6, RG 75, NA; Mann to The Reverend Henry Westroll, January 4, 1915, Miscellaneous Letters Sent, BIA, Box 1, RG 75, NA; *Star*, April 25, 1924, 1; Ora Padgett, PITS Superintendent, to Charles H. Burke, Commissioner of Indian Affairs, August 24, 1923, Letters Received from the Commissioner of Indian Affairs, BIA, Box 1, RG 75, NA; AIRP Tape no. 1026.

43. Harris to James T. McCleary, Minnesota Congressman, August 11, 1899, Miscellaneous Letters Sent, BIA, Box 1, RG 75, NA.

44. Charles H. Burke, Commissioner of Indian Affairs, "To All Indians," February 24, 1923, Letters received from the Commissioner of Indian Affairs, BIA, Box 1, RG 75, NA; James W. Balmer, PITS Superintendent, to Charles H. Burke, Commissioner of Indian Affairs, December 28, 1925, Letters Received, BIA, Box 1, RG 75, NA; Prucha, *The Great Father*, 272–77; Hoxie, *A Final Promise*, 112–13, 233–36.

45. Meritt to Padgett, March 2, 1922, Letters Received from the Commissioner of Indian Affairs, BIA, Box 1, RG 75, NA; Balmer to Virginia Sperlick, September 26, 1933, Decimal Correspondence Files, BIA, Box 9, RG 75, NA; Balmer to Josephine Lee, December 8, 1937, Decimal Correspondence Files, BIA, Box 9, RG 75, NA; Balmer to Joseph Balmer, Zurich, Switzerland, December 6, 1938, Decimal Correspondence Files, BIA, Box 12, RG 75, NA.

46. Harris to Jones, July 4, 1902, Letters to the Commissioner of Indian Affairs, BIA, Box 1, RG 75, NA; Harris to McLeary, August 11, 1899, and April 10, 1900, Miscellaneous Letters Sent, BIA, Box 1, RG 75, NA (emphasis in original).

47. *Star*, March 30, 1906, 3, July 6, 1906, 1, and March 22, 1907, 1.

48. Mann to Sells, October 19, 1915, Letters to the Commissioner of Indian Affairs, BIA, Box 2, RG 75, NA; Mann to Mary B. Felix, PITS Assistant Matron, March 19, 1918, Miscellaneous Letters Sent, BIA, Box 6, RG 75, NA; Pipestone, *The Charter of the City of Pipestone, Adopted April 1, 1913* (Pipestone: n.p., 1913), chapter 1, section 2; Mann to the Superintendents of the Indian Service, August 15, 1917, Miscellaneous Letters Sent, BIA, Box 5, RG 75, NA; Mann to George P. Gurley, Pipestone Patriotic Rally Committee Representative, April 21, 1917, Miscellaneous Letters Sent, BIA, Box 5, RG 75, NA.

49. J. G. Steinmeyer, *History of the St. Paul's Evangelical Lutheran Congregation, Pipestone, Minnesota, Commemorating the Forty-Fifth Anniversary* (n.p., 1937); The Pipestone Leader, *In the World War, 1917–1918–1919: An Honor Roll Containing a Pictorial Record of the Gallant and Courageous Men from Pipestone County, MN, U.S.A., who served in the Great War, 1917–1918–1919* (Pipestone: The Leader Publishing, 1919). For an examination of civic and racial nationalism, see Gary Gerstle, *American Crucible: Race and Nation in the Twentieth Century*.

50. Balmer to Huron H. Smith, August 18, 1924, Miscellaneous Letters Sent, BIA, Box 8, RG 75, NA; Balmer, to W. R. Handley, February 21, 1925, Decimal Correspondence, BIA, Box 12, RG 75, NA; Balmer, to W. H. Shawnee, August 4, 1924, Miscellaneous Letters Sent, BIA, Box 8, RG 75, NA; Balmer to David F. Kagey, August 13, 1924, Miscellaneous Letters Sent, BIA, Box 8, RG 75, NA.

51. Robert Gessner, *Massacre: A Survey of Today's American Indian,* 191–93; J. M. Bradley, "Visit to Pipestone School," *The American Indian* (The Official Publication of the Society of Oklahoma Indians) 2, no. 6 (March 1928); Meyer, *History of the Santee Sioux,* 344–45. Gessner's exposé journalism rarely complimented federal government actions or facilities. A 1931 brochure for Picnic Day at the school bore the slogan, "A Friendly School Operated by a Friendly Government"; General Collections, PCHS. As assimilation efforts declined, off-reservation boarding schools lost favor after their popularity peaked in 1915. Carlisle closed in 1918, and others began to receive less funding. See Adams, *Education for Extinction,* 320–25.

CHAPTER FOUR

1. In his article "Culture as Nature," Derek Bousé analyzes the "failure in the United States to internalize the historic experience of Native Americans as a part of what has been called 'the American Experience,'" (81). See also Deloria, *Playing Indian,* 71, and Lowenthal, *Possessed by the Past,* 180–83.

2. Of all the subjects related to the quarries, Pipestone National Monument has received the most thorough scholarly examination. The most extensive historical work includes Corbett's master's thesis, "A History," and his articles "The Red Pipestone Quarry" and "Pipestone: The Origin and Development of a National Monument." Most recently, the National Park Service (hereafter NPS) commissioned Rothman's *Managing the Sacred.* Robert Murray's work for the NPS—*A History of Pipestone National Monument, Minnesota*—preceded Rothman's study and is available for purchase by visitors to the national monument. Although Rothman's work is largely administrative, it examines the relationship between the federal government and the town of Pipestone more thoroughly than the other studies.

3. *Star,* February 21, 1890, 5.

4. Catlin, *Letters and Notes,* 2:261–63. For an insightful analysis of Catlin's ideas within a larger national and historical context, see Bousé, "Culture as Nature."

5. Many scholarly works have examined the behavior of tourists at attractions and noted the tendency of tourists to "mark" a site as a means of making the experience real to them. See John A. Jakle, *The Tourist: Travel in Twentieth-Century North America,* 26; Donald L. Redfoot, "Touristic Authenticity, Touristic Angst, and Modern Reality"; and Dean MacCannell, *The Tourist: A New Theory of the*

Leisure Class (New York: Schocken, 1976), and "Staged Authenticity: Arrangements of Social Space in Tourist Settings." The quarries' attraction and promotion bore similarities, though on a smaller and more localized scale, to the development of places such as Niagara Falls and the Grand Canyon. Preservation efforts were predicated on cultural values and beliefs projected onto the sites, and they involved an expectation of government support. For similar analyses, refer to Patrick V. McGreevy, *Imagining Niagara: The Meaning and Making of Niagara Falls* (Amherst: University of Massachusetts Press, 1994), and Pyne, *How the Canyon Became Grand.*

6. J. H. Mitchell, "The Pipestone Quarry or Restoring an Ancient Indian Shrine"; *Star,* August 18, 1893, 4; Murray, *History,* 44. The school personnel chose to lower the falls and to build the dam in order to control drainage and to increase workable acreage on the reservation.

7. For discussions of the interest and market in perceived tribal antiquity, see Robert W. Righter, "National Monuments to National Parks: The Use of the Antiquities Act of 1906"; Curtis M. Hinsley Jr., "Authoring Authenticity," and "Zunis and Brahmins"; and Bousé, "Culture as Nature," 77, 80–81.

8. Murray, *History,* 37–39; Kelley, "The Pipestone Quarries," 131–35. For a discussion of the American reverence for Indians firmly ensconced in the past and similar cultural tendencies, see Rosaldo, "Imperialist Nostalgia"; Dilworth, *Imagining Indians;* Root, *Cannibal Culture;* Crosby, "Construction of the Imaginary Indian"; Peter Bishop, *The Myth of Shangri-La: Tibet, Travel Writing and the Western Creation of Sacred Landscape* (London: Athlone Press, 1989); and Lowenthal, "The Place of the Past" and *Possessed by the Past,* 29, 135–39, 183.

9. Kammen, *Mystic Chords,* 153–56, 299.

10. Hal K. Rothman, *Preserving Different Pasts: The American National Monuments,* xi, 7–11, 36–38, 119; Righter, "National Monuments to National Parks," 282–85; Bousé, "Culture as Nature," 82–86, 91–95.

11. *Star,* November 15, 1895, 2, November 22, 1895, 1, and February 16, 1912, 1; Rothman, *Managing the Sacred,* 53. As with many women's and men's church groups, each of the Inter-Church Federation's meetings focused on a selected theme of local or regional interest and its applicability in daily life. The group meeting presented a typical small-town forum for discussion of popular topics.

12. Ralph J. Boomer, "Pipestone Reservation Park: A Park Development for Pipestone Indian Reservation"; *Star,* June 30, 1916, 1.

13. *Star,* June 17, 1919, 1, January 20, 1920, 1, August 5, 1921, 1, and August 19, 1921, 1; Murray, *History,* 44–47.

14. *Minnesota Historical Bulletin* 5, no. 3 (August 1923): 222, and 5, no. 6 (May 1924): 434; *Star,* October 23, 1923, 1.

15. Minnesota Highway Department, *Proposed Development for Pipestone State*

Park, Pipestone, Minnesota; W. E. Stoopes, "Report to the Honorable R. P. Chase, State Auditor."

16. Hoxie, *A Final Promise,* 231–38.

17. Hoover, *The Yankton Sioux,* 40–48; Rothman, *Managing the Sacred,* 47–48; Corbett, "The Red Pipestone Quarry," 111–13; Kelley, "The Pipestone Quarries," 133; *Star,* January 27, 1928, 1.

18. PCHS, *History,* 4; Corbett, "The Red Pipestone Quarry," 113–16; Rothman, *Managing the Sacred,* 48–50; Brian W. Dippie, *The Vanishing American: White Attitudes and U.S. Indian Policy,* 273–74.

19. PCHS, *History,* 159–60; Bartlett, "Pipestone County," 784–87.

20. Polly Welts Kaufman, *National Parks and the Woman's Voice: A History* (Albuquerque: University of New Mexico Press, 1996); Holly Beachley Brear, *Inherit the Alamo: Myth and Ritual at an American Shrine;* Kammen, *Mystic Chords,* 262–77.

21. Allie H. Davies, Regent Catlinite Chapter D. A. R., to James Balmer, April 24, 1925, Miscellaneous Letters Received, BIA, Box 8, RG 75, NA; Balmer to Davies, April 27, 1925, Miscellaneous Letters Received, BIA, Box 8, RG 75, NA; Balmer to Burke, April 27, 1925, Miscellaneous Letters Received, BIA, Box 8, RG 75, NA; Murray, *History,* 17, 46–47; *Star,* October 23, 1923, 1. Nicollet carved his name as J. N. Nicollet and Frémont his initials, J. E. F.

22. *Star,* April 24, 1925, 1, and March 4, 1932, 1. For a study of similar actions by the Daughters of the Republic of Texas in preserving a historical interpretation of the Alamo as an Anglo shrine, see Brear, *Inherit the Alamo,* 23–53, 153–57. For an analysis applicable to the DAR mentality, see also James M. Mayo, "War Memorials as Political Memory," *Geographical Review* 78, no. 1 (January 1988): 62–75.

23. PCHS, *History,* 90; PISA, *The Pipestone Indian Shrine.*

24. AIRP Tape no. 1026; Bartlett, "Pipestone County," 787; Rothman, *Managing the Sacred,* 58–59.

25. AIRP Tape no. 1026. Although Bartlett had witnessed the Yankton acting competently on their own behalf in the settlement case and in their relations with the federal government, she remained convinced that preserving the quarries was the duty of the Shrine Association.

26. PCHS, *History,* 90; AIRP Tape no. 1026; PISA, *The Pipestone Indian Shrine,* 5–7. Bartlett recalled that so few Indians came to quarry by the 1930s that the townspeople assumed they had no active interest in the quarries. In the booklet, she wrote that the local people had cooperated with the tribes to prevent vandalism and to preserve the site, suggesting local acknowledgment of shared economic circumstances.

27. AIRP Tape no. 1026; Rothman, *Managing the Sacred,* 59–60.

28. AIRP Tape no. 1026; Rothman, *Preserving Different Pasts,* 84–91, 119.

29. AIRP Tape no. 1026; Prucha, *The Great Father,* 326–33; Dippie, *The Vanishing American,* 304–9. Collier stated his approval of a park or monument at the quarries in November 1933.

30. Edward A. Hummel, "Report on Historical Field Investigation Proposed Area for National Monument: Pipestone Indian Shrine," Box 193—History, General Records of the NPS, RG 79, NA; Hummel to Regional Officer, Region IV, August 31, 1935, Box 193, NPS, RG 79, NA. David Glassberg observes the Park Service tendency to continue to describe tribal pasts as prehistory that serves as a timeless prelude to the national narrative of history (*Sense of History,* 3–6).

31. PCHS, *History,* 90; Rothman, *Managing the Sacred,* 61–68; *Star,* March 2, 1934, 1, May 8, 1934, 1, and January 29, 1937, 1. Rothman provides a detailed analysis of the position of the NPS in the 1930s and the legal problems surrounding discussions in Congress.

32. For an analysis of the role of references to the creation of place, see Yi-Fu Tuan, "Language and the Making of Place: A Narrative-Descriptive Approach," *Annals of the Association of American Geographers* 81, no. 4 (1991): 684–96. See also Bishop, *The Myth of Shangri-La,* 9–35, for a discussion of ways in which predominantly Protestant, industrialized societies locate sacred spaces in remote cultures, accepting travel narratives as empirical rather than subjective and literary. Brear discusses references to the Alamo as a shrine within the context of an American tendency to revere certain historical narratives as sacred texts, in *Inherit the Alamo,* 18–20.

33. Corbett, "Pipestone," 87–88; Rothman, *Managing the Sacred,* 67–68.

34. *Star,* July 5, 1932, 1, August 16, 1932, 1, August 30, 1932, 1, September 23, 1932, 1, December 13, 1932, 1, March 23, 1934, 1, June 12, 1934, 1, and June 25, 1937, 1; *Pipestone Farmers' Leader,* June 4, 1936, 1, and September 10, 1936, 1. Pipestone also promoted itself indirectly, for example by giving a carved pipe to the Minneapolis Civic and Commerce Association to bestow on the president of General Motors, Alfred P. Sloan Jr. (*Pipestone Farmers' Leader,* May 28, 1936, 1). For an extended analysis of the nontribal American use of tribal dress and mimicry, see Deloria, *Playing Indian,* 103–27. Deloria does not discuss "peace pipe–smoking" rituals among nontribal people, a practice that was not uncommon in the nineteenth and early twentieth centuries as a public form of celebrating an agreement.

35. Mitchell, "The Pipestone Quarry," 25–28; *Star,* March 27, 1934, 1. In a May 15, 1934, article on its front page, the *Star* used every typical descriptor for the team's activities—"Historic Ground Being Beautified: Work Progressing on Pipestone National Shrine in Sacred Quarry Region."

36. Rothman, *Managing the Sacred,* 69–71; Murray, *History,* 48–51; Corbett, "Pipestone," 88; PCHS, *History,* 8, 90; *Star,* August 6, 1937, 1, August 10, 1937, 1,

August 24, 1937, 1, and August 31, 1937, 1; *Pipestone Farmers' Leader,* August 26, 1937, 1. Senator Shipstead kept residents of Pipestone informed of congressional activities through telegrams. Other examples of national monuments with historical value created in the 1930s include Homestead National Monument in Nebraska, Ocmulgee National Monument in Georgia, and Jefferson National Expansion Memorial in St. Louis; see Rothman, *Preserving Different Pasts,* 188–209.

37. PCHS, *History,* 90; *Star,* November 30, 1937, 1.

38. Rothman, *Managing the Sacred,* 73–79; Righter, "National Monuments to National Parks," 287–88.

39. For more detailed description of the issues involved and Park Service policy, see Rothman, *Managing the Sacred,* 73–79.

40. Carroll H. Wegemann, Regional Geologist, Memorandum, August 5, 1938, Box 193, Inspections 1938–1952, NPS, RG 79, NA; Thomas J. Allen, Regional Director, NPS, to Balmer, October 14, 1940, BIA, Box 12 RG 75, NA; Arno Cammerer, NPS Director, to John Collier, Commissioner of Indian Affairs, February 2, 1940, BIA, Box 12, RG 75, NA; Acting Assistant to the Commissioner, to Balmer, February 8, 1940, BIA, Box 12, RG 75, NA; Donald B. Alexander, Acting Regional Director, November 27, 1939, Box 193, NPS, RG 79, NA. Moses Crow (Santee) from Niobrara, Nebraska, and Estella Pearsall (Santee) from Granite Falls, Minnesota, had both attended the Pipestone Indian School and returned to town in 1927 when Moses took work at the school. Moses's sister, Julia, was married to Joseph Taylor, who lived in Flandreau and quarried seasonally. PCHS, *History,* 169, 314; http://www.pipestone-dakota.com, accessed on February 10, 2004.

41. Rothman, *Managing the Sacred,* 80–81; G. A. Troskey, Acting Director NPS, to Region II, November 19, 1940, Box 193, NPS, RG 79, NA; Albert F. Drysdale, Annual Report, October 1, 1941, Box 193, Reports–General, September 1940–June 1951, NPS, RG 79, NA.

42. Wegemann, Inspections Report, August 5, 1938, Box 193, NPS, RG 79, NA; Drysdale, Memorandum to Regional Director Baker, July 23, 1940, and Hummel, handwritten response, Box 193, NPS, RG 79, NA; Drysdale, Memorandum to Regional Director, April 22, 1947, Box 193, NPS, RG 79, NA; Drysdale, Narrative Report, June 3, 1944, Box 193, NPS, RG 79, NA; Drysdale, Annual Report, October 1, 1941, Box 193, NPS, RG 79, NA; Howard W. Baker, Memorandum for the Files, August 10, 1948, Box 193, NPS, RG 79, NA; *Star,* April 18, 1941, 1. Drysdale noted that the custodian's shelter and the latrines often had been kicked in or defaced in his absence.

43. Minnesota Federal Writers' Project of the Works Projects Administration, *Minnesota: A State Guide* (New York: Viking Press, 1938), 11, 34–38, 100, 115, 132. The section on mining is in the "Manufacturing" chapter.

44. Ibid., 341–42. See also the WPA Writers' Project, Annals of Minnesota, which contains the historical records survey completed by the project (WPA Files, Manuscripts Collection, MHS), and Mabel S. Ulrich, "Salvaging Culture for the WPA," *Harper's Monthly* 178 (May 1939): 653–64. Ulrich directed the Writers' Project in Minnesota, which included such notable authors as Meridel LeSueur.

45. U.S. National Park Service, *Pipestone National Monument, Minnesota* (NPS, 1941); Winifred Bartlett to Hummel, Regional Supervisor of Historic Sites, December 30, 1940, History, Box 193, NPS, RG 79, NA.

46. Drysdale to Region II, January 23, 1940, Museums, Box 195, NPS, RG 79, NA; NPS Regional Director, Region II, to Drysdale, January 25, 1940, Box 195, NPS, RG 79, NA; Albert Drysdale to Region II, February 2, 1940, Box 193, NPS, RG 79, NA; Walter G. Benjamin, to Newton B. Drury, NPS Director, July 16, 1949, Box 195, NPS, RG 79, NA; A. E. Demarary, NPS Acting Director, to Benjamin, July 28, 1949, Box 195, NPS, RG 79, NA; *Pipestone Farmers' Leader,* March 8, 1940, 1; Rothman, *Managing the Sacred,* 85–87.

47. W. L. Wilson, Civic and Commerce Association President, to PITS, April 17, 1950, Box 193, NPS, RG 79, NA; NPS, "Self-Guiding Leaflet for Circle Trail: Pipestone National Monument, Minnesota," Box 193, NPS, RG 79, NA; Louis H. Powell to Hubert H. Humphrey, July 27, 1949, Box 195, NPS, RG 79, NA; Stanley C. Joseph, Region II Administrative Assistant, Memorandum for Files, December 22, 1948, Box 193, NPS, RG 79, NA. Powell's letter to Humphrey included the recommendation that the proposed museum give attention to the "famous early explorers who visited the region and Bishop Whipple who made valiant efforts to encourage the Indians to continue manufacturing pipestone materials." Bishop Henry Whipple, an Episcopal clergyman, was an Indian reformer in the mid-nineteenth century who advocated on behalf of the Minnesota Dakota during the Dakota Conflict of the 1860s. His intercession with President Abraham Lincoln stayed the execution of almost three hundred Dakota convicted by a state court after the 1862 war.

48. Lyle K. Linch, "The History of the Pipestone Indian Shrine and National Monument," 1954, Box 193, NPS, RG 79, NA; Rothman, *Managing the Sacred,* 88–92; Corbett, "Pipestone," 88–89; Murray, *History,* 53–55. The broad prairie would indeed seem monotonous to someone accustomed to the Black Hills or the Rocky Mountains.

49. Linch, Memorandum to Region II, June 16, 1950, Box 193, NPS, RG 79, NA; Joseph, Memorandum for the files, December 22, 1948, Box 193, NPS, RG 79, NA; Baker, Memorandum for the files, September 27, 1950, Box 194, NPS, RG 79, NA; Linch, Memorandum to Region II, June 1, 1950, Box 193, NPS, RG 79, NA.

50. Olaf T. Hagen, NPS Regional Historian, Memorandum to the Files, November 30, 1948, Box 193, NPS, RG 79, NA; Linch, Memorandum to Regional Director, August 22, 1949, Box 193, NPS, RG 79, NA; Linch, Memorandum to Regional Director, June 26, 1949, Box 193, NPS, RG 79, NA; Linch, "Pipestone National Monument," 1949, Box 195, NPS, RG 79, NA; Linch, Memorandum to Regional Director, July 1, 1949, Box 193, NPS, RG 79, NA. In her 1976 interview, Winifred Bartlett remembered Linch as someone who "wanted to make good here" and got involved with the local community to an extent that made his supervisors uncomfortable. Her impression of him included a sense that he wanted to impress people with his newspaper column, for which he often asked her to teach him big words. She also noted that he too often said what he thought, which offended local residents. See AIRP Tape no. 1026.

51. Linch, Memorandum to the Director, June 26, 1949, Box 193, NPS, RG 79, NA; Linch, Memorandum for the Files, September 27, 1948, Box 193, NPS, RG 79, NA.

52. "Are Indians Egyptians? Pipestone Holds 'Key,'" *Minneapolis Sunday Tribune,* August 20, 1950, 3, and "Pipestone Indian Cult from Egypt?" *Minneapolis Sunday Tribune,* September 17, 1950, 15; Lass, *Minnesota,* 48–53; Michael W. Hughey and Michael G. Michlovic, "'Making' History: The Vikings in the American Heartland." Interest in the rune stone has waxed and waned but has remained part of the state's identity.

53. Director, Region II, to Linch, September 3, 1950, Box 193, NPS, RG 79, NA; Jerome C. Miller to Linch, August 31, 1950, Box 195, NPS, RG 79, NA; Merrill J. Mattes to Linch, September 21, 1950, Box 193, NPS, RG 79, NA.

54. Linch, Memorandum for Director, August 1, 1949, Box 193, NPS, RG 79, NA; George Bryan, National Monument News, August 18, 1949, Box 193, NPS, RG 79, NA; Linch, Memorandum for Director, August 22, 1949, Box 193, NPS, RG 79, NA; AIRP Tape no. 1027, Anonymous Chippewa, interviewed by William Corbett, 1976; *Minneapolis Morning Tribune,* October 25 and October 26, 1949, 16; PCHS, *History,* 169.

55. Hummel, Memorandum to the Director, June 5, 1940, Box 193, NPS, RG 79, NA; Drysdale, Superintendent's Annual Report, October 1, 1941, Box 193, NPS, RG 79, NA; Balmer to Lawrence C. Merriam, Regional Director, November 23, 1945, Box 193, NPS, RG 79, NA; Rules and Regulations, Pipestone National Monument, National Park Service, 1946, Box 193, NPS, RG 79, NA.

56. Linch, Memorandum for Director, March 21, 1948, Box 193, NPS, RG 79, NA; Drysdale, Memorandum for Director, November 6, 1947, Box 193, NPS, RG 79, NA; Drysdale, Memorandum for Director, September 23, 1943, Box 193, NPS, RG 79, NA.

CHAPTER FIVE

1. Linch, Superintendent's Report, July 1952, Box 195, NPS, RG 79, NA.

2. Krech and Hail, *Collecting Native America*. In his chapter "Rudolf F. Haffenreffer and the King Philip Museum," Shepard Krech describes a collector with a similarity to Bennett, a businessman interested in the "legends" of his locality and in Native American stories told by Washington Irving, who used collecting to promote generalized Indian imagery of his place of residence (*Collecting Native America, 1870–1960*, 105–38).

3. Drysdale to Region II, January 23, 1940, Museums, Box 195, NPS, RG 79, NA; NPS Regional Director, Region II, to Drysdale, January 25, 1940, Box 195, NPS, RG 79, NA; Drysdale to Region II, February 2, 1940, Box 193, NPS, RG 79, NA; Benjamin to Drury, NPS Director, July 16, 1949, Box 195, NPS, RG 79, NA; Demarary, NPS Acting Director, to Benjamin, July 28, 1949, Box 195, NPS, RG 79, NA; *Pipestone Farmers' Leader*, March 8, 1940, 1; Rothman, *Managing the Sacred*, 85–87.

4. Krech and Hail, *Collecting Native America*; Smith, *Reimagining Indians*, 8–15, 119–27; Carter Jones Meyer and Diana Royer, eds., *Selling the Indian: Commercializing and Appropriating American Indian Cultures*; Erika Marie Bsumek, "Making 'Indian Made': The Production, Consumption and Construction of Navajo Ethnic Identity, 1880–1935."

5. *Star*, July 20, 1928, 1, and December 7, 1937, 1.

6. PCHS, *History*, 122; Bartlett, "Pipestone County," 790; *Pipestone Farmers' Leader*, September 16, 1937, 1. The sources claim that the Roe collection was the largest of its kind in North America. For analyses on regional markets for tribal goods, see Ruth B. Phillips, *Trading Identities: The Souvenir in Native North American Art from the Northeast, 1700–1900*, which includes discussion of Ojibwe markets along the Great Lakes; Dilworth, *Imagining Indians;* and Chris Wilson, *The Myth of Santa Fe: Creating a Modern Regional Tradition*. For examples of the interest in and commodification of tribal cultures of the Pacific Northwest, see Root, *Cannibal Culture*.

7. Roe's Indian Trading Post brochures, ca. 1940, Pipestone County Museum general collections and my own collection. Drysdale to NPS Regional Director, Region II, September 23, 1943, Box 193, NPS, RG 79, NA.

8. Roe's Indian Trading Post brochures; Private Holdings, Box 194, NPS, RG 79, NA. For an examination of similar promotional activities in another small town, see Bonnie Christensen, *Red Lodge and the Mythic West: Coal Miners to Cowboys*, 139–43.

9. Pipestone Telephone Directory, November 1949, Alan Woolworth private collection. The Park Service received half a line in a short paragraph, whereas the

Indian Training School merited a lengthy paragraph to itself. The directory also featured a map with the "Shrine National Park" and Winnewissa Falls labeled.

10. Roe's Indian Trading Post brochures, 1930s–1940s, and Civic and Commerce Association brochures, 1940s, Pipestone County Museum general collections. Sources from which descriptive phrases were excerpted include White, "A Trip to the Great Red Pipestone Quarry"; Hayden, "Sketch of the Geology"; Catlin, *Letters and Notes,* 2:164–68; PISA, *The Pipestone Indian Shrine,* 1–2.

11. *Star,* December 23, 1948, 1, December 18, 1950, 1, August 5, 1948, 1, and June 28, 1951, 1; Pipestone County, Minnesota, Statehood Centennial Committee, *Pipestone,* 30. The pipe no doubt seemed appropriate to the colonel, given the Air Force motto "Peace Is Our Profession." Reportedly, Winifred Bartlett sent a carved pipe to India after receiving a request in 1933.

12. *Star,* October 18, 1948, 1, and February 16, 1950, 1; Science Museum of Minnesota, "Pipes and Pipestone," Indian Leaflets 11 and 12 (St. Paul: Science Museum of Minnesota, 1955).

13. The poem's early stanzas read:

> On the Mountains of the Prairie
> On the great Red Pipe-stone Quarry
> Gitche Manito, the mighty
> He the Master of Life, descending
> On the red crags of the quarry
> Stood erect and called the nations
> Called the tribes of men together.
>
> From his footprints flowed a river
> Leaped into the light of morning
> . . .
> From the red stone of the quarry
> With his hand he broke a fragment
> Moulded it into a pipe-head
> Shaped and fashioned it with figures.
> . . .
> Smoked the calumet, the Peace-Pipe
> As a signal to the nations
> . . .
> All the warriors drawn together
> By the signal of the Peace-Pipe,
> To the Mountains of the Prairie,
> To the Great Red Pipe-stone Quarry
> (Longfellow, *The Song of Hiawatha,* 23–28)

14. AIRP Tape no. 1026; Beal, *I Have a Story,* 52–54; *Star,* July 18, 1913, 2, and June 12, 1914, 3; Bradley, "Visit to Pipestone School"; *Star,* May 17, 1932, 1, and May 27, 1932, 1. For an overview of the historical pageantry movement, see David Glassberg, *American Historical Pageantry: The Uses of Tradition in the Early Twentieth Century.* Glassberg identifies the Northeast and Midwest as the loci of pageant activity (132). Michael McNally has a forthcoming *American Quarterly* article about Native Americans participating in such productions, titled "The Indian Passion Play: Contests for the Real Indian in Song of Hiawatha Pageants."

15. *Star,* January 18, 1924, 1.

16. AIRP Tape no. 1026; George F. Ingalls, Regional Chief of Land and Recreational Planning, and Mattes, Memorandum to the Files, September 2, 1950, Box 193, NPS, RG 79, NA. National Exchange Club, *The Soul of Exchange: An Interpretation of the Ideals, Spirit, and Purposes of the Exchange Clubs of the United States.* Linch belonged to several fraternal groups in town and participated voluntarily in community activities, and he hoped that a successful pageant in Pipestone would attract additional visitors to the national monument.

17. AIRP Tape no. 1026; Beal, *I Have a Story,* 54–55. Owens purchased the land from R. L. Palmer. Moore ceased extracting quartzite in the late 1800s.

18. *Star,* May 12, 1949, 1, June 9, 1949, 1, and June 16, 1949, 1; AIRP Tape no. 1026; AIRP Tape no. 1027; "Song of Hiawatha" program, early 1950s, Box 193, NPS, RG 79, NA. As part of the preparation of the grounds, the city sprayed the area with DDT.

19. AIRP Tape no. 1026; AIRP Tape no. 1027; "Song of Hiawatha" program, early 1950s, Box 193, NPS, RG 79, NA.

20. *Star,* June 9, 1949, 1, and August 11, 1949, 1; Linch, Memorandum for the Director, June 26, 1949, Box 193, NPS, RG 79, NA; "Pipestone Exchange Club presents its second annual pageant" program, 1950, Box 194, NPS, RG 79, NA.

21. AIRP Tape no. 1026; "Song of Hiawatha" program, early 1950s, Box 193, NPS, RG 79, NA; Linch, Memorandum to the Director, July 1952, Box 193, NPS, RG 79, NA; *Star,* July 17, 1950, 1, July 24, 1950, 1, April 26, 1951, 1, July 23, 1951, 1, August 6, 1951, 1, July 13, 1953, 1, July 20, 1953, 1, and January 15, 1954, 1.

22. "Song of Hiawatha" program, early 1950s, Box 193, NPS, RG 79, NA; Hiawatha Club, "The Hiawatha Club presents its annual pageant," 1957, MHS, serial 242; Trachtenberg, "Singing Hiawatha," 1–19. Ethnologists immediately criticized Longfellow's work, and some accused him of borrowing the rhyme scheme and structure from the *Kalevala,* but the reading public steadfastly ignored their objections to the poem's representations of tribal life and myth. The poem remained popular in the state. In public school in the 1960s, I had to memorize stanzas of it, and while doing my initial research in the 1990s, I encountered Minnesotans of all ages who could also recite parts of the verse. In Minneapolis statues

of Longfellow and of Hiawatha with Minnehaha grace Minnehaha Park, where Minnehaha Creek—near Lakes Hiawatha and Nokomis—falls dramatically and runs into the Mississippi River just south of the Longfellow neighborhood.

23. "Song of Hiawatha" program, early 1950s, Box 193, NPS, RG 79, NA; Hiawatha Club, "The Hiawatha Club presents its annual pageant," 1957, MHS, serial 242; Trachtenberg, "Singing Hiawatha"; AIRP Tape no. 1026. Generations of scholars have analyzed the issues of authenticity and tourism and the particularly American tendency to prefer the contrived and artificial "authentic" to any unstructured experience. See Daniel J. Boorstin, *The Image: A Guide to Pseudo-Events in America*, 37–40, 78–99; Jakle, *The Tourist*, 23–28, 46–48, 286; Hinsley, "Authoring Authenticity"; Brear, *Inherit the Alamo*, 55–66; and Hughey and Michlovic, "'Making' History." For works that focus specifically on issues of the authentic in representations of Native Americans, see Katie Johnson and Tamara Underiner, "Command Performances: Staging Native Americans at Tillicum Village," in Jones and Royer, eds., *Selling the Indian*, 44–61; Gretchen M. Bataille, ed., *Native American Representations: First Encounters, Distorted Images, and Literary Appropriations;* S. Elizabeth Bird, "Constructing the Indian, 1830s–1990s"; Peter Geller, "'Hudson's Bay Company Indians': Images of Native People and the Red River Pageant, 1920," in *Dressing in Feathers: The Construction of the Indian in American Popular Culture*, ed. S. Elizabeth Bird (Boulder, CO: Westview Press, 1996), 1–12, 65–77; and Deloria, *Playing Indian*, 34–37, 101–3, 135–42.

24. Hiawatha Club, "The Hiawatha Club presents its annual pageant," 1957, MHS, serial 242.

25. Rothman, *Managing the Sacred*, 100–103. Visits to the national monument increased from approximately 5,000 in 1945 to over 52,000 in 1955, a change attributable partly to postwar prosperity and also to gradual improvements at the site, as well as to the promotional efforts of Pipestone and the success of the pageant.

26. Weldon W. Gratton to Ingalls, April 25, 1950, Box 194, NPS, RG 79, NA; Robert S. Owens to Linch, April 19, 1950, Box 194, NPS, RG 79, NA; Ingalls and Mattes, Memorandum to the Files, September 11, 1950, Box 194, NPS, RG 79, NA; Rothman, *Managing the Sacred*, 100.

27. *Star*, June 19, 1951, 1, July 6, 1950, 1, July 17, 1950, 1, and July 23, 1953, 1. For analyses of parades in American culture, see April R. Schultz, *Ethnicity on Parade: Inventing the Norwegian American through Celebration* (Amherst: University of Massachusetts Press, 1994), and Mary Ryan, "The American Parade: Representations of the Nineteenth-Century Social Order," in *The New Cultural History*, ed. Lynn Hunt (Berkeley: University of California Press), 1989, 131–53.

28. Glassberg, *American Historical Pageantry*, 114, 140, 152–56; Geller, "'Hudson's Bay Company Indians,'" 67–70.

29. Lenore A. Stiffarm and Phil Lane Jr., "The Demography of Native North America: A Question of American Indian Survival," in *The State of Native America: Genocide, Colonization, and Resistance*, ed. M. Annette Jaimes (Boston: South End Press, 1992), 23–53; Prucha, *The Great Father*, 340–56; Deloria, *Playing Indian*, 125–27.

30. Pipestone County, Minnesota, Statehood Centennial Committee, *Pipestone*, 73.

31. Ibid., 76–78. The time line included Yankton leader Struck-by-the-Ree's encounter with Lewis and Clark, which added a romanticized historical element to the tribe's reputation for peaceful coexistence, as well as the tribe's signing of the 1858 treaty. For a tribal analysis of white uses of history, see Donald A. Grinde Jr., "Historical Narratives of Nationhood and the Semiotic Construction of Social Identity: A Native American Perspective," in *Issues in Native American Cultural Identity*, ed. Michael K. Green (New York: Peter Lang, 1995), 201–22.

32. For an analysis of tourists' expectations, see Jakle, *The Tourist*, 4–8, 18–34.

33. *Star*, June 26, 1950, 1, and August 6, 1951, 1; Minneapolis Public Schools, *A Summer Vacation Guide: Nature and Science* (Minneapolis, MN: Board of Education, 1937); Bertha L. Heilbron, "Some Sioux Legends in Pictures," and "The Minnesota Pipestone Quarries."

34. *Worthington Daily Globe*, May 9, 1958, 12; PCHS, *History*, 80–81; Rothman, *Managing the Sacred*, 95–97. The school facilities eventually became a technical/vocational training school and a long-term care facility for elderly residents.

35. AIRP Tape no. 1026; Rothman, *Managing the Sacred*, 101–3. Bartlett stated the group's intentions were "to support the Indians" and "to keep it as authentic as possible."

36. Deloria, *Playing Indian*, 123. Tribal members participated in a variety of Indian events staged by whites; see David O. Born, "Black Elk and the Duhamel Sioux Indian Pageant," *North Dakota History* 61, no. 1 (Winter 1994): 22–29; Johnson and Underiner, "Command Performance," 48–54, and Barbara A. Hail, "Museums as Inspiration: Clara Endicott Sears and the Fruitlands Museums," in *Collecting Native America*, 172–202.

37. Lowenthal, *Possessed by the Past*, 241–45. For scholarly examinations of the appropriation of tribal spirituality by nontribal cultures, see Laurie Anne Whitt, "Indigenous Peoples and the Cultural Politics of Knowledge," in Green, *Issues in Native American Cultural Identity*, 223–71; Rayna Green, "The Tribe Called Wannabe: Playing Indian in America and Europe," and Wendy Rose, "The Great Pretenders: Further Reflections on White Shamanism," in Jaimes, *The State of Native America*, 403–21.

CONCLUSION

1. Colleen Sundvold Hofelman, *It's News to Me: With Help from My Friends and 25 Years On-the-Job Training*, 27–31; Rothman, *Managing the Sacred*, 148–51, 210–12; Hughes, *Perceptions of the Sacred*, 4.

2. Alvin R. Zephier, Yankton Tribal Chair, to Tim Giago, May 19, 1987, and Letter to Senator Daniel K. Inouye and Senate Select Committee on Indian Affairs, June 7, 1987, and Donald Gurnoe, St. Paul American Indian Center, to Roger Head, Minnesota Indian Affairs Council, June 27, 1987, Minnesota State Archives, Indian Affairs Council, Subject Files, Box 6, Yankton Sioux Tribe, 1987 Folder, MHS; Hughes, *Perceptions of the Sacred*, 3–4, 31–47; Rothman, *Managing the Sacred*, 153–60.

3. Gulliford, *Sacred Objects*, 170. See also http://littlefeather.50megs.com, accessed on February 11, 2004; http://www.pipekeepers.org, accessed on December 30, 2003; and http://wwwsacredland.org/pipestone.html, accessed on February 12, 2004.

4. Letter from Members of the Pipestone Indian Community to Donald Gurnoe, July 23, 1987, Minnesota State Archives, Indian Affairs Council, Subject Files, Box 6, Yankton Sioux Tribe, 1987 Folder, MHS; Letter from Betty Mc-Swain, Park Ranger, Pipestone National Monument, to author, June 21, 1996; Rothman, *Managing the Sacred*, 155–66.

5. Hofelman, *It's News to Me,* 27; "Welcome to Pipestone Minnesota: Home of the Peace Pipe," Minnesota State Archives, Indian Affairs Council, Subject Files, Box 4, Pipestone Indians Folder, 1979, MHS.

6. Letter from Christopher Roelfsema-Hummel, former director of the Pipestone County Historical Museum, to author, April 1, 1999; Stanley Fishman Associates, Inc., *Pipestone Preservation: A Study for the Conservation of Historic Resources of Pipestone, Minnesota* (St. Paul, MN: Stanley Fishman Associates, Inc., Architects and Planning Consultants, 1977), 2–8, 48–65; MHS, Division of Field Services, Historic Sites and Archaeology, *Historic Preservation in Minnesota,* The Annual Preservation Program, 1972, xxi, and 1975–76, 60 (St. Paul: Minnesota Historical Society); U.S. Department of the Interior, National Park Service, National Register of Historic Places Inventory—Nomination Form (St. Paul: State Historic Preservation Office, Minnesota Historical Society); AIRP Tape no. 92, Anonymous Yankton, interviewed by Richard Loder, 1968. In 1964 John H. Roe offered the store for sale; after the inventory was briefly owned by a local funeral director, the Glenbow Museum in Calgary, Alberta, purchased and took possession of much of the Roe's collection. PCHS, *History,* 122.

BIBLIOGRAPHY

ARCHIVAL COLLECTIONS OF UNPUBLISHED DOCUMENTS

Bureau of Indian Affairs, Record Group 75, National Archives–Central Plains Region, Kansas City, Missouri

General Collections, Minnesota Historical Society, St. Paul, Minnesota (includes Manuscripts Collection, Pamphlet Collection, and Minnesota State Archives)

General Collections, Pipestone County Historical Society, Pipestone, Minnesota

General Collections, Southwest Minnesota Regional History Center, Marshall, Minnesota

James J. Hill Papers, James J. Hill Reference Library, St. Paul, Minnesota

National Park Service, Record Group 79, National Archives–Central Plains Region, Kansas City, Missouri

South Dakota Oral History Center, American Indian Research Project, Institute of American Indian Studies, University of South Dakota, Vermillion, South Dakota

NEWSPAPERS

Chippeway Herald
Jasper Journal
Minneapolis Tribune (including *Morning Tribune* and *Sunday Tribune*)
Pipestone County Star
Pipestone Farmers' Leader
Pipestone Republican
St. Paul Dispatch
Svenska Amerikanska Posten
Worthington Daily Globe

THESES AND DISSERTATIONS

Boomer, Ralph J. "Pipestone Reservation Park: A Park Development for Pipestone Indian Reservation." BS thesis, Iowa State University, 1916.

Bsumek, Erika Marie. "Making 'Indian Made': The Production, Consumption, and Construction of Navajo Ethnic Identity, 1880–1935." PhD diss., Rutgers, The State University of New Jersey, 2000.

Child, Brenda Joyce. "A Bitter Lesson: Native Americans and the Government Boarding School Experience, 1890–1940." PhD diss., University of Iowa, 1993.

Corbett, William P. "A History of the Red Pipestone Quarry and Pipestone National Monument." MA thesis, University of South Dakota, 1976.

Davis, John Wayne. "A History of the Pipestone Reservation and Quarry." MA thesis, University of Colorado, 1934.

Kelley, Paul A. "The Pipestone Quarries: An Historical Geography." MA thesis, University of Nebraska, 1997.

Nicholas, Lisa Jane (aka Liza). "Culture and the Cowboy State: The Making of Westerners." PhD diss., University of Utah, 2001.

Reed, James P. "The Role of an English Land Company in the Settlement of Northwestern Iowa and Southwestern Minnesota: A Study in Historical Geography." MA thesis, University of Nebraska at Omaha, 1974.

Reynolds, Gaylord V. "The History of Pipestone Indian School." MA thesis, University of South Dakota, 1952.

ARTICLES, BOOKS, AND PUBLISHED DOCUMENTS

Adams, David Wallace. *Education for Extinction: American Indians and the Boarding School Experience, 1875–1928.* Lawrence: University of Kansas Press, 1995.

Ahern, Wilbert H. "Indian Education and Bureaucracy: The School at Morris, 1887–1909." *Minnesota History* 49 (Fall 1984): 82–98.

Allen, J. L. "Horizons of the Sublime: The Invention of the Romantic West." *Journal of Historical Geography* 18, no. 1 (1992): 27–40.

Ambler, Cathy. "Small Historical Sites in Kansas: Merging Artifactual Landscapes and Community Values." *Great Plains Quarterly* 15, no. 1 (Winter 1995): 33–48.

Anderson, Benedict. *Imagined Communities: Reflections on the Origins and Spread of Nationalism.* London: Verso, 1983.

Anderson, Gary Clayton. *Kinsmen of Another Kind: Dakota-White Relations in the Upper Mississippi Valley, 1650–1862.* Lincoln: University of Nebraska Press, 1984.

Anderson, Kay, and Fay Gale, eds. *Inventing Places: Studies in Cultural Geography.* Melbourne, Australia: Longman Cheshire, 1992.

Archuleta, Margaret L., Brenda J. Child, and K. Tsianina Lomawaima, eds. *Away from Home: American Indian Boarding School Experiences, 1879–2000.* Phoenix, AZ: Heard Museum, 2000.

Armstrong, Moses K. *History and Resources of Dakota, Montana, and Idaho.* Yankton, Dakota Territory: G. W. Kingsbury Printers, 1866.

Athearn, Robert G. *The Mythic West in the Twentieth Century.* Lawrence: University of Kansas Press, 1986.

Bartlett, Winifred. "Pipestone County." In *Who's Who in Minnesota.* Minneapolis: Minnesota Editorial Association, 1941.

Bataille, Gretchen M., ed. *Native American Representations: First Encounters, Distorted Images, and Literary Appropriations.* Lincoln: University of Nebraska Press, 2001.

Beal, Wanita. *I Have a Story to Tell about Pipestone.* Pipestone, MN: Dennis Hansen Associates, 1991.

Berkhofer, Robert F., Jr. *The White Man's Indian: Images of the American Indian from Columbus to the Present.* New York: Vintage Books, 1979.

————. "White Conceptions of Indians." In *History of Indian-White Relations,* vol. 4, ed. Wilcomb E. Washburn, 522–47. Washington, DC: Smithsonian Institution, 1988.

Bird, S. Elizabeth. *Dressing in Feathers: The Construction of the Indian in American Popular Culture.* Boulder, CO: Westview Press, 1996.

Blodgett, Peter J. "Visiting 'The Realm of Wonder': Yosemite and the Business of Tourism, 1855–1916." *California History* 69, no. 2 (Summer 1990): 118–33.

Bodnar, John. *Remaking America: Public Memory, Commemoration, and Patriotism in the Twentieth Century.* Princeton, NJ: Princeton University Press, 1992.

Boorstin, Daniel J. *The Image: A Guide to Pseudo-Events in America.* New York: Vintage Books, 1992.

Bousé, Derek. "Culture as Nature: How Native American Cultural Antiquities Became Part of the Natural World." *Public Historian* 18 (Fall 1996): 75–98.

Bowden, Martyn J. "The Invention of American Tradition." *Journal of Historical Geography* 18, no. 1 (1992): 3–26.

Bray, Edmund C., and Martha Coleman Bray, eds. and trans. *Joseph N. Nicollet on the Plains and Prairies: The Expeditions of 1838–39, with Journals, Letters, and Notes on the Dakota Indians.* St. Paul: Minnesota Historical Society Press, 1993.

Brear, Holly Beachley. *Inherit the Alamo: Myth and Ritual at an American Shrine.* Austin: University of Texas Press, 1995.

Bremer, Richard G. *Indian Agent and Wilderness Scholar: The Life of Henry Rowe Schoolcraft.* Mount Pleasant: Clarke Historical Library, Central Michigan University, 1987.

Carnes, Mark C. "Middle-Class Men and the Solace of Fraternal Ritual." In *Meanings for Manhood: Constructions of Masculinity in Victorian America,* ed. Mark C. Carnes and Clyde Griffen, 37–52. Chicago: University of Chicago Press, 1990.

Carter, Paul. *The Road to Botany Bay: An Essay in Spatial History.* London: Faber and Faber, 1987.

Catlin, George. *Letters and Notes on the Manners, Customs, and Conditions of North American Indians.* Vol. 2. 1844. Reprint, New York: Dover Publications, 1973.

Chapman, Charles A. *South Western Minnesota: The Best Farming Section in the World.* Mankato: Southwestern Minnesota Land and Immigration Association, 1882.

Child, Brenda Joyce. *Boarding School Seasons: American Indian Families, 1900–1940.* Lincoln: University of Nebraska Press, 1998.

Christensen, Bonnie. *Red Lodge and the Mythic West: Coal Miners to Cowboys.* Lawrence: University Press of Kansas, 2002.

Clawson, Mary Ann. *Constructing Brotherhood: Class, Gender, and Fraternalism.* Princeton, NJ: Princeton University Press, 1989.

Cohen, Erik. "Authenticity and Commoditization in Tourism." *Annals of Tourism Research* 15 (1988): 371–86.

Coleman, Michael C. *American Indian Children at School, 1850–1930.* Jackson: University Press of Mississippi, 1993.

Corbett, William P. "The Red Pipestone Quarry: The Yankton Defend a Sacred Tradition, 1858–1929." *South Dakota History* 8 (Spring 1978): 99–116.

———. "Pipestone: The Origin and Development of a National Monument." *Minnesota History* 47 (Fall 1980): 83–92.

Cronon, William. *Nature's Metropolis: Chicago and the Great West.* New York: W. W. Norton, 1991.

Danbom, David B. *Born in the Country: A History of Rural America.* Baltimore, MD: The Johns Hopkins University Press, 1995.

Davies, E. W., and Company. *Pipestone County and a Glimpse of Pipestone, Minnesota.* Pipestone, MN: E. W. Davies, 1895.

Davies, Richard O. *Main Street Blues: The Decline of Small-Town America.* Columbus: The Ohio State University Press, 1998.

Debo, Angie. *A History of the Indians in the United States.* Norman: University of Oklahoma Press, 1970.

Deloria, Philip J. *Playing Indian.* New Haven: Yale University Press, 1988.

Dilworth, Leah. *Imagining Indians in the Southwest: Persistent Visions of a Primitive Past.* Washington, DC: Smithsonian Institution Press, 1996.

Dippie, Brian W. *The Vanishing American: White Attitudes and U.S. Indian Policy.* Lawrence: University Press of Kansas, 1982.

———. *Catlin and His Contemporaries: The Politics of Patronage.* Lincoln: University of Nebraska Press, 1990.

———. "This Bold but Wasting Race: Stereotypes and American Indian Policy." *Montana: The Magazine of Western History* 23 (January 1993): 2–13.

Engler, Mira. "Drive-Thru History: Theme Towns in Iowa." *Landscape* 32 (1993): 8–18.

Ewers, John C., ed. *Indian Art in Pipestone: George Catlin's Portfolio in the British Museum.* Washington, DC: Smithsonian Institution Press, 1979.

———. "The Emergence of the Plains Indian as the Symbol of the North American Indian." In *American Indian Stereotypes in the World of Children: A Reader and Bibliography,* 2nd ed., ed. Arlene Hirschfelder, Paulette Fairbanks Molin, and Yvonne Wakin, 11–23. Lanham, MD, and London: Scarecrow Press, 1999.

Ferris, Jacob. *The States and Territories of the Great West.* New York: Miller, Orton, and Mulligan, 1856.

Francis, Daniel. *The Imaginary Indian: The Image of the Indian in Canadian Culture.* Vancouver, BC: Arsenal Pulp Press, 1992.

Frow, John. "Tourism and the Semiotics of Nostalgia." *October* 57 (Summer 1991): 123–51.

Gerstle, Gary. *American Crucible: Race and Nation in the Twentieth Century.* Princeton, NJ: Princeton University Press, 2001.

Gessner, Robert. *Massacre: A Survey of Today's American Indian.* New York: J. Cape and H. Smith, 1931.

Gjerde, Jon. *The Minds of the West: Ethnocultural Evolution in the Rural Midwest, 1830–1917.* Chapel Hill: University of North Carolina Press, 1997.

Glassberg, David. *American Historical Pageantry: The Uses of Tradition in the Early Twentieth Century.* Chapel Hill: University of North Carolina Press, 1990.

———. "Monuments and Memories." *American Quarterly* 43, no. 1 (March 1991): 143–56.

———. *Sense of History: The Place of the Past in American Life.* Amherst: University of Massachusetts Press, 2001.

Goetzmann, William H. *Exploration and Empire: The Explorer and the Scientist in the Winning of the American West.* New York: Vintage Books, 1966.

Goetzmann, William H., and William N. Goetzmann. *The West of the Imagination.* New York: W. W. Norton, 1986.

Green, Michael K., ed. *Issues in Native American Cultural Identity.* New York: Peter Lang, 1995.

Green, Rayna. "The Tribe Called Wannabe: Playing Indian in America and Europe." *Folklore* 99, no. 1 (1988): 30–39.

Gulliford, Andrew. *Sacred Objects and Sacred Places: Preserving Tribal Traditions.* Boulder, CO: University Press of Colorado, 2000.

Gurney, George, and Therese Thau Heyman, eds. *George Catlin and His Indian Gallery.* New York: W. W. Norton for the Smithsonian American Art Museum, 2002.

Haas, Lisbeth. *Conquests and Historical Identities in California, 1769–1936.* Berkeley: University of California Press, 1995.

Hall, Stuart. "The Question of Cultural Identity." In *Modernity and Its Futures*, 274–316. Cambridge: Polity Press, 1992.

Handler, Richard, and Jocelyn Linnekin. "Tradition, Genuine or Spurious." *Journal of American Folklore* 97, no. 385 (1984): 273–90.

Haralson, Eric L. "Mars in Petticoats: Longfellow and Sentimental Masculinity." *Nineteenth-Century Literature* 51, no. 3 (December 1996): 327–55.

Harmon, Alexandra. *Indians in the Making: Ethnic Relations and Indian Identities around Puget Sound.* Berkeley: University of California Press, 1998.

Harnack, Curtis. *Gentlemen on the Prairie.* Ames: Iowa State University, 1985.

Hauptman, Laurence M. *Tribes and Tribulations: Misconceptions about American Indians and Their Histories.* Albuquerque: University of New Mexico Press, 1995.

Hayden, Ferdinand V. "Sketch of the Geology of Northeastern Dakota, with a Notice of a Short Visit to the Celebrated Pipestone Quarry." *American Journal of Science,* 2nd series, 43, no. 127 (January 1867): 15–22.

Heilbron, Bertha L. "Some Sioux Legends in Pictures." *Minnesota History* 36 (March 1958): 18–23.

———. "The Minnesota Pipestone Quarries." *Minnesota Archaeologist* 24 (January 1962): 42–44.

Hine, Robert V. *Community on the American Frontier: Separate but Not Alone.* Norman: University of Oklahoma Press, 1980.

Hinsley, Curtis M., Jr. "Zunis and Brahmins: Cultural Ambivalence in the Gilded Age." In *Romantic Motives: Essays on Anthropological Sensibility,* ed. George W. Stocking Jr., 169–207. Vol. 6 in the History of Anthropology series. Madison: University of Wisconsin Press, 1989.

———. "Authoring Authenticity." *Journal of the Southwest* 32, no. 4 (Winter 1990): 462–78.

Hodge, Frederick Webb. *Handbook of the American Indians North of Mexico.* Smithsonian Institution Bureau of American Ethnology, Bulletin 30, Part 1. Washington, DC: U.S. Government Printing Office, 1912.

Hofelman, Colleen Sundvold. *It's News to Me: With Help from My Friends and 25 Years On-the-Job Training.* N.p., 1994.

Holley, Frances Chamberlain. *Once Their Home or Our Legacy from the Dakotahs.* Chicago: Donohue and Henneberry, 1890.

Holmquist, June Drenning, ed. *They Chose Minnesota: A Survey of the State's Ethnic Groups.* St. Paul: Minnesota Historical Society Press, 1981.

Hoover, Herbert T. *The Yankton Sioux,* with Leonard R. Bruguier. New York: Chelsea House Publishers, 1988.

Hoover, Herbert T. "Yankton Sioux Tribal Claims against the United States, 1917–1975." *Western Historical Quarterly* 7, no. 2 (April 1976): 125–42.

Hoxie, Frederick E. *A Final Promise: The Campaign to Assimilate the Indians, 1880–1920*. New York: Cambridge University Press, 1989.

Hughes, David T. "Perceptions of the Sacred: A Review of Selected Native American Groups and Their Relationships with the Catlinite Quarries." Manuscript written for the National Park Service, Lincoln, Nebraska, 1995.

Hughey, Michael W., and Michael G. Michlovic. "'Making' History: The Vikings in the American Heartland." *Politics, Culture, and Society* 2, no. 3 (Spring 1989): 338–60.

Hyde, Anne Farrar. *An American Vision: Far Western Landscape and National Culture, 1820–1920*. New York: New York University Press, 1990.

———. "Cultural Filters: The Significance of Perception in the History of the American West." *Western Historical Quarterly* 24, no. 3 (August 1993): 351–74.

Jackson, Charles T. "Catlinite or Indian Pipe Stone." *American Journal of Science*, first series, 35 (1839): 388.

Jackson, John Brinckerhoff. *The Necessity for Ruins and Other Topics*. Amherst: University of Massachusetts Press, 1980.

Jaimes, M. Annette, ed. *The State of Native America: Genocide, Colonization, and Resistance*. Boston: South End Press, 1992.

Jakle, John A. *The American Small Town: Twentieth-Century Place Images*. Hamden, CT: Archon Books, 1982.

———. *The Tourist: Travel in Twentieth-Century North America*. Lincoln: University of Nebraska Press, 1985.

Johnston, Basil. *The Manitous: The Spiritual World of the Ojibway*. New York: HarperCollins Publishers, 1995.

Judd, Mary Catherine. *Wigwam Stories Told by North American Indians*. Boston: Ginn, Athenaeum Press, 1906.

Kammen, Michael. *Mystic Chords of Memory: The Transformation of Tradition in American Culture*. New York: Vintage Books, 1993.

Krech, Shepard III, and Barbara A. Hail, eds. *Collecting Native America, 1870–1960*. Washington, DC: Smithsonian Institution Press, 1999.

Landsman, Gail H. "The 'Other' as Political Symbol: Images of Indians in the Woman Suffrage Movement." *Ethnohistory* 39, no. 3 (Summer 1992): 247–78.

Larson, Paul Clifford, with Susan M. Brown, eds. *The Spirit of H. H. Richardson on the Midland Prairies: Regional Transformations of an Architectural Style*. Minneapolis: University Art Museum, University of Minnesota Press, 1988.

Lass, William E. *Minnesota: A Centennial History*. 2nd ed. New York: Norton, 1998.

Lears, Jackson. *No Place of Grace: Antimodernism and the Transformation of American Culture, 1880–1920*. New York: Pantheon, 1981.

Lewis, Peirce F. "Small Town in Pennsylvania." *Annals of the Association of American Geographers* 62 (June 1972): 323–51.

Lewis, Samuel, after William Clark. "A Map of Lewis and Clark's Track." In Nicholas Biddle and Paul Allen, *History of the Expedition under the Command of Captains Lewis and Clark to the Sources of the Missouri. . . .* Philadelphia: Bradford and Inskeep, 1814. Geography and Maps Division, Library of Congress.

Lindsey, Donal F. *Indians at Hampton Institute, 1877–1923.* Urbana and Chicago: University of Illinois Press, 1995.

Lomawaima, K. Tsianina. *They Called It Prairie Light: The Story of Chilocco Indian School.* Lincoln: University of Nebraska Press, 1995.

Longfellow, Henry Wadsworth. *The Song of Hiawatha.* 1855. Reprint, Rutland, VT, and Tokyo: Charles E. Tuttle, 1975.

Lopez, Barry. *About This Life: Journeys on the Threshold of Memory.* New York: Vintage Books, 1998.

Lowenthal, David. "Past Time, Present Place: Landscape and Memory." *Geographical Review* 65, no. 1 (January 1975): 1–36.

———. *The Past Is a Foreign Country.* Cambridge: Cambridge University Press, 1985.

———. *Landscape Meanings and Values.* London: Allen and Unwin, 1986.

———. "Identity, Heritage, and History." In *Commemorations: The Politics of National Identity,* ed. John R. Gillis, 41–57. Princeton, NJ: Princeton University Press, 1994.

———. *Possessed by the Past: The Heritage Crusade and the Spoils of History.* New York: Free Press, 1996.

Lowenthal, David, and Martyn J. Bowden, eds. *Geographies of the Mind: Essays in Historical Geosophy.* New York: Oxford University Press, 1976.

MacCannell, Dean. "Staged Authenticity: Arrangements of Social Space in Tourist Settings." *American Journal of Sociology* 79, no. 3 (1979): 589–603.

Marx, Leo. *The Machine in the Garden: Technology and the Pastoral Ideal in America.* New York: Oxford University Press, 1964.

Medina, Laurie Kroshus. "Commoditizing Culture: Tourism and Maya Identity." *Annals of Tourism Research* 30, no. 2 (2003): 353–68.

Meyer, Carter Jones, and Diana Royer, eds. *Selling the Indian: Commercializing and Appropriating American Indian Cultures.* Tucson: University of Arizona Press, 2001.

Mihesuah, Devon A. *Cultivating the Rosebuds: The Education of Women at the Cherokee Female Seminary, 1851–1909.* Urbana and Chicago: University of Illinois Press, 1993.

———, ed. *Natives and Academics: Researching and Writing about American Indians.* Lincoln: University of Nebraska Press, 1998.

Milner, Clyde A., II. "The View from Wisdom: Region and Identity in the Minds of Four Westerners." *Montana: The Magazine of Western History* 41, no. 3 (Summer 1991): 2–17.

Minnesota Board of World's Fair Managers. *Final Report of the Minnesota Board of World's Fair Managers.* St. Paul: Minnesota Board of World's Fair Managers, 1894.

Minnesota Federal Writers' Project of the Works Projects Administration. *Minnesota: A State Guide.* New York: Viking Press, 1938.

Minnesota Highway Department. *Proposed Development for Pipestone State Park, Pipestone, Minnesota.* St. Paul, MN: Commissioner of Highways, 1924.

Mitchell, J. H. "The Pipestone Quarry, or Restoring an Ancient Indian Shrine." *Indians at Work* 2, no. 8 (December 1, 1934): 25–29.

Montgomery, Charles. *The Spanish Redemption: Heritage, Power, and Loss on New Mexico's Upper Rio Grande.* Berkeley: University of California Press, 2002.

Moulton, Gary E., ed. *The Journals of the Lewis and Clark Expedition, August 25, 1804–April 6, 1805,* vol. 3. Lincoln: University of Nebraska Press, 1987.

Murray, Robert A. *A History of Pipestone National Monument, Minnesota.* Pipestone, MN: National Park Service and the Pipestone Indian Shrine Association, 1965.

National Exchange Club. *The Soul of Exchange: An Interpretation of the Ideals, Spirit, and Purposes of the Exchange Clubs of the United States.* Toledo, OH: National Exchange Club, n.d.

Nelson, Dana. *National Manhood: Capitalist Citizenship and the Imagined Fraternity of White Men.* Durham, NC: Duke University Press, 1998.

Nelson, Paula M. *After the West Was Won: Homesteaders and Town-Builders in Western South Dakota, 1900–1917.* Iowa City: University of Iowa Press, 1986.

Nicholas, Liza. "Wyoming as America: Celebrations, a Museum, and Yale." *American Quarterly* 54, no. 3 (2002): 437–65.

Nicollet, Joseph N. "Report Intended to Illustrate a Map of the Hydrological Basin of the Upper Mississippi River." Senate Report 237, 26th Cong., 2nd sess., February 16, 1841.

Nobles, Gregory H. *American Frontiers: Cultural Encounters and Continental Conquest.* New York: Hill and Wang, 1997.

Nora, Pierre. "Between History and Memory: Les Lieux de Mémoire." *Representations* 26 (Spring 1989): 7–25.

Norris, Philetus W. *The Calumet of the Coteau, and Other Poetic Legends of the Border.* Philadelphia: J. B. Lippincott, 1883.

Northrup, Jim. *Rez Road Follies: Canoes, Casinos, Computers, and Birch Bark Baskets.* New York: Kodansha International, 1997.

O'Gorman, James F. *H. H. Richardson: Architectural Forms for an American Society.* Chicago: University of Chicago Press, 1987.

———. *ABC of Architecture.* Philadelphia: University of Pennsylvania Press, 1998.

Osborn, Chase S., and Stellanova Osborn. *Schoolcraft-Longfellow-Hiawatha.* Lancaster, PA: Jacques Cattell Press, 1942.

Parker, Donald Dean, ed. *The Recollections of Philander Prescott: Frontiersman of the Old Northwest, 1819–1862.* Lincoln: University of Nebraska Press, 1966.

Parker, John, ed. *The Journals of Jonathan Carver and Related Documents, 1766–1770.* St. Paul: Minnesota Historical Society Press, 1976.

Phillips, Ruth B. *Trading Identities: The Souvenir in Native North American Art from the Northeast, 1700–1900.* Seattle: University of Washington Press, 1998.

Pipestone County Genealogical Society. *Biographies of the Civil War Veterans Who Came to Pipestone County, Minnesota.* Pipestone, MN: Pipestone Publishing, 1991.

Pipestone County Historical Society. *A History of Pipestone County.* Dallas, TX: Taylor Publishing, 1984.

Pipestone County, Minnesota, Statehood Centennial Committee. *Pipestone.* Pipestone, MN: Statehood Centennial Committee, 1958.

Pipestone Indian Shrine Association. *The Pipestone Indian Shrine, Pipestone, Minnesota: Indian Legends and Historical Facts Regarding the Red Pipestone Quarry, Winnewissa Falls, and the "Twin Maidens."* Pipestone, MN: The Pipestone Leader, 1932.

Pohl, Frances K. "Old World, New World: The Encounter of Cultures on the American Frontier." In *Nineteenth-Century Art: A Critical History,* ed. Stephen Eisenman, 144–62. London: Thames and Hudson, 1994.

Pomeroy, Earl. *In Search of the Golden West: The Tourist in Western America.* Lincoln: University of Nebraska Press, 1957.

Poulsen, Richard C. *The Landscape of the Mind: Cultural Transformations of the American West.* New York: Peter Lang, 1992.

Powell, J. M. *Mirrors of the New World: Images and Image-Makers in the Settlement Process.* Fothestone, Kent, UK: Dawson-Archon Books, 1977.

Powell, J. W. Letter to Commissioner of Indian Affairs W. A. Jones, quoted in "Title of Yankton Indians to the Pipestone Reservation in Minnesota," Senate Document 55, 57th Cong., 1st sess., vol. 2, April 12, 1898.

Pratt, Mary Louise. *Imperial Eyes: Travel Writing and Transculturation.* London: Routledge, 1992.

Pretes, Michael. "Tourism and Nationalism." *Annals of Tourism Research* 30, no. 1 (2003): 125–42.

Prown, Jules David, ed. *Discovered Lands–Invented Pasts: Transforming Visions of the American West.* New Haven: Yale University Press, 1992.

Prucha, Francis Paul. *Americanizing the American Indians: Writings by the "Friends of the Indian," 1880–1900.* Lincoln: University of Nebraska Press, 1973.

———. *The Great Father: The United States Government and the American Indians.* Lincoln: University of Nebraska Press, 1986.

Pyne, Stephen J. *How the Canyon Became Grand: A Short History.* New York: Viking Penguin, 1998.

Radzilowski, John. *Prairie Town: A History of Marshall, Minnesota, 1872–1997.* Marshall, MN: Lyon County Historical Society, 1997.

Rau, Charles. "Red Pipestone." Annual Report of the Smithsonian, House Miscellaneous Document 107, 42nd Cong., 3rd sess., 1872.

Redfoot, Donald L. "Touristic Authenticity, Touristic Angst, and Modern Reality." *Qualitative Sociology* 7, no. 4 (Winter 1984): 291–309.

Righter, Robert W. "National Monuments to National Parks: The Use of the Antiquities Act of 1906." *Western History Quarterly* 20 (August 1989): 281–301.

Riney, Scott. *The Rapid City Indian School, 1898–1933.* Norman: University of Oklahoma Press, 1999.

Roberts, Randy, and James S. Olson. *A Line in the Sand: The Alamo in Blood and Memory.* New York: Free Press, 2001.

Rodriguez, Richard. *Days of Obligation: An Argument with My Mexican Father.* New York: Viking Penguin, 1992.

Root, Deborah. *Cannibal Culture: Art, Appropriation, and the Commodification of Difference.* Boulder, CO: Westview Press, 1996.

Rosaldo, Renato. *Culture and Truth: The Remaking of Social Analysis.* Boston: Beacon Press, 1989.

Rose, Arthur P. *An Illustrated History of the Counties of Rock and Pipestone, Minnesota.* Luverne, MN: Northern History Publishing, 1911.

Rothman, Hal K. *Preserving Different Pasts: The American National Monuments.* Urbana: University of Illinois Press, 1989.

———. *Managing the Sacred and the Secular: An Administrative History of Pipestone National Monument.* Omaha, NE: U.S. National Park Service, Midwest Region, 1992.

———. *Devil's Bargains: Tourism in the Twentieth-Century American West.* Lawrence: University Press of Kansas, 1998.

Said, Edward W. "Invention, Memory, and Place." *Critical Inquiry* 26, no. 2 (Winter 2000): 175–92.

Scheckel, Susan. *The Insistence of the Indian: Race and Nationalism in Nineteenth-Century American Culture.* Princeton, NJ: Princeton University Press, 1998.

Schoolcraft, Henry Rowe. *Historical and Statistical Information Respecting the History, Condition and Prospects of the Indian Tribes of the United States.* Philadelphia: Lippincott, Grambo, 1851–1857.

———. *Personal Memoirs of a Residence of Thirty Years with the Indian Tribes of the American Frontiers.* Philadelphia: Lippincott, Grambo, 1851.

Scott, Joan W. "Fantasy Echo: History and the Construction of Identity." *Critical Inquiry* 27 (Winter 2001): 284–304.

Sears, John F. *Sacred Places: American Tourist Attractions in the Nineteenth Century.* New York: Oxford University Press, 1989.

Sibley, Henry H. Letter to the Legislative Council of Minnesota Territory, September 11, 1849. In *Journal of the Council, during the First Legislative Assembly of the Territory of Minnesota.* St. Paul, MN: McLean and Owens, 1850.

Sigstad, John S. "A Field Test for Catlinite." *American Antiquity* 35, no. 3 (July 1970): 377–82.

Skinner, Charles M. *Myths and Legends of Our Own Land.* Vol. 2. Philadelphia: J. B. Lippincott, 1896.

Smith, Sherry L. *Reimagining Indians: Native Americans through Anglo Eyes, 1880–1940.* New York: Oxford University Press, 2000.

Starr, Frederick. *American Indians.* Boston: D. C. Heath, 1899.

Stoopes, W. E. "Report to the Honorable R. P. Chase, State Auditor." St. Paul, MN: n.p., 1924.

Susman, Warren J. *Culture as History: The Transformation of American Society in the Twentieth Century.* New York: Pantheon, 1973.

Takaki, Ronald. *Iron Cages: Race and Culture in Nineteenth-Century America.* New York: Oxford University Press, 1990.

Trachtenberg, Alan. *The Incorporation of America: Culture and Society in the Gilded Age.* New York: Hill and Wang, 1982.

———. "Singing Hiawatha: Longfellow's Hybrid Myth of America." *Yale Review* 90, no. 1 (January 2002): 1–19.

Truettner, William H. *The Natural Man Observed: A Study of Catlin's Indian Gallery.* Washington, DC: Smithsonian Institution Press, 1979.

———, ed. *The West as America: Reinterpreting Images of the American Frontier, 1820–1920.* Washington, DC: Smithsonian Institution Press, 1991.

Tuan, Yi-Fu. *Topophilia: A Study of Environmental Perception, Attitudes, and Values.* Englewood Cliffs, NJ: Prentice-Hall, 1974.

———. *Space and Place: The Perspective of Experience.* Minneapolis: University of Minnesota Press, 1977.

Vecsey, Christopher. *Imagine Ourselves Richly: Mythic Narratives of North American Indians.* New York: Crossroads Publishing, 1988.

White, Charles A., M.D. "A Trip to the Great Red Pipestone Quarry." *American Naturalist* 2 (1869): 644–53.

Wiebe, Robert H. *The Search for Order, 1877–1920.* New York: Hill and Wang, 1967.

Williams, Cecil B. *Henry Wadsworth Longfellow.* New York: Twayne Publishers, 1964.

Wilson, Chris. *The Myth of Santa Fe: Creating a Modern Regional Tradition.* Albuquerque: University of New Mexico Press, 1997.

Winchell, Newton H. *The Geological and Natural History of Minnesota,* Sixth Annual Report. Minneapolis, MN: Johnson, Smith, and Harrison, 1878.

Wing, C. L., comp. *Pipestone County Directory.* Kingsley, IA: Press of the Kingsley Times, 1898.

Wrobel, David M., and Patrick T. Long, eds. *Seeing and Being Seen: Tourism in the American West.* Lawrence: University Press of Kansas, 2001.

Wub-e-ke-niew. *We Have the Right to Exist: A Translation of Aboriginal Indigenous Thought.* New York: Black Thistle Press, 1995.

Zelinsky, Wilbur. "Where Every Town Is above Average: Welcoming Signs along America's Highways." *Landscape* 30, no. 1 (1988): 1–10.

INDEX

American Indian Movement (AIM), 144,
146
American Indian Religious Freedom Act
(1978), 146
Americanism: patriotism in World War
I, 86; sense of after Civil War, 33, 50;
sense of during Cold War, 9, 113, 121
Andrus, W. D., 51
ankh, 116–17, 139. *See also* Linch, Lyle K.
Antiquities Act (1906), 93–94, 103
antiquity: North American archaeology/
geology as evidence of, 16, 106, 139
architecture and symbolism. *See* buildings
Armstrong, Moses, 26
Atkins, J. D. C., 52
attitudes, American cultural: ambivalence toward Indians, 3–4, 14, 40,
53–55, 92–93, 109–10, 118–19, 138; ambivalence toward modernity, 4, 14, 33,
50, 63, 75, 93, 123; antebellum, 13, 17,
22, 24; Cold War–era, 113, 121,
127–28, 135, 138; early twentieth-century, 92–93; post–Civil War, 4, 33, 50,
62–63; toward federal government,54,
63, 65–69, 82, 84–85, 88–89, 93,
103–4, 138; toward future, 4, 44, 46,
62–63; toward past, 7–8, 25, 50, 63,
98–100, 126–27; toward place, 7, 14;
toward preservation, 92–94, 98–99
authenticity: Catlin's certificates of authenticity, 20; as commodity, 109,
118–19, 134–37; as tourist expectation,
108–9, 118, 132–35, 147; as value in
identity, 64, 134–35, 147
authority, cultural: accepted authority of
explorers and writers, 12–13, 125, 148;
claimed by local residents, 8–10, 12,
33, 35, 82–83, 108, 119–20, 123,
134–42; role of experts and eyewitnesses, 12–14, 22, 25, 102, 134–35,
139–40; scientists as, 26–27, 104, 135,
139–40

Baker, Howard W., 110, 115
Balmer, James, 79, 86–87, 99–100, 103,
105, 108–9, 113, 118
Bartlett, G. Winifred: background, 101;
preservation activities, 101–4, 120;
reputation as expert on quarries,
101–3, 108, 114, 117, 120, 122, 134
Benjamin, Walter, 113
Bennett, Adelaide George, 37–38, 41–42,
49, 148
Bennett, Charles H.: beliefs and values,
63–65; death, 98, 112; early civic roles,
including as historian, 36, 42–43; initial visit to quarries, 32, 98, 140; interest in protecting the quarries, 89–91,
94, plate 3; marriage, 37–38; origins,
36; owner of quartzite deposits, 43–44;
promotional uses of pipestone, 54,
59–60, 72–74, 98, 122–23, 128–29, 148;
store, 36, 50, 72, 122–24
Berkhofer, Robert F., Jr., 7, 17, 25, 154n11
Boomer, Ralph J., 95–96
Bousé, Derek, 172n1
Briggs, Henry, 37, 47
Bryan, George (Standing Eagle): as employee at PNM, 118–19, 128, 141–42;
as participant in pageant, 132, 135, 142
buildings, quartzite: Bennett block, 44;
Calumet Hotel, 47, 71, 115; contribution to local identity, 44–46, 70–72,
plate 5; courthouse, 72, 123; descriptions of, 43–45, 112; Ferris Opera
House, 44, 79; historic preservation
of, 147; Indian school, 70–71; library,
72; Pipestone County Historical Museum, 147; Richardsonian Romanesque, 43–44, 70–72; Syndicate
block, 44
Bureau of Ethnology, 28, 60
Bureau of Indian Affairs (also Indian
Affairs, Indian Office), 60, 66, 78, 81,
89, 98, 103–4, 108–9

Burke, Charles, 83
Burns, Bea (Nokomis), 133, 135, 142

Campbell, Willard S., 85
Carpenter, Herbert, 39, 52. *See also*
  squatters
Carver, Jonathan, 14–15
Catlin, George: artistic images, 3–5, 8,
  21–22; Indian Gallery, 22; *Letters and
  Notes*, 19, 89–90; literary representations, 3–5, 19–21, 115; "mystic horizon," 3, 20; "Pipestone Quarry"
  painting, 21–22; promotion of own
  image, 20–22; town's uses of name
  and fame, 37, 56, 74–75, 89, 101–2,
  112, 125, 127, 130; visit to quarries
  (1836), 3, 12, 14, 17–21, 90, 111, 127
catlinite, 22, 140, 156n20
churches, 59, 70–72, 74, 81, 86, 132, 137
Civic and Commerce Association, 106,
  113, 125–27, 133–34, plate 10
Claussen, August, 39. *See also* squatters
Close brothers, 46–49, 66, 106, 125, 128
Collier, John, 104–6
commodification: of tribal artifacts,
  50–51, 68, 73, 78, 82–83, 106–8, 112,
  123–25, 128–29, 141–42, 144–46, 149;
  of Indian imagery, 19–20, 37, 40–41,
  48–49, 66, 102–6, 111, 124–27,
  147–48; of Indian past, 37, 50, 83–84,
  121–22, 124–27, 135, 139–41, 147–49
Côteau des Prairies, 1–2, 17–18, 21–22,
  34, 56–57, 112
Crandall, Clinton J., 72, 75, 79, 84
Crow, Clara, 118
Crow, Moses and Estella, 108–9, 118, 142
cultural appropriation: definition, 5,
  8–10, 20, 155n16

Dakota Conflict (1862), 31
Daughters of the American Revolution
  (DAR), 98–100, 104
Davies, Allie, 99–100
Davies, E. W., 35, 37, 58–59, 71, 99
Deloria, Philip J., 8, 17, 20, 56, 89, 107, 142
Department of the Interior, 77, 91, 108,
  118, 136, 141
Derby, Chuck, 145
Dippie, Brian, 19
Dorchester, Daniel, 68, 71
Downs, D. Ivan, 48, 66, 163n31
Drysdale, Albert F., 109–12, 114, 119

Eastman, Seth, 22
exhibitions of Indian culture: at fairs,
  59–60, 72; at PNM, 118–19, 141–42,
  145; at quarries, 39–40, 47–48, 51–52,
  83, 90–92, 110; prohibition on dancing, 83. *See also* Burke, Charles
exploration of lands in West, 13–18
expositions and world's fairs: exhibits of
  pipestone at, 59–60, 62, 72–74

Federal Writers' Project, 111–12
Ferris, Allen D., 44, 56, 63
Ferris, Gratia, 34, 44
Ferris, Jacob, 26
Flandreau: Indian school, 66–67,
  69–70; Santee Dakota (Wahpeton
  and Sisseton), 47–48, 51, 54 64, 82,
  97, 108, 142
Fort Pipestone, 147
Francis, Daniel, 7
Frémont, John, 17, 74, 99

Gardner-Sharp, Abigail, 57, 74, 96, 113
General Allotment (Dawes) Act, 52, 76
Gitche Manito, 23–24, 54, 56, 59, 121,
  132, 180n13
Glassberg, David, 8, 152n6
Goodnow, Charles C., 52–54
Grand Army of the Republic (GAR), 36,
  73–74, 147

Hagen, Olaf T., 115
Hard, A. D., 75
Harris, DeWitt, 82–85, 110
Hart, Isaac L., 36, 38–39, 53, 63, 66, 89
Hart, Ralph G., 94
Hayden, Ferdinand, 8, 27, 50
heritage: definition of, as distinct from
  history, 8, 128; as experienced, 7–10;
  as useful, 8, 98–99, 123–24
Hiawatha, tale of, 23, 75
Hiawatha Club, 134–35, 149
Hill, James J., 49, 91
historical landscape: DAR examples,
  98–100; local or popular sense of,
  2–3, 50, 96–97, 102–3, 106, 136–37
history, uses of, 8–10; American "history"
  as different from Indian "legend," 26,
  96, 99, 101–2, 105, 112, 124–28,
  139–40
Hodge, Frederick Webb, 75
Howard, Charles B., 80

Hummel, Edward A., 104, 110
Humphrey, Hubert, 113, 123

identity: active participation in, 32–33, 44, 90–93; as cumulative process, 4, 8, 62, 88–89, 92, 102, 106, 122, 134–37; expression of national identity through local, 10, 33, 45–46, 55–56, 59–60, 64–65, 92, 109–11, 137–38, 149; use of history and sense of past to create, 2–3, 8, 20, 42, 55–56, 90, 102, 104, 122–27, 130; interplay of local and American, 2–4, 10, 33, 36, 46, 55–56, 59–60, 92, 108, 126–27, 132–37, 139–41; use of landscape and place to create, 2–3, 12–13, 16, 44–46, 88–89, 100, 105, 122, 136–37; local, creation and expression of, 9–10, 33, 148–50, 121–22, 139–41; local need for national validation of, 8–10, 33, 46, 60, 62, 71, 108, 119–20, 134–37, 140–41; national, creation and contribution to, 4, 43, 46, 123–27, 150; post–Civil War search for unifying identity, 4, 9, 33; repetition of imagery in creation of, 2, 8, 33, 62–63, 89–90, 92, 125–27, 134–35, 148–50
imagery of "Indian": as American heritage, 3–4, 8, 16–17, 25–26, 55–56, 92–94, 124–28; culture as uniform, static, pantribal, 5, 16–17, 20, 22–23, 30, 58, 68–69, 78, 93, 138; dissonance between ideal and perceived real, 39–41, 53–55, 64, 109–10, 118–19; as extractable, 3–5, 9–10, 20, 25–26, 50, 60, 90–93, 134–35, 142; as good/bad, Noble/Savage, 14, 23, 39–41, 53–58, 64, 79–81, 109, 138; as impediment to settlement of southwestern Minnesota, 31, 34; as part of nature, natural landscape, 25, 40, 56, 89, 93–94, 102, 106; as peaceful, pacified, 3, 24–25; Plains tribes as archetypal, 14, 90, 106–7, 115, 118, 128; popular interest in, 2–5, 8–10, 20–25, 64–65, 108, 117–19, 129, 133–35, 140–41; as prehistory, part of past, 3, 16, 21, 55, 89, 92–93, 99–101, 105, 111–12, 119, 134, 139; as premodern and uncorrupted, 4, 16, 23, 25, 102, 134, 137–38; as representative of America, 19, 93; as part of timeless past, 3, 16, 20–23, 58, 92–93, 111, 134, 149; tribal opposition to, 144–46; tribal participation in creating, 30–31, 38–40, 51–53, 56, 79–81, 109, 118–19, 135, 142; as unable to preserve own heritage, 9–10, 20, 92–93, 96, 101–2; as vanishing, 13–14, 20, 55, 57, 123–24, 138; as part of West, 14, 91
"imaginary Indians," 5, 40, 56–58, 79, 106–7, 115, 118, 132, 135, 142
immigrants to southwestern Minnesota, 36–37, 41, 46–47, 79
Indian Appropriation Acts (1892, 1897), 77
Indian Citizenship Act (1924), 96
Indian Claims Commission, 97
Indian education: assimilation effort, 63–70, 78–81; Carlisle as model school, 63–66, 69. See also Flandreau; Pipestone Indian Training School (PITS)
Indian New Deal, 103–7; Indian Emergency Conservation Work at quarries, 104, 107
Indian policy, national: antebellum, 24, 30–31; late-nineteenth-century, 64, 66–69, 78–81, 83, 91–92, 96; mid-twentieth-century, 138, 141; Pipestone residents as aligned with, 9–10, 51–52, 62–64, 81, 94, 103–5; twentieth-century reform movement, 92–94, 96, 105–6
Indians as tourist attraction, 38–40, 47–48, 73, 78, 83, 92, 108–9, 118–19, 140, 142, 145
Indian-themed park, 53, 67, 69, 89, 94, 100, 105, 147
Inkpaduta, 31, 57, 113
Inter-Church Federation, 94–95

Jackson, Charles, 22, 27
Jones, William, 84
Judd, Mary Catherine, 75

Keepers of the Sacred Tradition of Pipemakers, 145
Kvale, Paul, 105, 107

Laframboise, Joseph, 17
Lake Manito/Lake Hiawatha, 82, 91
landscape at quarries, 1–2, 18, 21–22, 70

legends: creation stories, 4–5, 56–57, 112; dehistoricized, 3–4, 8, 21–22, 125–27, 137; marketed by town residents, 9–10, 48–51, 66, 71, 90, 96, 102, 106, 125–27, 137–38, 147; about origin and uses of pipe, 4–5, 21–25; used by Park Service, 104, 111–12, 119; associated with quarries, 3–5, 18, 21–24, 112
"Legends of the Pipestone Quarries" (brochure), 48–51, 66, 125
Lewis and Clark Expedition/Corps of Discovery, 2, 8, 15–16, 20, 30
Linch, Lyle K.: background, 114; interpretive activities, 116–19, 121–22, 131–34, 136; personality, 114–16, 178n50
Lind, John, 66–68, 76
Little Feather Interpretive Center, 145
Longfellow, Henry Wadsworth: descriptions of Indian culture, 3, 7–8, 23–26; invited to visit Pipestone, 38, 41; name used to promote quarries, 48, 50, 66, 90, 94, 102, 112, 125, 129–30, 134–35; role in developing American culture, 23, 25, 36, 129–30, 134–35
Lowenthal, David, 1, 8, 89

Mann, F. T., 80, 82, 84–86
Mattes, Merrill J., 117
McCleary, James, 74, 84–85, 94
McLaughlin, James, 77, 82, 97
Meritt, E. B., 78, 83
Minneapolis Tribune, 74, 106, 116, 118
Minnesota: Pipestone's imagery used to promote, 29, 45, 96, 128, 140; settlement and statehood, 34, 62, 65, 96; territory, 1, 30, 34, 131
Minnesota Historical Society, 96, 140
Moore, Leon H., 43–44, 73–74, 131
Morgan, Thomas Jefferson, 68, 71, 167n10
Murray, Robert, 7
museum stores, 113, 122–28, 130, 147

National Congress of American Indians (NCAI), 144
National Exchange Club, 131–32, 134, 136
National Park Service (NPS, also Park Service): creation in 1916, 94; management of national monuments, 103–5, 107–11, 135; policies, 108–11, 115, 117–19, 141–43, 146
neighboring towns, 43, 59, 66–67

Nelson, Knute, 95
newspapers. See Minneapolis Tribune; Pipestone County Farmers' Leader; Pipestone County Star; Saint Paul Daily Globe; Saint Paul Pioneer Press
Nicollet, Joseph: description of quarries, 1–2, 17–18; exploration of Côteau, 17–19, 74, 89, 96, 99, 127; rock with carved initials, 99, 116, plate 7
Norris, Philetus W. (Calumet of the Coteau), 56–57
Northrup, Jim, 170n33, 170n37
nostalgia: as antimodern, 50, 93, 123; as idealization of preindustrial past, 25–26; as shaping attitudes about Indian past, 13–14, 25–26, 93

Old Settlers Society, 42, 49, 112, 123
orders, fraternal and sororal, 36, 59, 86, 98, 114, 137
Owens, Robert, 131, 136–37

Padgett, Ora, 82, 86, 99
pageant. See Song of Hiawatha, The (pageant)
parades, 56, 137
past: as usable foundation for identity, 3–5, 8–10, 148–50
"peace pipe": description and image of, 3–5, 16, 23–24, 44, 73, 128; image used for promotion, 38, 44, 48, 50, 59, 66, 79, 106–7, 124, 128–29, 134
pipe ceremonies, 5–6, 13, 15, 23–24
pipestone (catlinite or inya sa): description of, 2, 21; naming, 27; samples used for promotion, 37–38, 45, 48, 50, 54, 68, 73, 82–85, 102–3, 106, 124–25, 141–42, 144–47; tribal trading of, 13, 16, 140
Pipestone (town): characteristics of town founders, 8, 33; as county seat, 35; early development, 34, 41–42; efforts to create Indian museum, 112–13, 122–23; founders' promise to respect quarries, 35, 53, 78; founding, 3, 32–34; population of, 10, 35, 112; residents' proprietary stance toward area, 59, 70, 83, 100–103, 109–12, 123–26, 134–37; types of settlers, 35–37; uses of imagery, 62–63, 106, 122, 126–27, 134–35, 148–49; Yankee values of town, 36, 47, 63–65

Pipestone Businessmen's Association, 95, 98

Pipestone County Farmers' Leader, 64

Pipestone County Star: comments on Close Brothers, 47; descriptions of buildings, 42, 44–45; descriptions of Yankton, 39–40, 64; established as a booster paper, 35; expressions of local ambivalence toward tribes, 39–40, 53–55, 64, 80; expressions of local attitudes toward quarries, 94–95, 110, 115, 132–33; Linch's Tepee Smoke column, 114–15, 118, 131

Pipestone Dakota (Tiospaye) community, 70, 108–9, 118, 142, 145

Pipestone Indian Shrine Association (PISA): goal of public education, 102–3; images used by, 101–3, 105, 107; mission as quarries' guardian, 101–3, 108; reorganized at PNM, 141–42; tribal opposition to, 145–46

Pipestone Indian Training School (PITS): actions of pupils, 78–81; closure, 141; curriculum, 69, 78–79; economic benefits to town, 69–72; federal legislation regarding, 68, 76; growth and construction, 70–71; performance of Indian plays, 79, 130; superintendents' federal authority at quarries, 77–78, 81–86, 91, 108–9; tensions with town, 80, 82–86; town efforts to establish, 64–68, 76, 141; town identification with, 68–71, 80–81, 84–86, 91, 93

Pipestone National Monument (PNM): interpretation of tribal culture and past, 112–14, 117–19, 122, 144, 146, plate 11; legislation to establish, 104–7; popularity of, 133, 141, 147–48, 182n25; regulation of stone extraction, 6, 107–9, 118–19; relations with town, 109–111, 114–15, 117–18, 122, 130, 135–38; relations with tribes, 108–9, 118–19, 145–47

Pipestone National Park Federation, 100

Poorbaugh, John, 70

Powell, John Wesley, 8, 28, 104

powwows and tribal ceremonies at quarries, 56, 106, 140, 145–46

Prescott, Philander, 17

preservation of quarries: townspeople as guardians, 65, 6971, 88–91, 93–96, 100–102, 123, 125–27; women leaders in, 9, 88–89, 98–100, 149

promotion of town, 3, 9–10; by railroads, 47–49; by residents, 35–36, 41–42, 50–51, 64–65, 71–73, 90–92, 106, 108, 110, 121–22, 128–30, 134–37; by state, 96, 139

quarries: diversity of tribal views about, 6–7, 144–46; geological/historical attributes of, 2, 5, 16, 21–22, 90, 119; tribal control of, 6, 52–53, 76–78, 97–98; tribal extraction of stone from, 6, 30–31, 38–40, 51, 64, 82–83, 90–92, 97, 108–9, 118–19, 141–42; visited annually by tribes, 16, 48, 127; white extraction of stone from, 29, 37–38, 50–52, 59–60, 73, 82, 92, 119, 164n36

quarries, descriptions of: as celebrated or famous, 27–28, 45, 111, 127; "classic ground," 21, 28, 41, 90, 115; "fountain of the pipe," 20–21; "Indian Eden," 5, 12, 20, 102, 108, 116, 139, 148; as Indian shrine or peace shrine, 9, 102–3, 105, 108, 113–15, 121, 126–28, 132, 138; mountain of stone, 14, 23; place of peace, 2, 15, 33, 64, 75, 102, 111, 113, 125, 138; sacred to all tribes, 2, 15, 26, 40, 58, 64, 67–68, 74, 102, 108, 122, 125; significant part of American heritage, 3–4, 26, 33, 55–56, 63, 89, 90, 92, 94–96, 102–5, 125–28, 136–38, 148–50; timeless, 1, 3, 20, 28, 50, 58, 105, 126; unique, 3, 5, 20, 27–28, 86, 92, 113, 127. *See also* legends

quartzite, Sioux: composition of, 42–43, 161n22; confusion with catlinite, 45, 58, 163n27; description of bluffs at quarries, 2, 21; economic benefit of deposits, 42–43, 68–72; uses of, 43–45, 67–71. *See also* buildings

railroads: Burlington, Cedar Rapids, and Northern Railroad, 49, 76; Chicago, Milwaukee, and St. Paul Railroad, 41, 49; excursion trains, 47, 73; Great Northern Railway, 49, 91; importance of, 34, 41–42, 49, 65, 149; St. Paul and Sioux City Railway, 41–42; Southern Minnesota Railroad Company, 41–42

Rau, Charles, 28
recreation at quarries: dual role of National Park Service, 103–4; graffiti and vandalism, 60, 82, 90–92, 103, 111, 172n5; local residents' activities, 55–56, 80, 82–83, 91–92, 95, 106–7, 110–11, 115, 131, plate 4; school children's actions, 80, 131; tourists, 91–92, 109–11
Richardson, Henry H. *See* buildings
Rodriguez, Richard, 26, 157n25
Roe, Ethelyn, John H., and John S., 124–25
Roe's Trading Post, 124–26, 140, 142, 147, plates 8, 9, 12
Root, Deborah, 155n16. *See also* cultural appropriation
rune stone, Kensington, 116–17, 139

sacred: as generalized Indian spirituality, 4–5; landscape as, 4, 6–8, 50; secular uses of (pilgrimage), 4, 74–75, 105; sense of in American culture, 149
Saint Paul Daily Globe, 67
Saint Paul Pioneer Press, 79
salvage ethnographers: Bartlett, Winifred, 101–2; Bennett, Charles, 60, 73, 90, 98, 112, 122–24, 131, plate 3; Catlin, George, 19–21, 60, 90; Collier, John, 104; National Park Service, 108, 112; Pipestone Indian Shrine Association, 101–2
salvage ethnography, 9, 20, 90, 155n16
Schoolcraft, Henry Rowe, 8, 16–17, 22–23, 75, 101, 112, 135
Science Institute/Museum of Minnesota, 113, 116, 129, 140
Scott, Joan W., 8, 152n6
Shipstead, Henrik, 104–5
Sibley, Henry, 29
Smithsonian Institution, 22, 28, 60, 75
Song of Hiawatha, The (pageant): Indian School production, 79, 130; elsewhere in U.S., 129–30; as assertion of local authority about past, 134–37; as expression of town identity, 130, 133–39, in promotion, 4, 131–39, 143, 144, reinforcing identity, 4, 39, 149
The (poem): national 129, 134, 137,

181n22; opening verses and summary of, 23–25, 180n13; part of developing American literature, 23, 134–35; uses of verses in Pipestone promotion, 37, 48–50, 54–55, 59, 96, 102, 112, 129, 134, 137–38. See also *Song of Hiawatha, The* (pageant)
southwestern Indian sites, 92–94, 118, 125
squatters: on reserved quarry land, 39–40, 52–53
Stoopes, W. E., 96
Struck-by-the-Ree, or Old Strike, 30, 39, 48, 51
Sweet, Daniel, 32, 35–37, 52, 54, 60, 64–65, 147
Swenning, Eli H., 124

Taylor, Ephraim (Looking Eagle), 119
Taylor, Joseph, 109
Three Maidens, 5, 22, 59, 112, 121, 131–32, 136–37, plate 6
tourism and tourists: pageant attendance, 121, 132–22, 135–36; tours of quarries, 47–48, 73–74, 106, 111, 118
treaties, 13; Traverse des Sioux (1851), 30; Washington (1858), 6, 30–31, 39, 52, 76, 82, 97, 131, 146

Washburn, W. D., 71
White, Charles, 27–28
Whitehead, D. C. and Job, 32, 36, 65
Winchell, Newton H., 28–29
Winnewissa Falls, 36, 48, 50, 91, 116, 125, 130
Works Projects Administration (WPA), 111–12
world's fairs, 59–60, 62, 72–74

Yankton (Ihanktonwan Nakota) tribe: 1858 treaty establishment of reserved land at quarries, 30; 1928 claims settlement, 89–91, 97–98, 106; early control of quarries, 6; efforts against marketing of pipestone, 6, 144–46; efforts to prevent illegal quarrying, 51–52, 76–78; preferences for peaceful relations, 30–31, 76–77; reservation on Missouri River, 30–31, 75–76, 92, 142; uses of U.S. legal system, 30, 38–39, 76–78, 106
Yellowstone National Park, 56, 90–91, 105